Ben Bradford's book expands our understanding of the role of the police and adds significantly to the police powers debate in the UK. As one would expect, the empirical research is comprehensive, stimulating, accessible and makes an original contribution to the stop and search literature.

Jenny Fleming, *Professor of Criminology, University of Southampton, and Editor-in-Chief of Policing & Society, an international journal of research and policy*

The use of stop and search is one of the most contentious issues in policing and Bradford provides invaluable analysis in an area where debates are often shallow and simplistic. The rich and detailed evidence is combined with fascinating discussion of the wider role and status of police in contemporary society. This book makes an important contribution to vital debates in criminology and police studies.

Michael Rowe, *Professor of Criminology, Northumbria University*

Stop and search is amongst the most controversial of policing issues, above all because of the huge disparity in its use against different groups. Ben Bradford has produced a penetrating, provocative state-of-the-art review of the history, use, and potential of the stop and search power. It is a rare combination of sophisticated theoretical and empirical analysis, combining a wealth of detailed data with a comprehensive critique of the fundamental interdependence of stop and search – and indeed policing more generally – with both security and inequality. It is a must-read for anyone with a concern about policing and social justice.

Robert Reiner, *Emeritus Professor of Criminology, London School of Economics*

Stop and Search and Police Legitimacy

'Stop and search' is a form of police–citizen interaction that is confrontational, often stressful for those involved, and potentially damaging to the relationship between police and public. The extent to which police officers use their power to stop and perhaps search members of the public is intimately linked not only to the present-day context of policing but also to longer-term patterns in the aims of policing, the methods used to achieve them, and ultimately to the ideology of policing in England and Wales.

Stop and Search and Police Legitimacy draws upon both police-administrative and survey-based data to examine what has for many years been one of the most highly charged and contested aspects of police practice. Taking a decidedly quantitative, empirical approach, this book examines the patterning of police stops over social and geographic space, the problem of ethnic disproportionality, and the evidence concerning how people experience and react to being stopped by police – particularly in relation to issues of fairness, legitimacy, cooperation and compliance. A further important concern is the extent to which this form of police practice shapes and re-shapes the identities of those affected by it.

This ground-breaking study is a comprehensive resource for students and scholars in the fields of criminology, sociology, social policy, ethnic and racial studies and human rights. It will also be of special interest to police leaders and policy-makers.

Ben Bradford is Departmental Lecturer in Criminology in the Faculty of Law, University of Oxford, UK. He has collaborated with the London Metropolitan Police, the College of Policing, Police Scotland and other agencies on research projects concerned with improving police understanding of public opinions and priorities.

Routledge Frontiers of Criminal Justice

29 Punishing the Other
The social production of immorality revisited
Anna Eriksson

30 International Developments and Practices in Investigative Interviewing and Interrogation
Volume 1: Victims and witnesses
Edited by David Walsh, Gavin Oxburgh, Allison Redlich and Trond Myklebust

31 International Developments and Practices in Investigative Interviewing and Interrogation
Volume 2: Suspects
Edited by David Walsh, Gavin Oxburgh, Allison Redlich and Trond Myklebust

32 Improving Criminal Justice Workplaces
Translating theory and research into evidence-based practice
Paula Brough, Jennifer Brown and Amanda Biggs

33 Experiencing Imprisonment
Research on the experience of living and working in carceral institutions
Edited by Carla Reeves

36 Restorative Justice in Transitional Settings
Edited by Kerry Clamp

37 Prisoner Radicalization and Terrorism Detention Policy
Institutionalized fear or evidence-based policy-making?
Tinka M. Veldhuis

38 Drugs, Evidence, and Policy
The shaping of Belgian drug policy, 1996–2003
Julie Tieberghien

39 Restorative Policing
Concepts, theory and practice
Kerry Clamp and Craig Paterson

40 The Penal Voluntary Sector
Philippa Tomczak

41 Transforming Summary Justice
Modernisation in the lower criminal courts
Jennifer Ward

42 Stop and Search and Police Legitimacy
Ben Bradford

43 Young Offenders and Open Custody
Tove Pettersson

Stop and Search and Police Legitimacy

Ben Bradford

Routledge
Taylor & Francis Group
LONDON AND NEW YORK

First published 2017 by Routledge

2 Park Square, Milton Park, Abingdon, Oxfordshire OX14 4RN
52 Vanderbilt Avenue, New York, NY 10017

Routledge is an imprint of the Taylor & Francis Group, an informa business

First issued in paperback 2019

British Library Cataloguing-in-Publication Data
A catalogue record for this book is available from the British Library

Library of Congress Cataloging in Publication Data
Names: Bradford, Ben, author.
Title: Stop and search and police legitimacy / Ben Bradford.
Description: New York, NY : Routledge, 2017. | Series: Routledge frontiers of criminal justice ; 42 | Includes bibliographical references and index.
Identifiers: LCCN 2016028735| ISBN 9780415708647 (hardback) | ISBN 9781315885940 (ebook)
Subjects: LCSH: Police–Great Britain. | Searches and seizures–Great Britain. | Police-community relations–Great Britain. | Crime prevention–Great Britain.
Classification: LCC HV8195.A3 B73 2017 | DDC 363.25/2–dc23
LC record available at https://lccn.loc.gov/2016028735

ISBN: 978-0-415-70864-7 (hbk)
ISBN: 978-0-367-22619-0 (pbk)

Typeset in Times New Roman
by Wearset Ltd, Boldon, Tyne and Wear

Contents

Figures

Tables

Acknowledgements

This book brings together a number of things I have been working on for some time. In 2009, I started to look at issues around ethnic profiling with Rebekah Delsol and Mike Shiner and their colleagues at the Open Society Foundation (OSF) and Stopwatch. Since then I have collaborated with several others, too, on reports, book chapters and journal articles directly relevant to the material covered here and upon which the discussion frequently draws. In addition to Rebekah and Mike, I am grateful in particular to Mike Hough, Ian Loader and Jon Jackson. Without this group of people many of the ideas sketched herein would never have come to fruition, and I am hugely in their debt. It goes without saying that all the mistakes, errors and omissions are entirely my own. I should also note that I first produced some of the datasets and analysis used in this book while working as a consultant for OSF. I was given complete academic freedom at the time, and the views laid out below are not endorsed or influenced by the OSF in any way (although I hope the people there will find them interesting and useful).

A number of people have also helped me with comments on chapters, discussion and sometimes arguments over the course of several years. I am very grateful for the help and advice provided by Katrin Hohl, Jouni Kuha, Richard Martin, Kath Murray, Andy Myhill, Alpa Parmar, Paul Quinton, Betsy Stanko and Matteo Tiratelli. I hope I have not left anyone off that list.

Finally, thanks also to Amra. This is for you (plus one).

1 Introduction

This is a book about a specific police power. It is concerned with the nature, distribution and consequences of the ability of police in England and Wales to stop, and perhaps search, members of the public in public spaces or on the public highway. It is also a book about police power in a more general sense – what it is for and in particular the types of people against whom it is deployed – and about the ways the policed experience this power. What lessons do citizens take from their encounters with police, and what are the implications of these lessons for public trust, police legitimacy and the relationship between police and policed?

Police stops are moments where a certain vision of order is invoked and asserted. Efforts to 'fight crime' and deal with disorder are both practiced and demonstrated by police who interdict, question and search people in public spaces. Such activity has normative and symbolic power as well as an instrumental purpose, holding multiple layers of meaning for police, suspect and onlookers alike. Stop/search and associated practices can stand for the wider means and ends of police, representing a particular way policing can be 'done' – broadly speaking, via the firm and proactive assertion of investigative and regulatory power – *and* the purposes toward which police power is directed, namely the identification, deterrence, control and disciplining of those who threaten the safety of others and the 'good order' of society. In all such moments the legitimacy of the police is asserted and tested. Officers conducting a stop are making a claim as to the rightfulness of the authority vested in them – that they are empowered to treat citizens in this way and that the nature and extent of their use of power is justified (Huq *et al.* 2016). The people stopped, on the other hand, make judgements about these claims. Are the actions of the police justified, in this and similar cases? Is the officer acting proportionately and with the right intentions, or is he or she motivated by bias or prejudice? Are the laws on which this method of policing is based themselves justified, in terms of the aims they represent and the fairness with which they are applied (Bradford and Jackson 2016: 222)?

Street, traffic and other forms of police stop are also among the most controversial modes or applications of police power. Debate, contest and conflict surrounds stop and search, in particular, like almost no other aspect of policing in England and Wales – and the picture is often little different in other developed democracies where similar powers exist, notably of course the United States. To the proverbial incoming alien this might seem somewhat strange. What could be more basic to the process of policing as it is understood in a liberal democracy than officers deciding, based on criteria at least partially constrained in law, to apprehend citizens, ask them to account for themselves in some way, and possibly make a search of their person, without requiring recourse to the more coercive tool of arrest? Given the professed – and widely accepted – aims of policing, effort oriented toward 'fighting crime', maintaining order and 'keeping the peace', such activity seems essential, and particularly so if avoidance of more intrusive interventions is desired.

Yet stop and search remains one of the most highly charged, contested, and in many ways problematic aspects of police practice, and has been now for many years. There are, broadly speaking, two reasons for this. First, police activity is in an important sense *always* highly charged, contested and problematic. The police are empowered to use non-negotiable force to deal with an essentially limitless set of potential problems (Bittner 1990: 121–122) which, nevertheless, frequently involve dispute, the weighing of divergent public and/or private interests and, not least, the ability of the state to compel its citizens to undertake or refrain from activities they may otherwise have wished to avoid or perform. Under such conditions, disputes over the actions and omissions of police officers are inevitable, and these seem particularly likely to emerge in moments of face-to-face interaction where the power of the state, embodied by the police officer, is instantiated and made real in people's lives. Many forms of police activity represent in a tangible and direct way the ability of the state to interfere in the lives of its citizens, and such activity will thus always be a locus of debate and often discord. Stops, searches and cognate activities are thus, in some senses at least, merely examples of the broader practice of policing (at least in as much as this is conducted by uniformed, public police).

Second, however, there appears to be something specific to stop and search, certainly in England and Wales and perhaps more widely, which above and beyond the generally 'difficult' nature of policing sets it apart and elevates it to a special position socially, culturally and institutionally. Ethnic and other disproportionalities in the experience of police stop and search activity are in many ways *the* key factor driving this phenomenon. Stop and search in England and Wales has been a controversial issue for many years because it has consistently be shown to have been unevenly applied: across different social or class boundaries; in different parts of the city (and indeed the country); and particularly across different ethnic groups (Smith and Gray 1985; Keith 1993; Bowling and Phillips 2002, 2007; Ariza 2014; Delsol and Shiner 2015; Bradford and Loader 2016). People from some ethnic groups are much more likely to be stopped and/or searched than those from others, with the difference between people with black and white ethnicities being especially stark. In 2014/2015, for example, black people were four times more likely to be stopped than white people, down from six times in 2010/2011 (Home Office 2015); figures that merely continue a long run of similar annual data.

Such ethnic disproportionality is, when it occurs and is not justified in terms of variation in levels of offending, unfair procedurally and distributively. It is equally unfair in a normative (or objective) sense and from the empirical (or subjective) viewpoint of those affected. It is for this reason that the question of legitimacy lies at the heart of the debate that revolves around stop and search (Bowling and Phillips 2007; Bradford and Jackson 2016; Delsol and Shiner 2006, 2015; Jackson *et al.* 2013). A significant body of research supports the idea that personal contacts between police and citizens are important moments in which public trust and the legitimacy of the police is tested, reproduced or undermined (Bradford *et al.* 2009; Mazerolle *et al.* 2011, 2012; Skogan 2006; Jackson *et al.* 2012; Tyler and Fagan 2008; Tyler *et al.* 2015). A consistent finding of this research has been that on average such encounters damage trust and legitimacy. In particular, people who have recently experienced contact with police initiated by the officers concerned typically evince significantly lower levels of trust in police, and are typically less likely to indicate that they hold the police legitimate. It seems that stop and search almost inevitably presents a challenge to legitimacy.

Herein lies a conundrum that shapes much of the discussion to follow. On the one hand, police are tasked with dealing with issues of crime and disorder, and more broadly with maintaining social order and the general fabric of society. Organizational, institutional and socio-cultural pressures converge in promoting a proactive approach to these tasks. Police in England and Wales are expected and expect themselves to be 'out on the streets', addressing crime, confronting potential instances of disorder, and providing a reassuring, assertive, presence. Such an approach is both deeply inscribed in occupational culture (Reiner 2010) and resonant with the preferences of many sections of the public (Girling *et al.* 2000; Harkin 2014). The political pressure on police to live up to this image is constant – as Home Secretary Theresa May pronounced shortly after coming to power in 2010, the mission of the police is 'it is to cut crime. No more, and no less' (Home Office 2010) – and while some policy innovations have been recognizant of the wider role of police (Stanko and Bradford 2009) the idea that officers are first and foremost crime-fighters is usually foremost in any discussion of policy and practice. Stopping people, questioning and perhaps searching them can be an important way for police both to do the things expected of them (and that they wish in any case to do) and to *demonstrate* this in a highly visible manner.

On the other hand, those who are objects of this kind of police attention – which many years of research has identified as primarily the young, the marginal, the excluded, and those from ethnic and other minorities – want what is ostensibly a quite different style of policing, one that recognizes their right to use public space unhindered, treats them with dignity and respect, and as the equals of others in society and, in many cases, simply leaves them alone. The political, social and cultural pressures that predispose police toward proactive, interdictory modalities, that is, come at a cost, which is experienced in the first instance by those on the receiving end of such practices. Importantly, though, this cost can also be borne by the police. The damage done to relations with such individuals and groups inhibits the ability of officers to function effectively in some areas and communities. The costs of stop activity can also be borne by the wider community, not least to the extent that social tension is generated and exacerbated by institutional practice experienced as exclusionary and discriminatory.

Stop and search therefore brings to light a somewhat underexplored facet of the relationship between police and public – the gap between how people would like to be policed themselves, and how they would like the police to behave in relation to others. Research suggests that while those from marginalized and excluded communities and social groups desire forms of policing aligned with those they see others receiving (Brunson and Miller 2006; Carr *et al.* 2007), there is much also to imply that significant sections of the 'majority' population desire, or will at least tolerate, forms of policing that attempt to 'crack down' on high crime areas and those living there (Girling *et al.* 2000; Harkin 2014; Pickett 2016). Visible police activity likely contributes significantly to legitimacy among many of those observing it, if not among those directly caught up in it (Sindall and Sturgis 2013).

Legitimacy may be both enhanced and undermined by the kind of proactive policing style exemplified by stop and search. Stop and search is on some accounts (certainly those of many police officers) a vital weapon in the police's crime fighting armoury. Such activity represents attempts to fight crime and maintain order, and police enjoy trust and legitimacy to the extent that they embody and defend order (Jackson *et al.* 2013) and, albeit to a lesser, more contingent degree, fight crime (Bradford *et al.* 2014; Sindall *et al.* 2012; Tankebe 2009). Yet, trust and legitimacy are premised also on the extent to which police activity is experienced by the policed as fair, and indeed on the extent to which people retain a general notion that police behave in a normatively desirable manner (Jackson *et al.* 2012; Tyler 2006; Tyler and Huo 2002). Police legitimacy, contingent and subject to a continuous ('dialogic' – Bottoms and Tankebe 2012) process of debate and contest, is challenged when people feel activities such as stop and search are unfair – which they often do. This is a practice that seems to be inherently contradictory, and productive of multiple tensions and anomalies.

Another part of the puzzle is this: from a purely practical perspective stop and search can indeed be a useful tool of policing. This is true from a common sense perspective – how else would police operating in public spaces go about their business if they could not stop, question and perhaps search people they suspect of committing a crime – and from an academic or evidence-based perspective. There is much to suggest that stop and search activity can have a significant impact on crime in the short to medium term, particularly when it is part of a targeted package of interventions (see Chapter 2 below). Yet, despite the widespread belief inside and outside the police service that stop and search and associated practice is a highly effective use of time and resource, a key fact shaping the social and political difficulties that swirl around this topic is that the *strength* of the association between stop and search and crime and disorder is contested, difficult to prove, and probably weak (Apel 2016; Delsol 2015). While there is no doubt that stop and search in England and Wales makes *some* contribution to addressing issues of crime and disorder – it certainly produces a significant number of arrests – the extent and implications of this contribution are far from clear. Very little research has considered, for example, the marginal effect of stop and search activity on crime rates. Moreover, as shown in Chapters 5 and 6 below the distribution of police stops in local neighbourhoods and across Police Force Areas has relatively little to do with the distribution of crime or victimization. This is not a practice that necessarily tracks closely the phenomena it is intended to inhibit (McCandless *et al.* 2016). In sum, while it would be facile to suggest police stops have nothing to do with crime, its distribution or its prevention, this is a power and a practice that seems to be at least as much, and arguably more, concerned with some other set of goals.

Stop and search is a 'wicked issue' (Fleming and McLaughlin 2010: 201): 'complicated and demanding … (and) premised upon other tricky psycho-social concepts, namely, perceptions, sentiments, opinions, expectations, judgements, satisfaction, trust, and legitimacy'; a list to which might be added an equally tricky range of criminological, sociological and political concepts: race, ethnicity, marginality, social exclusion, offending and deterrence. It is within this remarkably difficult political, social and cultural space that stop and search is located and within which questions about it must be explored. Is it possible to reconcile the imperative *to* police – to intervene, to assert control, to order – with the imperative to act in ways that do not undermine the legitimacy *the* police need to fulfil these roles? Can tensions between the need to demonstrate effectiveness in the 'fight against crime' and to act in as procedurally and distributively fair ways as possible be overcome? What are the implications arising from the concentration of police attention on particular social groups and categories? While police cannot possibly satisfy all of the people, all of the time, to what extent can they be expected to provide the type of policing that everyone wants, for themselves if not for others, in the face of such tensions? To be sure, only very contingent and partial answers to these questions will be provided in the pages that follow, but they run through the book in many important ways.

Stop, police

As in the discussion thus far, much academic and policy discourse – and legal intervention – in this area has revolved primarily around the issue of stop and search, whether this be framed in terms of the suspicion-based powers such as Section 1 PACE or the even more controversial suspicion-less powers such as Section 60 of the Criminal Justice and Public Order Act 1994. However these are only a subset of a much wider 'family' of police powers and practices that is strikingly varied in nature.

There are, first, other legal powers that police can draw upon to stop people going about their business, perhaps most importantly those established by the

Road Traffic Act 1988, which allow officers to stop motorized vehicles or bicycles using the highway. Second, there is 'stop and account', which might be best described as a 'sub-legal' power. While police in England and Wales have no formal legal power to stop and merely question people in the street, for example about what they are doing or where they are going, and cannot detain a person in order to do so, it is clear that they maintain a wider, or perhaps deeper, ability to engage in such behaviour that is founded in the symbolic and material power vested in them as police officers. Moreover, while the formal powers of stop and search cannot be invoked in order to enable a conversation through which sufficient suspicion might be developed to allow a search, it is equally clear that officers often start conversations with people, develop suspicion, and then invoke a formal power in order to conduct a search (naturally, such legal niceties will often be invisible, irrelevant or both to the person stopped). The importance of such encounters, and their link to stop and search, was recognized by the requirement, placed on police in the aftermath of the Stephen Lawrence enquiry, to record stop and accounts in the same way as stop and searches are recorded. While this requirement has now been dropped (see Chapter 2) it serves to reinforce the idea that stop and account exists in a legal grey zone somewhere between a formal power and a simple 'chat'.

Third, there are, precisely, simple 'chats'. Due again to the symbolic and material power of police, what might often seem like a brief conversation, exchange of views or 'intelligence gathering' to a police officer might feel like something much more intrusive or even coercive to a citizen. This is not to claim that police cannot and do not have friendly chats with people, because of course they do, but merely that a proportion of such encounters will be experienced by the non-police party in ways akin to more formal stop/searches.

Stop and search is an 'iconic' police power that both provides a name for and shapes understanding of the subject matter covered in this book (as well as its name). Yet the discussion that follows is as much concerned with the wider family of practices outlined above as it is with the specific powers to 'stop and search'. In widening the lens to include a greater number of police–public interactions I consider all contacts between police and public occurring in public or quasi-public spaces, instigated by police, wherein officer(s) stop people going about their business and direct, question and/or search them in some way. Stop and search falls squarely into this category, but so do many other police–public interactions. Involving mainly experiences defined by members of the public, the discussion therefore revolves around not a legal but rather a sociological definition of this form of policing. Seen in such terms the police power to 'stop' is much broader than that established by specific pieces of legislation, and can be envisaged as existing along a continuum, with the formal legal powers at one end (arguably the most coercive) and informal chats nevertheless experienced as intrusive by citizens at the other (arguably the least coercive). The legal power does not neatly delimit this form of police activity, and it would stretch credulity of breaking point to argue that legally mandated stop/searches exhaust the form, quantity, meaning and implication of such encounters. Police officers have much more power than that, and it is important to paint as rounded a picture of this power as possible.

Widening the lens in this way does create a small difficulty or room for confusion in terminology, which is resolved thus. The term 'police stops', or simply 'stops', is used to refer to the wider family of activities outlined above, which includes stop and search but also other types of activity. When it appears the phrase 'stop and search' can, therefore, be taken to refer to the specific powers granted to police under PACE and associated legislation.

The aims of this book

In light of the definition provided above, this book will provide an empirical investigation of the social and geographic distribution, experience and consequences of police stop activity. Using both administrative- and survey-based data, the chapters that follow will examine such activity both as a specific set of practices and as representative, and arguably symbolic, of the wider effort of policing. Positioning police stops within a wider understanding of the nature of police power, and of the ends toward which this power is directed, three key areas of research provide sensitizing concepts and questions.

The first concerns the question of disproportionality in police stop activity. As with others before me (MVA and Miller 2000; Waddington *et al.* 2004), a primary question guiding the analysis is whether ethnic disproportionality in the experience of stops can be considered 'real'. Are people from ethnic minority groups really more likely to be stopped (and searched) than their majority-group (white) counterparts *because* they are from a minority group? Many would claim this must in an almost definitional sense be true – indeed, this position can often appear almost as an article of faith. Yet there is a significant counter-argument, which holds that disproportionality can be accounted for by other factors, such as the age of the ethnic minority population, the geographic distribution and/or differential behaviour patterns of ethnic groups. These arguments cannot be taken into account in analysis of the police data most commonly used to explore the question of disproportionality because these contain very little detail on the characteristics and behaviours of the individuals concerned. Using data from the Crime Survey of England and Wales (CSEW) to address this question, I also consider whether there are other inequalities in the experience and distribution of stop and search. Are people from some other social groups or categories disproportionally subject to this aspect of police power, and if so why?

The experience of policing among people from ethnic minority groups is then fundamental to much of what follows. This raises some important conceptual and definitional issues that, while not central to the discussion, must be addressed at the outset. I use, primarily, the language of ethnicity rather than race, mainly because the binary categorization of race exported from the United States into many research contexts is a very poor measure of the complexity of the social reality in, for example, the present day United Kingdom (Wimmer 2013). This is not to downplay the relevance of *racism*. Nor is it to elide the concept of intersectionality – the ways in which multiple aspects of people's social selves interact with each other to shape and predict particular opportunities, experiences and/or modes of oppression. Relatedly, while I privilege the concept of ethnicity and therefore of self-assignment to mutable and shifting social categories, people's physical appearance is, plainly, relevant when considering their experience of police stops. One's skin tone may be an important factor predicting one's chances of contact with the police; but so, equally, might be the way one dresses or behaves. I therefore frequently fall back on the standard terminology of Black and Minority Ethnic group (BME) to describe a particular subset of the population who are (likely to be) visibly ethnically different from the majority white British population. As a corollary I tend to group together all those who self-identify as 'white', an approach not entirely without difficulties since it lumps in those who may resemble majority group members physically and yet be identifiably ethnically different – for example people from Roma or Irish traveller communities. These compromises are inevitable, if not always desirable. Finally, since this book is based entirely on analysis of quantitative data, ethnic group classifications are restricted to those provided by the surveys used, a further inevitable compromise. In recognition of this the text will refer, for example, to people with 'black African ethnicities' – this is to acknowledge that individuals who ticked the same 'black African' box in a survey may come from very different ethnic groups.

The second area of research is the effect of police stops on public trust and the legitimacy of the police. Drawing on Tyler and colleagues procedural justice theory (Lind and Tyler 1988; Tyler 2006; Tyler and Huo 2002) to conceptualize the relationships involved, I explore issues of trust and legitimacy at the individual level, and attempt to draw some lessons in terms of police–community relations in a wider sense. On this account the legitimacy of the police is premised most importantly on public perceptions that officers and organization behave in open, respectful and transparent ways that respect the dignity of those with who police interact. Police stop activity will damage trust and police legitimacy when, and to the extent that, it is experienced as unfair and disrespectful by those stopped. People who do not trust police, who do not hold them legitimate, are less likely to respect, cooperate with and defer to officers, and another aim of this aspect of the book is to think about these issues in terms of the extent to which they interfere with the professed crime-fighting ends of police. In addition, as an important representative of superordinate social categories such as nation, state and community, police behaviour can communicate to people their status, worth and belonging within these groups (Bradford 2014; Bradford *et al.* 2014; Tyler and Blader 2000; Blader and Tyler 2009). One reason procedural justice is important to people is that it carries identity relevant information, and people use this information to shape and reproduce their identities and sense of belonging. Police behaviour can shift not only people's relationships with the police but also their relationships with others in their community, and a further important set of questions concerns the power and effect of such processes.

The third main area of interest is an exploration of police power in a wider sense. This aspect of the book picks up and expands on issues outlined above. What is the distribution of police stop activity – what factors predict greater or lesser use of the power of police to interfere in people's lives? What does the way this power is used say about the *ends* of policing towards which the *means* of stops and searches are directed? Developing arguments first made elsewhere (Bradford and Loader 2016), in addressing these questions I will draw on a concept of 'police' that is older than its current association with the uniformed state police organization we know today. Markus Dubber (2005) describes *police power* as comprising and encompassing efforts to maintain a diffuse notion of social order defined by existing power relations and extant normative conceptions of propriety and right. In doing so he harks back to pre-nineteenth-century understandings, where 'police' was simply part of the activity, if not *the* activity, of the state (see also Dubber and Valverde 2008; Neocleous 2000). To police was moreover not only to regulate and control subjects/citizens, although this was an important end toward which this power was directed. 'Police', or policing, was also directed toward promoting the happiness, commerce and good relations among the population (Reiner 2010: 5). It aimed to ensure conformity to good manners, neighbourliness, decency, industriousness and above all established norms of behaviour (Dubber 2005: xii). To police is to (attempt to) produce and reproduce both good order and 'orderly people', to patrol the boundaries of what constitutes this order, and to maintain appropriate power relations and social hierarchies.

'Police' in this literature thus means something much broader than the currently dominant usage of the term would allow. Yet this broader concept is, I think, a useful frame of reference when thinking about the activity of 'the police' in general and police stops in particular. 'The police' are uniformed specialists dedicated to the function of 'police', and represent this wider state practice in important ways. Moreover, if policing is to do with the endless task of asserting a particular version of social order, then police stops are and probably always have been an important part of this effort (Bradford and Loader 2016). From the seventeenth century onwards police and police regulations were concerned with controlling flows of people into, out of and within the city, and with maintaining a sense of order conducive to commerce and 'good governance'.

Yet the police power was also centrally concerned with those who threatened such order, most importantly the poor, the landless, beggars and vagrants, with the primary aim of making these groups and individuals into productive – and disciplined – members of society. Neocleous (2000: 17) describes the situation in seventeenth- and eighteenth-century France thus:

> The police distinguished between groups according to the degree of danger they appeared to pose to the common good – domestic labourers, prostitutes, the young, religious and political groups – but the most significant part of this enemy was the growing class of poverty (and its social cousin, the 'class' of vagrants), which was most in need of being mobilized for work.

Intercepting people, asking them to account for themselves, temporarily detaining them, searching them for illicit goods and substances were fundamental to such efforts, and are 'deeply inscribed in institutional structure and organizational behaviour (and) part … of the DNA of policing' (Bradford and Loader 2016: 254). The primary aim of this third aspect of the book is to consider the extent to which groups and individuals defined as economically unproductive, disorderly or marginal, and/or who challenge, transgress or undermine existing social norms and categories, are the special targets of police. In what ways do police respond to, and indeed help constitute, such 'problematic' categories? (cf. Choongh 1997; Waddington 1999).

To anticipate…

As the text progresses some of the questions posed above are answered in ways that will resonate strongly with those familiar with this area of research or, indeed, anyone with a passing acquaintance with the policy, legal and popular debates around stop and search. In relation to the issue of ethnic disproportionality, in particular, analysis appears to confirm – and extend – the results of earlier studies. I conclude that there is a level of ethnic disproportionality that cannot be 'explained away' by other factors. Yet I present other results less commonly discussed. There are a number of other consistently identifiable disproportionalities in the experience of this aspect of police practice. The unemployed, those with living in socially rented accommodation, those in poor health, victims of crime and the young are all more likely to be stopped by police, as are those who use illegal drugs. Many of the same groups or categories of person are also more likely to be searched once they have been stopped. It seems this is indeed a power regularly directed towards people from marginalized, and perhaps stigmatized, social groups defined in ways other than ethnicity. The concentration of policing on the marginal finds expression both in individual-level stop data derived from the CSEW and in police-recorded stop and search data, which show variation in the use of stop and search across different police force areas. In the latter case, those forces serving areas with higher levels of social deprivation tend to use the power more, irrespective of the level of crime. It would appear that police stops are indeed as much about controlling marginality as they are about fighting crime.

I also present findings that support the idea police stops often serve to undermine police legitimacy among those who experience them. This has significant implications for both the individuals concerned, who experience a loss of trust and a sense of social dislocation, for the police, as people's propensities to assist and cooperate with them decline, and perhaps also for the wider community involved, which may suffer as a result of these and related processes. Particularly important here is the extent to which police activity experienced as unfair does damage to and may shift an individual's sense of self. Because police stops are often experienced as unfair this seems to be a practice that symbolically (as well as materially) excludes many of those who experience it, with significant consequences for their sense of belonging to wider society. Positioned thus police stops don't just inhibit or prevent – they also create and constitute particular objective and subjective positions and experiences. They also continuously throw up challenges to the legitimacy of the police.

The structure of the book

Having summarized the conceptual framework of the book this introductory chapter concludes with an outline of its structure. Chapter 2 immediately follows. First, the historical development of the power to stop and search is sketched out, the current picture across England and Wales considered, and questions of effectiveness raised. The discussion then moves on to place this particular police power within a wider consideration of police stops and the role of the police in 'fighting crime' and reproducing order. Following the work of many police scholars I conclude that the primary purpose of police is not, in fact, to deter and detect crime but to secure a wider notion of order that rests in the final analysis on the maintenance existing social, economic and administrative hierarchies. Police stops must be understood within this wider context and cannot be separated from it.

Chapter 3 introduces the concept of legitimacy, and outlines the approach taken to this concept in the current volume. This chapter attends not only to what makes the police legitimate in the eyes of the policed but also to what may be important in shaping police officer's sense of their own legitimacy and, importantly, the types of broader legitimating claims made by police organizations (Bottoms and Tankebe 2012). These, I argue, form an important basis for understanding why police continue to use stop and search in the face of the obvious problems it creates.

The next two chapters motivate and then present analysis of the CSEW. Having laid the empirical and conceptual groundwork in the previous chapters, I turn in Chapter 4 to a theoretical treatment of the distribution of police stop activity, concentrating on the issue of ethnic disproportionality but also widening the net to consider the potential for a wider set of impacts on different types and groups of individuals. Chapter 5 picks up the theory and confronts it with data. Using three waves of data from the survey, I first investigate the social and spatial distribution of foot and traffic stops. Second, I explore the question of who is searched once they have been stopped. Using multi-level regression models to take into account individual and area-level correlates, this chapter represents one of the key contributions of this book, and is framed by one overarching question – can the ethnic disproportionality in the experience of police stops be explained by other factors?

Switching the level of analysis, Chapter 6 presents results from analysis of stop and search data recorded at the Police Force Area (PFA) level. Numbering 43 in total, PFAs are the primary unit of policing in England and Wales, and each returns data on the use of stop and search powers each year. The use of stop and search varies substantially across PFAs, as does the level of ethnic disproportionality, and this chapter considers both issues, with a particular emphasis on whether it is crime, or deprivation, that might explain this variation.

Turning to the effect of police stops on public trust and police legitimacy, Chapter 7 consider in some depth the likely effects of police contact, and stops in particular, on both aspects of public opinion. Key issues include the consistency of any such effect (essentially, do people tend to react in a similar to being stopped) and the extent to which stop and search may undermine public cooperation and encourage, rather than discourage, offending. Chapter 8 then picks up some of the wider implications of procedural justice theory to explore the effect experiences of police unfairness may have on people's sense of social embeddedness and belonging. Drawing out the links between procedural justice and labelling theories, it considers police behaviour as classificatory action and the implications for individuals of being assigned by police to marginal, excluded or denigrated social categories.

Chapter 9 concludes the book with, first, a recap and expansion of the overall argument and second an attempt to draw some policy lessons from the discussion.

Some disclaimers

Finally, I should note at the outset what is *not* covered in this book. Perhaps most importantly, this is an account of experiences of police stops among the policed. Although it would be impossible to consider this topic without some reference to the experiences of police officers themselves, I have relatively little to say on this important subject and rely on the accounts of others and theoretical conjecture to address this issue. Second, I do not consider in any real depth the instrumental effectiveness of stop and search, or indeed the wider category of police stops, as they are currently practiced. While Chapter 2 summarizes research in this area there is no further empirical investigation of this question.

Third, this is an avowedly parochial book. While I have no doubt that many of the issues discussed here will resonate in non-UK contexts (see, for example, Weber and Bowling 2012) the empirical aspects of the text are confined almost entirely to England and Wales, although Scotland also puts in an appearance. The reason for this is simple. The controversy surrounding stop and search and cognate practices is such that it seemed important that every argument was as well supported by empirical evidence as possible – and not only is England and Wales the context that I know best but it is also currently one of the few places around the world where good quality data on the issues in which I am interested exists. There are exceptions, of course, most obviously in the United States (see for example Epp *et al.* 2014; Geller and Fagan 2010; Geller *et al.* 2014; Tyler and Fagan 2008) and also elsewhere (e.g. Añón *et al.* 2013; Mazerolle *et al.* 2011, 2012; Wortly and Owusu-Bempah 2011), but a resource such as the CSEW remains highly unusual in international terms. With this in mind some of the wider claims made in the chapters that follow might perhaps be seen as challenges to those working in comparative contexts. Is the structure and implications of police stop activity described in the pages that follow replicated in other contexts, and if not, why not?

References

Añón, J.G., Bradford, B., Sàez, J.A.G., Cuenca, A.G. and Ferreres, A.L. (2013). *Identificación policial po perfil étnico en España*. Valencia: Tirant lo Blanch.

Apel, R. (2016). On the deterrent effect of stop, question and frisk. *Criminology and Public Policy* 15(1): 57–66.

Ariza, J.J.M. (2014). Police-initiated contacts: young people, ethnicity, and the 'usual suspects'. *Policing and Society* 24(2): 208–223.

Bittner, E. (1990). *Aspects of Police Work*. Boston, MA: Boston University Press.

Blader, S. and Tyler, T.R. (2009). Testing and expanding the group engagement model. *Journal of Applied Psychology* 94: 445–464.

Bottoms, A. and Tankebe, J. (2012). Beyond procedural justice: A dialogic approach to legitimacy in criminal justice. *Journal of Criminal Law and Criminology* 102: 119.

Bowling, B. and Phillips, C. (2002). *Racism, Crime and Justice*. Harlow: Pearson Education.

Bowling, B. and Phillips, C. (2007). Disproportionate and discriminatory: Reviewing the evidence on police stop and search. *Modern Law Review* 70: 936–961.

Bradford, B. (2014). Policing and social identity: Procedural justice, inclusion, and cooperation between police and public. *Policing and Society* 24(1): 22–43.

Bradford, B. and Jackson, J. (2016). Enabling and constraining police power: On the moral regulation of policing, in Jacobs, J. and Jackson, J. (eds) *Routledge Handbook of Criminal Justice Ethics*. Oxford: Routledge.

Bradford, B. and Loader, I. (2016). Police, crime and order: The case of stop and search, in Bradford, B., Jauregui, B., Loader, I. and Steinberg, J. (eds) *The SAGE Handbook of Global Policing*. London: SAGE.

Bradford, B., Huq, A., Jackson, J. and Roberts, B. (2014). What price fairness when security is at stake? Police legitimacy in South Africa. *Regulation and Governance* 8(2): 246–268.

Bradford, B., Jackson, J. and Stanko, E.B. (2009). Contact and confidence. Revisiting the impact of public encounters with the police. *Policing and Society* 19: 20–46.

Bradford, B., Murphy, K. and Jackson, J. (2014). Officers as mirrors: Policing, procedural justice and the (re)production of social identity. *British Journal of Criminology* 54(4): 527–550.

Brunson, R.K. and Miller, J. (2006). Young black men and urban policing in the United States. *British Journal of Criminology* 46: 613–640.

Carr, P.J., Napolitano, L., and Keating, J. (2007). We never call the cops and here is why: A qualitative examination of legal cynicism in three Philadelphia neighbourhoods. *Criminology* 45(2): 445–480.

Choongh, S. (1997). *Policing as Social Discipline*. Oxford: Clarendon Press.

Delsol, R. (2015). Effectiveness, in Delsol, R. and Shiner, M. (eds) *Stop and Search*. Basingstoke: Palgrave Macmillan.

Delsol, R. and Shiner, M. (2006). Regulating stop and search: A challenge for police and community relations in England and Wales. *Critical Criminology* 14: 241–263.

Delsol, R. and Shiner, M. (eds) (2015). *Stop and Search*. Basingstoke: Palgrave Macmillan.

Dubber, M.D. (2005). *The Police Power. Patriarchy and the Foundations of American Government*. New York: Columbia University Press.

Dubber, M.D. and Valverde, M. (2008). *The New Police Science. The Police Power in Domestic and International Governance*. Stanford: Stanford University Press.

Epp, C.R., Maynard-Moody, S. and Haidar-Markel, D. (2014). *Pulled Over. How Police Stops Define Race and Citizenship*. Chicago: University of Chicago Press.

Fleming, J. and McLaughlin, E. (2010). 'The public gets what the public wants?' Interrogating the 'public confidence' agenda. *Policing: A Journal of Policy and Practice* 4(3): 199–202.

Geller, A. and Fagan, J. (2010). Pot as pretext: Marijuana, race, and the new disorder in New York city street policing. *Journal of Empirical Legal Studies* 7(4): 591–633.

Geller, A., Fagan, J., Tyler, T.R., and Link, B. (2014). Aggressive policing and the mental health of young urban men. *American Journal of Public Health* 104(12): 2321–2327.

Girling, E., Loader, I. and Sparks R. (2000). *Crime and Social Change in Middle England.* London: Routledge.

Harkin, D. (2014). The police and punishment: Understanding the pains of policing. *Theoretical Criminology* 19(1): 43–58.

Home Office (2010). Theresa May's speech to the National Policing Conference, 29th June. Available at: www.gov.uk/government/speeches/police-reform-theresa-mays-speech-to-the-national-policing-conference. Accessed December 2015.

Home Office (2015). *Police Powers and Procedures England and Wales, Year Ending 31 March 2015*. London: Home Office.

Huq, A., Jackson, J. and Trinkner, R. (2016). 'Legitimating Practices: Revisiting the Predicates of Police Legitimacy', *British Journal of Criminology* Advance Access.

Jackson, J., Bradford, B., Hough, M., Myhill, A., Quinton, P. and Tyler, T.R. (2012). Why do people comply with the law? Legitimacy and the influence of legal institutions. *British Journal of Criminology* 52(6): 1051–1071.

Jackson, J. Bradford, B., Stanko, B. and Hohl, K. (2013). *Just Authority? Trust in the Police in England and Wales*. London: Routledge.

Keith, M. (1993). *Race, Riots and Policing: Lore and Disorder in a Multi-Racist Society.* London: UCL Press.

Lind, A.E. and Tyler, T.R. (1988). *The Social Psychology of Procedural Justice*. New York: Plenum Press.

Loader, I, and Mulcahy, A. (2003). *Policing and the Condition of England.* Oxford: Oxford University Press.

McCandless, R., Feist, A., Allan, J. and Morgan, N. (2016). *Do Initiatives Involving Substantial Increases in Stop and Search Reduce Crime? Assessing the Impact of Operation BLUNT 2*. London: Home Office.

Mazerolle, L., Bennett, S., Antrobus, E. and Eggins, E. (2011). *Key Findings from the Queensland Community Engagement Trial*. CEPS Briefing Paper June 2011.

Mazerolle, L., Bennett, S., Antrobus, E. and Eggins, E. (2012). Procedural justice, routine encounters and citizen perceptions of the police: Main findings from the Queensland Community Engagement Trial (QCET). *Journal of Experimental Criminology* 8(4): 343–366.

MVA and Miller, J. (2000). *Profiling Populations Available for Stops and Searches.* London: Home Office.

Neocleous, M. (2000). *The Fabrication of Social Order*. London: Pluto Press.

Pickett, J.T. (2016). On the social foundations of crimmigration: Latino threats and support for expanded police powers. *Journal of Quantitative Criminology* 32: 103–132.

Reiner, R. (2010). *The Politics of the Police* (4th edn). Oxford: Oxford University Press.

Sindall, K. and Sturgis, P. (2013). Austerity policing: is visibility more important than numbers in determining public confidence in the police? *European Journal of Criminology* 10(2): 137–153.

Sindall, K., Sturgis, P. and Jennings, W. (2012). Public confidence in the police: A time-series analysis. *British Journal of Criminology* 52(4): 744–764.

Skogan, W.G. (2006). Asymmetry in the impact of encounters with police. *Policing and Society* 16: 99–126.

Smith, D.J. and Gray, J. (1985). *Police and People in London: The PSI Report*. London: Policy Studies Institute.

Stanko, E.A. and Bradford, B. (2009). Beyond measuring 'how good a job' police are doing: the MPS model of confidence in policing. *Policing: A Journal of Policy and Practice* 3(4): 332–330.

Sunshine, J. and Tyler, T.R. (2003). Moral solidarity, identification with the community, and the importance of procedural justice: The police as prototypical representatives of a group's moral values. *Social Psychology Quarterly* 66(2): 153–165.

Tankebe, J. (2009). Public Cooperation with the police in Ghana: Does procedural fairness matter? *Criminology* 47: 1265–93.

Tyler, T. (2006). *Why People Obey the Law* (2nd edn). New Haven: Yale University Press.

Tyler, T.R. and Blader, S. (2000). *Cooperation in Groups: Procedural Justice, Social Identity, and Behavioral Engagement.* Philadelphia, PA: Psychology Press.

Tyler, T.R. and Fagan, J. (2008). Legitimacy and cooperation: Why do people help the police fight crime in their communities? *Ohio State Journal of Criminal Law* 6: 231–276.

Tyler, T.R. and Huo, Y. (2002). *Trust in the Law: Encouraging Public Cooperation with the Police and Courts.* New York: Russell Sage Foundation.

Tyler, T.R., Jackson, J. and Mentovich, A. (2015). The consequences of being an object of suspicion: Potential pitfalls of proactive police contact. *Journal of Empirical Legal Studies* 12(4): 602–636.

Waddington, P.A.J. (1999). *Policing Citizens: Authority and Rights*. London: University College Press.

Waddington, P.A.J, Stenson, K. and Don, D. (2004). In proportion: Race and police stop and search. *British Journal of Criminology* 44: 889–914.

Weber, L. and Bowling, B. (2012) *Stop and Search: Police Power in Global Context.* London: Routledge.

Wimmer, A. (2013) *Ethnic Boundary Making. Institutions, Power, Networks.* Oxford: Oxford University Press.

Wortley, S. and Owusu-Bempah, A. (2011). The usual suspects: police stop and search practices in Canada. *Policing and Society* 21(4): 395–407.

2 Police stops and the production of order

This chapter has three main aims. First, it will describe stop and search in general terms and, equally importantly, make the case that this is just one form of the wider, more diffuse police power to 'stop' citizens to direct, question and, perhaps, search them. Second, it will discuss whether this mode of policing can be considered effective, and indeed what effectiveness might mean in this context. The focus will then switch, third, to a much wider consideration of the function of police which will provide a framework for understanding police stops as the book progresses. As its title suggests, the over-arching message of the chapter is that this is a tool or modality of policing that aims above all to assert and reproduce a particular form of social order because this is, itself, a fundamental aim of policing. Although it has many worthwhile foundations and positive outcomes – not least the detection and prevention of crime – the ends of policing are premised in the final analysis on the maintenance of the already existing social order. Stop/search and related activities must be viewed with this in mind.

A brief history of stop and search

It is safe to say that the history of stop and search as a particular legal power in England and Wales is well known, and it is not my intention to repeat it here in any real depth (see, instead, Bowling and Phillips 2002, 2007; Bridges 2015; Sanders *et al.* 2010; Shiner and Delsol 2015). A number of points concerning this specific power and exemplar of the wider category of police stops are worth reiterating, however. These concern the history of the police power to 'stop and search'; the introduction of Police and Criminal Evidence Act (PACE) in 1984 and the powers it granted police; the recording of stop/searches by police; levels of stop and/or searches; and the issue of ethnic disproportionality. To these must also be added some consideration of the wider category of 'police stops', and the effectiveness of stop/search, and related practices, as tools of policing.

The history of the power

Prior to 1984 there was no *general* power for police to stop and search people in public places in England and Wales. Formal powers to stop and search people in relation to specific crimes were in place before then: in particular, the Misuse of Drugs Act 1971 and the Firearms Act 1968 both granted officers the ability, subject to reasonable suspicion, to stop and search people in public places if they suspected them of carrying drugs or firearms, respectively. More generally, though, a variety of laws and practices at both national and local levels enabled police officers to engage in activities that were essentially stop/searches as this form of police–public interaction is now understood. Most (in)famous of these was the so-called 'Sus' law, established by the Vagrancy Act 1824, which enabled police to stop and search anyone suspected of 'frequenting or loitering in a public place with intent to commit an arrestable offence' (Whitfield 2009: n.p.). This Act, along with other legislation and various 'ways and means' abilities vested in local forces, seems to have often meant that police could stop and search almost anyone they chose, at almost any time, particularly in as much as he or she could be defined as a potential vagrant, loiterer or miscreant.

While PACE is often presented as a watershed moment that signalled a profound shift in the ability of police to stop and/or search people in the streets the new raft of powers it introduced are thus more correctly seen as a 'rationalization and codification of hitherto haphazard statute and common law, or a legitimation of what was already police practice' (Reiner 2010: 213). This point becomes clearer when one considers that the 1824 Act and the other statutory and common law powers police had to interdict, question and search individuals were themselves continuations of earlier practice and legislation that aimed to control vagrants and other categories of 'misfits' (Weber and Bowling 2008: 356–358). The control of such populations by the *function* of police is a feature of legislation that, indeed, pre-dates by several centuries the existence of police organizations as they are now understood. Philip Rawlings (2002: 45–46) notes, for example, that in the wake of the plague in 1348 there was a shift in the emphasis of policing, which naturally then looked very different, in organizational and institutional terms, from its present day manifestation, toward control of the poor. A particular prominence was given to curtailing the freedom of movement of those classified as vagrants and 'valiant beggars', and pressing them into the service of the landed classes. A primary motivation of this shift was the labour shortage that arose in the wake of the plague and a concern to make such individuals economically productive.

Moving forward in time Dubber (2005: 51–54) catalogues a series of English and American laws, starting with Henry VIII's Act relating to Vagabonds in 1536, that sought to control the idle, the unattached, 'Egyptians' (Gypsies), 'rogues and vagabonds' and others who appeared detached from society. As described by Dubber the aim of these laws was, at least in relation to less serious 'offenders', to return those who appeared to be existing outside established structures of governance to a more regular condition that subjected them to the authority of family, lord and king, often by recourse to physical punishment (such as being whipped from town to town). Although others were of course subject to imprisonment and even execution, in keeping with the harsh penal practice of the time, the police power, as it was configured and operationalized at the time, was concerned to a significant extent with bringing these troubling individuals back into the fold, and it relied by definition on identifying and apprehending such individuals in order to return them to their correct physical (home town or village) and social location, and to useful employment (Neocleous 2000).

Moving forward again, Clive Emsley (2010: 60–61) discusses Henry Fielding's *Enquiry into the Causes of the late Increase of Robbers* (1751). Concerned with a breakdown in morality and social bonds in society, the effects of which he perceived right across the social spectrum, Fielding was nevertheless focused on the idle – and therefore crime-prone – poor and, once again, on the control and supervision of vagabondage and similar transgressions. Perhaps more tellingly, Patrick Colquhoun, founder of the Thames River Police (1798) published his *Treatise on the Policing of the Metropolis* in 1792. In it he similarly decried the breakdown of moral and religious values, particularly among the poor, and prescribed a more European system of police for London that would be concerned with the moral regulation of the poor, the idle and the itinerant (Emsley 2010: 64). Colquhoun's writing and work fed, of course, directly into the foundation of the London Metropolitan Police in 1829, and a concern with the need for moral regulation in the face of urbanization and rapid social change can be identified in many of the debates current at the time of the foundation of the modern police (Silver 1967).

This historical context is important because it is often tempting to see stop and search as a manifestation of police power that, as a practice intimately caught up with ethnic and racial tensions, inequalities and oppression, is in some definitional sense 'modern', at least to the extent that such aspects of social experience in the United Kingdom are primarily features of the post-war period. Yet it can be argued that the power to stop and search, both pre- and post-1984, builds on and is part of a much longer tradition of policing concerned primarily with the control of marginal populations.

The Police and Criminal Evidence Act 1984

Central in any discussion of the history of stop and search are the 1981 Brixton riots, the Scarman report, and the passing of the Police and Criminal Evidence Act 1984 (PACE). While disquiet about the Sus law had been growing for some time, particularly in relation to its use against black people living in London and the police racism involved (see, generally, Hall *et al.* 1978), the Brixton riots of 1981, and subsequent events in Liverpool and elsewhere, proved to be a pinch point and a catalyst of change. A key proximal cause of the events in Brixton was 'Swamp 81', a Metropolitan Police Service (MPS) anti-mugging initiative aimed primarily at young black men that involved heavy use of stop and search, although this 'trigger' would hardly have been effective in the absence of a long history of problematic relations between black communities and police in this and many other parts of London (Bowling and Phillips 2002, Chapter 6).

The riots themselves, and the subsequent Scarman report (1981), did not immediately result in change. Scarman concluded that racism was not an institution-level problem in the MPS, and did not recommend a change to stop and search laws (Bridges 2015: 10). As Bowling and Phillips (2002) note, aggressive police interventions into black communities continued throughout the 1980s. Yet the introduction in PACE of specific legislation governing the police power to stop and search, three years after the riots, is generally seen as flowing directly from these earlier events. PACE has been described by one leading police scholar as 'the most significant landmark in the modern development of police powers' (Reiner 2010: 212), and it built on the work of the earlier Royal Commission on Criminal Procedure (1981) to provide a 'statutory codification and rationalization of police powers and the safeguards over their exercise' (ibid.), with the stated aim of striking a balance between the rights of individuals suspected or accused of crimes and the need for the 'community' to deal effectively with issues of offending and disorder. Stop and search was at the heart of the Act, and covered in Part 1 of it.

A primary reason for the introduction of PACE and the regulation it placed around stop/search activity was therefore the need to respond to what was perceived to be a crisis in police legitimacy (Bridges 2015: 10). This crisis was instigated to a significant degree by the unfair application of the Sus law and, in a more general sense, by a feeling that police targeting of ethnic and other minority groups was unjustified, damaging and in some instances out of control. The aim was to corral and direct expressions of police power that appeared to many at the time to be both lacking in constraint and fundamentally misdirected (albeit that the extent to which codified rules are an effective restraint on the behaviour of police officers is open to significant doubt and debate (Dixon 1997)).

The content of PACE

Section 1 of PACE covers the general police power to stop and search people in public places. It is somewhat ironic, given the political impetus behind the introduction of PACE and the inclusion of stop and search within its framework, that these changes amounted to significant *extension* of the police power to stop and search (Bridges 2015; Reiner 2010). This is primarily because it introduced, precisely, a general power to stop and search. Whereas in the past such powers had either related to specific behaviours, illicit goods, or types of person, PACE established the ability of police to:

> stop and search a person, vehicle or anything in or on the vehicle in a public place where they have reasonable suspicion that the person is in possession of, or the vehicle contains, stolen goods or prohibited items (which) include offensive weapons, bladed instruments, prohibited fireworks or any article made, adapted or intended for use in burglary, theft, taking a motor vehicle without consent, obtaining property by deception or causing criminal damage.
>
> (Bridges 2015: 11)

This might from many perspectives be seen as an extraordinarily wide-ranging power. Here, police constables – and the level at which the power is regulated is important, in as much as it is left to the individual police officer 'on the ground' to decide who to search, when, and for what – are empowered to search any person or vehicle for 'stolen and prohibited articles' and to 'detain a person or vehicle for purpose of such a search' (Home Office 2015a). This amounts to a power of (usually very transient) arrest, or at least detention, the grounds for which can be suspicion of involvement in almost any property or drug crime and many types of violent crime (Bowling and Phillips 2007). As Bowling and Phillips insist, this is intended primarily as an *investigatory* power – as a way, that is, for police to investigate a crime they have cause for believing has already been committed (although there is of course good reason to believe it is also used for other aims).

Searches can only occur, however, if the constable has 'reasonable grounds for suspecting that he will find stolen or prohibited articles' – a phrase that has been the subject of much debate in the years since 1984 (Bridges 2015; Sanders *et al.* 2010). A code of practice – 'Code A' – governs the use by police of PACE and other powers of stop and search (e.g. those established by the Misuse of Drugs Act 1971 – see below) and is revised periodically. The 2015 version of the code of practice (Home Office 2015a: 6) states the following:

> Reasonable grounds for suspicion is the legal test which a police officer must satisfy before they can stop and detain individuals or vehicles to search them under powers such as section 1 of PACE.... This test must be applied to the particular circumstances in each case and is in two parts:
>
> (i) *Firstly*, the officer must have formed a *genuine* suspicion in their own mind that they will find the object for which the search power being exercised allows them to search...
> (ii) *Secondly*, the suspicion that the object will be found must be reasonable. This means that there must be an *objective* basis for that suspicion based on facts, information and/or intelligence which are relevant to the likelihood that the object in question will be found, so that a reasonable person would be entitled to reach the same conclusion based on the same facts and information and/or intelligence.
>
> Officers must therefore be able to explain the basis for their suspicion by reference to intelligence or information about, or some specific behaviour by, the person concerned.

While giving the appearance of a carefully constrained and regulated power, though, the reasonable suspicion test is in fact almost impossible to enforce after the fact (Dixon 1997; Sanders *et al.* 2010), since what is at stake is the subjective state of mind of the officer concerned. The radical discretion granted to individual police officers, which is upheld in PACE and the code of practice despite the appearance that they limit police activity, means the probability of individual stop/search decisions being challenged or second-guessed by supervisors or others further down the line is extremely small: all an officer needs to say is that 'I thought I saw him using drugs', or something similar, and that, in a sense, is that. Usually, in fact, such questions appear not even to be asked. Her Majesty's Inspectorate of Constabulary (HMIC), in its 2013 report on stop and search, noted that from a sample of 8,783 records of stop and searches (containing at least 200 from each police force in England and Wales) 27 per cent appeared to give insufficient grounds for the search – that is, were *prima facie* illegal. Yet there seems to be no evidence of any action being taken against any of the officers concerned, despite a requirement that supervisors (usually Sergeants) sign off each record of a stop and search provided to them by officers under their command.

The recording of stop/searches

The issue of the recording of stop/searches is, it seems to me, of sufficient interest to warrant its own section in this discussion. Originally part of the bureaucratic and administrative framework established by PACE and intended to provide the counter-weight to the extended powers it granted to police (Bridges 2015), the records police officers make of the stops they conduct have over the last 20 years taken on something of life of their own, and constitute a key node in the patterns of debate and discord that revolve around the power.

As originally specified by PACE an officer conducting a stop and search is required by law to produce a record of the encounter that includes such details as the date, time and place of the search, the grounds and power used, the name and address of the person searched, whether anything was found, and the name of the officer concerned. The person stopped is entitled to a copy of the record, either there and then or later if they make a request for one within 12 months.

Subsequent amendments to Code A have extended the recording requirements. Most notably, after the Criminal Justice Act 1991 established a requirement on the Home Office to publish regular statistics on race and the criminal justice system a duty was placed on police to record the ethnicity of the person stopped. Ethnicity was initially recorded by the officer involved using a simple Asian/black/white/other metric (a practice that many academics and activists found highly problematic – since ethnicity is a self-assigned categorization it amounts to a category error to have another define one's ethnicity). In recent years this has been changed – as a result of a recommendation from the Stephen Lawrence enquiry (Macpherson 1999) – to the self-assessed ethnicity of the subject of the search, captured by the 16-category classification used in the 2001 Census (which, to be sure, many find equally problematic).

Bridges (2015: 15) notes that these recording requirements serve, at least in theory, a number of purposes. They may provide individuals who have been stopped with assistance if they want to challenge the actions of the officer(s) concerned; they may enable or enhance the internal regulation and supervision of the use of the power by officers, units and indeed forces; and they allow for a more general enumeration and monitoring of the use of stop and search. While there is scant evidence that the forms are actually used much for the first two purposes – as witnessed for example by the HMIC report mentioned above – they have been used extensively to provide a picture of 'police-recorded' stop and search, both in official publications, such as the 'Race in the Criminal Justice System' series (e.g. MoJ 2011) academic publications (e.g. Borooah 2011; Miller 2010) and elsewhere. This police recorded data also provides a key source for the analysis presented in Chapter 6 of the current volume.

It is a fact not often remarked upon that the police are thus engaged, as far as is known quite faithfully, in a practice that regularly provides their critics with a stick with which to beat them. Some of the strongest critiques of ethnic disproportionality in the use of stop and search have relied almost entirely on data recorded by the police themselves (e.g. EHRC 2010; Release 2013). While there should rightly be caution in relation to the extent to which 'all' stops and searches make their way into the police-recorded data – it seems very doubtful that they do – it seems important, not least in terms of the need to retain democratic control over police, that such statistics are generated and made publicly available. The extent to which such recording practices enable debate is, I think, something to be celebrated in some small way.

This is not to claim of course that the police recorded statistics are entirely unproblematic. The usual provisos around the collection and use of administrative data apply; indeed, probably more so here than in other cases since the recording is done 'on the streets' and usually well away from any kind of supervisory control or oversight. There must be a 'dark figure' of unrecorded stop/searches, just as there is a dark figure of unrecorded crime. Moreover, the rules around recording can and do change, which can undermine clarity and continuity and provide forces with the opportunity to reduce or abolish recording. The most important example of this is the recording of stops that do not result in a search ('stop and accounts'), which was introduced in the aftermath of the Stephen Lawrence enquiry but then dropped, by most forces, as a result of changes to PACE Code A introduced by the new coalition government in 2011 (Home Office 2011). These changes, which also included a reduction in the amount of information required on the stop and search form, were optional – but most forces immediately stopped recording stop and accounts, in most cases without any form of consultation (Bridges 2015). An important exception was the MPS, which did consult on this change and which continues to record stop and account. An important source of information on the wider set of police practices of which stop and search is just one example was therefore lost almost overnight.

Widening the lens

Despite the frequent prominence of PACE in discussions around stop and search, a range of other legislation in England and Wales gives the police formal, and often sweeping, powers to stop and/or search members of the public. In addition to the Firearms Act 1968 and the Misuse of Drugs Act 1971, general powers to stop and/or search members of the public are also granted to police under the Road Traffic Act 1988 and the Criminal Justice and Public Order Act 1994. There are also a range of more specific powers relating to areas such as customs and excise, environmental protection, sporting events, aviation security and counter-terrorism. It is worth noting that although these are 'non-PACE' powers most are governed by Code A (a notable exception is the Terrorism Act 2000).

These powers to stop and search typically fall into one of two categories. Most rely on the same or similar reasonable suspicion tests as PACE – including those provided by the more esoteric and presumably less-used pieces of legislation, such as the stop/search provision in the Sporting Events (Control of Alcohol etc.) Act 1985. Others, however, are not subject to a reasonable suspicion test, and some of these are among the most high-profile and controversial powers vested in the British police today. Most notably, s.60 of the Criminal Justice and Public Order Act 1994 allows a senior officer (an Inspector, with subsequent checking/confirmation by a Superintendent) to nominate an area of a town or city, on the basis of a reasonable suspicion that violence has or is about to occur, as an area within which stop and search can be carried out *without* the need for reasonable suspicion. Section 44 of the Terrorism Act 2000 contained a similar provision, and as Shiner and Delsol (2015: 38) note, although s.44 stops 'could only be used when specifically authorized by the home secretary, (i)n practice, a series of rolling authorizations were issued, which meant that Section 44 was actively in place across London for the best part of a decade'. Schedule 7 of the Terrorism Act 2000 allows police and immigration and customs officials to stop, search and detain people on entry to or exit of the UK to determine whether they are engaged in terrorist activity: a reasonable suspicion test does not apply here, either.

As a result of the controversy around the 'suspicion-less' powers, legislation and practice has changed in recent years. After a long process of litigation in the Gillan and Quinton case, Section 44 of the Terrorism Act 2000 was struck down by the European Court of Human Rights in 2010, on the basis that such stops constituted interference with the right to a private life and that the power was insufficiently circumscribed (EHRC 2010: 43; see also Bridges 2015). Although not struck down or officially abandoned, the use of s.60 stops subsequently declined from a peak of around 150,000 a year in 2008/2009 to just 1,000 in 2014/2015 (Home Office 2015b). It is important to note that not only are the use of specific powers to stop, question and/or search people often contested, but the level at which they are used is also subject to significant change in the short to medium term.

Traffic stops comprise what is arguably the greatest unknown in terms of the extent of police stop activity. PACE specifically allows for the searching of vehicles as well as people. Yet, police are also empowered under section 163 of the Road Traffic Act 1988 to require people using a motor vehicle or bicycle on the highway to stop when ordered to – failure to then do so is an offence. While s.163 does not list the reasons why police can require someone to stop under such conditions – making this seem an extraordinarily wide-ranging power – it is obvious from the content of the rest of the Act and a moments reflection that police most commonly use this power to deal with dangerous driving and vehicles, and related issues. Section 6, for example, empowers police to 'require a person to cooperate with any one or more preliminary tests administered to the person by that constable or another constable' in order to ascertain whether she or he is under the influence of drink and/or drugs.

Shiner and Delsol (2015: 32) note that while traffic stops under s.163 – which do not require reasonable suspicion or recording by police – are probably becoming less common, not least because the number of police officers has been reduced since 2010, this power is extremely widely used. They cite Moon *et al.* (2011) who, using CSEW data, estimated that there were almost 5.5 million traffic stops in 2010/2011, a figure supported by the analysis presented in Chapter 5 below. It is of course not insignificant that this figure had to be derived via estimates from a population survey, and the lack of recording makes accurate data on these types of stops very hard to find. Compared with stop and search under PACE and associated legislation, traffic stops appear to be lightly regulated, if at all, seem to provoke far less debate and discord that other, ostensibly similar powers, and are not 'counted' in any centralized manner.[1] Yet their sheer number mean they form an important component of the 'background noise' of policing and the quotidian interaction between police and public. Equally, they are unlikely to be exempt from the problems associated with the other powers to stop and/or search described above.

Finally, there is the general power of police to intervene in people's lives and conduct more informal stops. In many ways it is this general power that is the real object of this book. It is diffuse, hard to pin down, largely unregulated and extremely widespread in its application. 'Stop and accounts', a term fixed in 2005 when the requirement to record stop and search was extended to encounters where the police stopped someone and asked them to 'account' for themselves in some way without conducting a search, provide instructive example pointing toward just how widespread 'police stops' are likely to be. Legally speaking, stop and accounts are different to stop and searches, in that the police have no formal power to detain a member of the public to simply ask them want they are doing (and even less to require them to answer). As research in Scotland has shown, however, this distinction is a fine one (Murray 2014), and it moreover seems likely that many people exposed to this type of police activity experience the stop in much the same way they would a stop and search, i.e. an unwanted but nevertheless impossible to refuse intrusion into their lives, backed by the power and authority of an important representative of the state.

The requirement to record stop and account was introduced in the aftermath of the Stephen Lawrence enquiry; in the face, that is, of continued concerns about the disproportionate attention paid by police to members of ethnic and other visible minorities. Data confirm this is a widely used 'power', or perhaps more correctly a very common police practice: in 2008/2009, for example, there were over 2.2 million such encounters recorded (Stopwatch 2011: 7–8). While the requirement to record stop and accounts was as noted dropped during the so-called 'bonfire of red tape' after the 2010 general election some forces have continued recording, notably the MPS, and in 2013/2014 there were around 332,000 stop and accounts in London, compared with around 289,000 stop and searches under s.1 PACE (although these figures are marked reductions from previous years).

If the number of stops under PACE, the Road Traffic Act and other legislation, and stop and accounts are added together, then, the figure is likely to be, even in the most recent years where the use of this type of police power seems to have declined, well in excess of five million. As shown in Chapter 5, it does not seem unreasonable to suggest that around one in 10 of the adult population experience some form of police stop each year, albeit that most are traffic stops rather than the more emblematic street or foot stops. Not only is this is the category of 'police stops' diffuse and wide-ranging, it constitutes an important part of people's experiences of policing.

Use of the power to stop and search

The extent and distribution of police stops are discussed in detail in Chapter 5. As an initial matter, though, it is worth considering what the police recorded data have to say about the use of stop and search specifically. It is these data, after all, that are most widely used in the debates that swirl around this issue. In line with the idea that PACE did not constrain police power but simply provided for regulation (and enumeration) of behaviours that were previously largely unregulated (and not counted), there is much evidence to suggest that the use of stop and search *grew* after PACE, particularly in the 1990s and again from the early 2000s onwards, reaching 1.2 million stops in 2010/2011 (Shiner and Delsol 2015). Despite the need for some caution about the extent of change from earlier periods – it is almost certain that recording practice improved over time and contributed to the apparent growth in overall numbers – this power has become one of the most widely used formal powers granted to the police in England and Wales, with instances almost equal to the number of arrests (of which there were 1.4 million in 2010/2011, for example).

Figure 2.1 plots the use of stop and search over the last decade and a half. It clearly shows the growth in stop and searches under PACE s.1 and other legislation (e.g. the Misuse of Drugs Act) from the early 2000s through to 2010/2011, and then a significant reduction in the latest years. This reduction corresponds with (a) the advent of the coalition government in 2010 and subsequent initiation of 'austerity', with consequences in terms of police budgets that have continued to the time of writing and (b) a significant uptick in the level of political debate surrounding stop and search. This was given impetus by the continued work of pressure groups such as Stopwatch (www.stopwatch.org) and Release (www.release.org) and a confluence of particular events and circumstances, including the death of Mark Duggan and the London riots in 2011, and the presence of a Home Secretary prepared, unlike many of her predecessors, to be openly critical

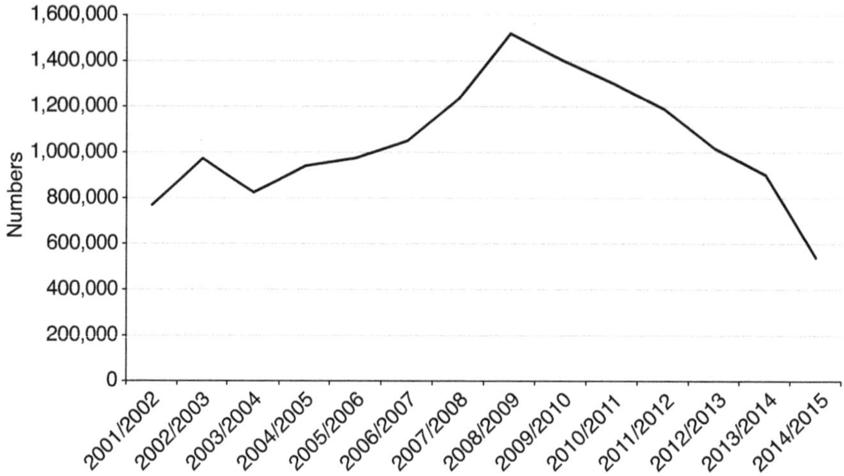

Figure 2.1 Trend in stop and search, 2001/2002 to 2014/2015.

Source: Home Office.

of police in general, and stop and search tactics, in particular. These events and circumstances seem to have created a particular political space and pressure on police that, in all likelihood in combination with reduced budgets and manpower, capped and then reversed the previously seemingly inexorable use of the power.

The correlation between numbers of police and use of stop and search is explored in more depth in Chapter 6; relevant at this stage is simply to note that the use if stop and search by police appears to be influenced not only be internal factors but also by external social and political pressures. Crucially, this is not the first time levels of stop and search have fallen in the way they have since around 2010 – in the aftermath of the report on the Stephen Lawrence inquiry in 1999 there was a similar reduction in the use of the power that is commonly ascribed to the scrutiny and pressure police felt themselves to be under at the time (Shiner and Delsol 2015). Indeed, it is the latter stages of this dip that are represented on the left hand side of Figure 2.1.

Ethnic disproportionality

The final issue to be raised in any overview of stop and search in England and Wales is, inevitably, that the use of stop and search has consistently been found to be ethnically disproportionate. People from ethnic minority groups, particularly black groups, have been shown to be much likely to be stopped and searched than their white majority group counterparts. Evidence for ethnic disproportionality in the application of this type of policing – albeit often little more than anecdotal – pre-dates PACE. Bowling and Phillips, for example (2002:

128–129), note a study of 34 African/Caribbean men conducted by All Faiths for One Race (1978) – over one-third reported at least one incident of police harassment or brutality, while more than half reported having a friend with such experiences. The extent to which police, throughout the 1970s, 1980s and into the 1990s targeted ethnic minority and particularly black individuals and communities is of course well known (Bowling and Phillips 2002: 129), and over this period police routinely focused particular types of attention on such people and places, leading to the now famous charge that they were 'over-policed and under-protected' (Macpherson 1999).

Striking though is the evidence that ethnic disproportionality in stop and search, specifically, *increased* from the turn of the Millennium up to 2009/2010 (see Figure 2.2), and while it has since fallen in line with the general reduction in the use of stop and search it has not been eliminated. The potential reasons behind this disproportionality are the subject of Chapters 4 and 5 that follow, but at the threshold Figure 2.2 illustrates neatly why stop and search continues to be such a contentious issue. Despite half a century's worth of efforts – starting with the Race Relations Act 1965 – aimed at making policing more equitable and improving relations between criminal justice agencies and Britain's minority communities, black people were in 2014/2015 still over four times more likely to be stopped and searched than white people.

It is also worth noting that the more sweeping s.60 and s.44 powers have tended to be even more ethnically disproportionate in their application than stops

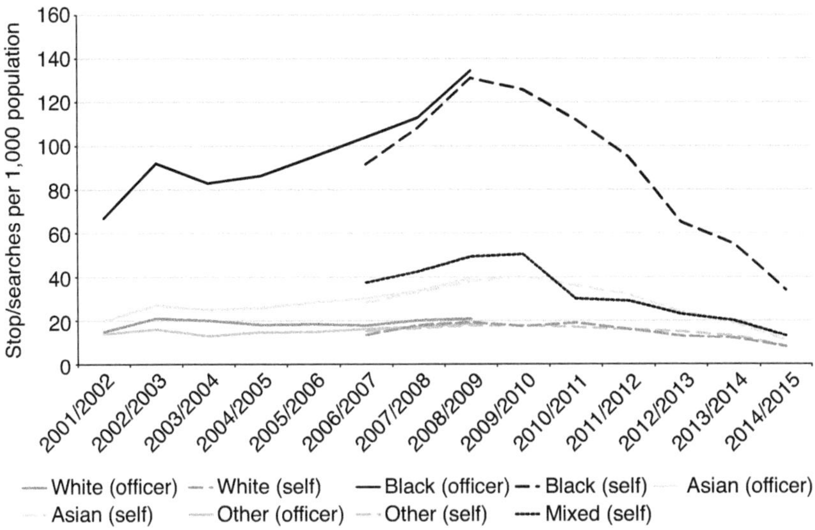

Figure 2.2 The level of ethnic disproportionality changes over time.

Source: Home Office.

Notes

'Officer' = officer-assessed ethnicity; 'self' = self-assessed ethnicity.

under PACE s.1, with Asian people the most badly affected (Quinlan and Derfoufi 2015). In 2010/2011, for example, overall 10 per cent of those stopped under PACE and associated legislation were from an Asian ethnic group, compared with 20 per cent of those stopped under s.60 (MoJ 2013); around 7.5 per cent of the population as a whole were from an Asian ethnic group. Similarly, in 2012/2013 some 22 per cent of those stopped under Schedule 7 were from an Asian ethnic group (Bridges 2015: 24), while fully 17 per cent were categorized as coming from an 'other' ethnic group, compared with 1 per cent of the general population. It seems highly likely many of this latter group were of Arab ethnicity or appearance.

The effectiveness of stop and search

Whether framed in terms of PACE and other specific pieces of legislation, or in terms of the broader and in a sense deeper power of police to intervene into people's lives, police stops constitute an important aspect of many officers' practice. This naturally raises the immediate question of how useful is this power. What is its effect in terms of, for example, detecting or deterring crime? How effective is stop and search, in particular, as a tool of policing? It continues to be something of a puzzle that these questions are only rarely explored, and very little is known about how effective stop/search is as a way of 'doing' policing (Bradford 2015; Delsol 2015). In this section I will concentrate primarily on stop and search, for the simple reason that this is where what research exists has been concentrated.

While there has been significant research into the existence, extent and implications of disproportionality (Ariza 2014; Borooah 2011; Bowling and Phillips 2007; Delsol and Shiner 2006; Miller 2010; MVA and Miller 2000; Waddington *et al.* 2004), there have until very recently been many fewer investigations into its effectiveness. Moreover, while disproportionality is a well-known and well-understood, albeit disputed, concept, it is much less clear what effectiveness *means* in the context of stop and search (see Miller *et al.* 2000). At the simplest level, stop and search may be effective when it *deters* crime (as envisaged by s.60 of the Criminal Justice and Public Order Act 1994 and s.44 of the Terrorism Act 2000) and/or when it *detects* crime (as envisaged in PACE, s.1 of which positions stop and search as a power for detecting crime). That is, it might be claimed that stop and search is effective when it is linked to both the absence of crime, because it has a deterrent effect, and conversely when it is linked to the presence of crime, because it aids in the detection and subsequent prosecution of offences, and thus their entry into the recorded crime statistics. The importance of this apparent contradiction should not be overlooked, not least because it provides a rhetorical device for proponents of stop and search to argue that it is successful when it is associated with and is apparently a contributory factor to either increases *or* decreases in levels of (recorded) crime.

Debate in this area has long been held back by a lack of research that might allow firm conclusions to be drawn on whether stop and search and related police tactics do, or not, produce desired outcomes. Careful experimental or longitudinal studies conducted at the local level might, for example, untangle the conundrum outlined above, one possible outcome, of course, being that stop and search 'produces' crimes – or rather detections – in the short term, but deters them in the long run. Few such studies are available, though, and there is as yet no conclusive evidence one way or the other. There have however been a number of pieces of research that offer suggestive, albeit inconclusive, findings. These have tended to cover two broad, interrelated areas: the effect of stop and search on levels of crime (and the potential for unintended consequences); and the extent to which police practice is associated with, or driven by, intelligence gathering and use.

Stop/search and arrests

On the basis of existing studies a number of loosely defined but still useful claims about the general effectiveness of stop and search can be made. First, stop and search makes a significant contribution to the numbers of arrests made by police (Fitzgerald 1999; Miller *et al.* 2000). Data from *Police Powers and Procedures England and Wales 2010 to 2011* (Home Office 2012), for example, show that 113,676 arrests were made as a result of a Section 1 PACE searches in 2010/2011, out of a total of 1,360,451 arrests for notifiable offences over the same period. By 2014/2015, the same publication (Home Office 2015b: 5) revealed that police had arrested 950,000 that financial year, of which 8 per cent (75,000) resulted from a stop and search.

However there seem to have been no studies which have examined the extent to which these are 'extra' arrests, i.e. arrests that would not be made if the police did not have the power to stop and search (or used it less), or whether some, at least, are substitutes for arrests that would have been made as a result of some other form of police activity. Moreover, Home Office data suggest the proportion of stop/searches resulting in an arrest is low and fell from the 1980s until recently. In 1986 some 17 per cent of stop and searches resulted in an arrest; by 2014/2015 this figure stood at 14 per cent (Home Office 2015b: 15), which was a significant improvement on the 9 per cent seen in 2009/2010 (see Delsol 2015: 87). It should be noted that specific forces often manage to generate significantly higher arrest rates – in 2012/2013 City of London Police had an arrest rate of 20 per cent, while in 2015 the MPS achieved a rate of 19 per cent across London as a whole (Delsol 2015: 88; MOPAC 2015). The corollary, however, is that some forces produce much *lower* arrest rates – the lowest arrest rate in 2014/2015, for example, was in Humberside, at just 1 per cent (Home Office 2015b: 23).

Arrests are a problematic measure of success, though. Not all arrests result in a charge, let alone a conviction, and therefore they cannot be used as a direct measure of success in detecting crime. There are other issues. On the one hand, police have a number of other disposals available to them, such as fixed penalty notices (FPNs), penalty notices for disorder (PNDs) and cannabis warnings, which may indicate the stop was a success. These are not currently recorded a fully systematic basis, but there are indications that they are used quite extensively. In September 2015, for example, the MPS reported that 15 per cent of stop and searches resulted in 'other action' (i.e. not an arrest but some other disposal); a year previously, in September 2014, this figure was 37 per cent (MOPAC 2015). The absence of an arrest does not necessarily indicate nothing was found, and it is likely that some part of the country at least the actual 'hit' rate is substantially higher than the arrest rate alone would indicate (HMIC 2013).

On the other hand, arrests may be created by the stop itself, for example if the person stopped becomes angry and verbally or physical abusive to the officer(s) involved: it is hard to see how an arrest in such circumstances is a positive outcome. The extent to which this is a significant problem is unclear, however, and most arrests resulting from stop and searches relate to stolen property, drugs, offensive weapons and going equipped (Home Office 2015b).

Despite these shortcomings arrest data are often one the few outcome measures available, and in the absence of alternatives offer at least some indication of success. For example, to be successful in *detecting* crime it seems fairly certain that stop/searches should, taken as a whole, produce significant numbers of arrests, and the fact that arrest rates rarely if ever exceed 20 per cent continues to be a concern, despite the use of other disposals.

Marginal utility

Despite the number of arrests stop and search undoubtedly produces evidence of the marginal utility of the power is hard to find. It remains unclear as to whether increasing the use of stop and search in a particular time and places has a negative effect on crime. What research there has been on the specific relationship between stop and search/frisk and crime has tended to use time series data and has produced very mixed results. For example Weisburd *et al.* (2015) used daily and weekly data on crime incident reports and stop-question-frisk (SQF) at the 'street segment' level (a very small unit of geographic aggregation) in New York. The authors concluded that when focused on crime hotspots SQF had a significant but modest negative effect on crime (ibid.: 46). By contrast Rosenfeld and Fornango (2014) used yearly precinct-level data from the same city and found few if any effects of stop/frisk activity on robbery and burglary. This appears if nothing else to be an example of the Modifiable Unit Areal Problem (MAUP – Openshaw and Taylor 1979), a well-known phenomenon whereby the correlation between two variables can vary simply as a function of the level of geographic aggregation of the data, thus obscuring the nature of the 'real' association between them.

A key challenge faced by such research is the problem of endogeneity. While these studies used stop/frisk rates to predict crime rates, it could equally be, and in fact very likely is, that crime rates predict stop/frisk (all else equal police are likely to conduct more stops in areas where there is more crime). As in the above cases this issue can be partially solved at the level of analysis, for example by using regression models with lagged effects, where crime rates at time t are regressed on stop rates at t–1, t–2 and so on.

A recent Home Office study used a slightly different approach (McCandless *et al.* 2016). Based around the implementation of 'Operation BLUNT 2' the study took advantage of what was essentially a natural experiment. It thus constitutes one of the very small number of such studies that are in existence. During the initiative London boroughs were split into three groups, and those with the highest levels of knife crime ('Tier 1' boroughs) were targeted for extensive use of weapons searches. The two other groups of boroughs (Tier 2 and Tier 3) also experienced an increase in weapons searches, but to a lesser degree. The authors were then able to use difference-in-difference regression analysis to examine whether the increase in stop and search in the Tier 1 areas had an effect on nine types of crime, including assault using sharp instruments, robbery and drug offences. Their conclusion was that there was 'no statistically significant crime-reducing effect from the large increase in weapons searches during the course of Operation Blunt 2' (ibid.: 2).

Another problem is perhaps thornier – the proposed mechanism linking stops with crime. This is most commonly envisaged as some combination of general and specific deterrence. People who have been stopped in the past and/or who are intending to commit a crime may be deterred, particularly when they know police activity in an area is high. More generally those who are aware of this activity might also be deterred from illegal acts. In both cases, though, and particularly perhaps in the latter it is unclear (a) how long police activity has to be 'higher' for anyone to notice and therefore change their behaviour; (b) whether higher levels of activity need to be maintained in order to continue to have an effect; and (c) if police stop activity is reduced (falls back to normal) after an increase, how long any deterrent effect on behaviour is likely to last. This uncertainty means it is hard to specify which lagged effects (e.g. one week, one month, six months) are appropriate for analysis, and, moreover, casts a general sense of doubt over research findings that show, for example, an effect of stops at t–2 on crime at time t, but no effect of stops at t–1 or t–3. Why should one lag be significant but not the others?

Notably, research on the deterrent threat of stop/search has tended to conclude that if the power does have such an effect it is probably weak (Miller *et al.* 2000; Apel 2016). An evaluation of the Tackling Knives and Serious Youth Violence Action Programme (TKAP), which included police forces that made most use of Section 60 searches, demonstrated no measurable impact on levels of knife crime. The second phase of TKAP was evaluated using a quasi-experimental methodology (Ward *et al.*, 2011), which found that while there were reductions in the number of victims and principal suspects in the target age group across England and Wales, these reductions were not proportionately greater in areas participating in the TKAP initiative (that is, those that were heavy users of Section 60). Similarly, hospital admissions for assault involving the target age group fell – but these reductions were only evident in the *non*-TKAP areas. The report authors (ibid.: 24) concluded that it was 'impossible to directly attribute reductions in the TKAP areas to Phase II activities' (i.e. stop and search).

Other research has suggested that not only might stop and search (and cognate practices) be unsuccessful in achieving desired ends, but it may also be actively counterproductive. For example, research on the use of SQF to police drug users in the United States suggests that many users, rather than being deterred by the threat of being stopped, merely alter their behaviour to reduce their chances of coming to the attention of the police (Ream *et al.* 2010). Furthermore, order maintenance policing that uses minor drug offences as a pretext for searches intended to uncover more serious crimes (e.g. guns) appear to be largely unsuccessful (Geller and Fagan 2010). Finally, when drugs and drug paraphernalia are seized during searches, drug users may often simply go and obtain more (Werb *et al.* 2008), with implications in terms of increased offending and also health risks (see Kerr *et al.* 2005). Taken together, this research suggests that, at least in relation to drug offences, stop and search may be ineffective in both a proximate and more general sense, as well as actually promoting harmful behaviour among some of the groups targeted. This seems a particularly important point, given that, quite consistently, around 50 per cent of all stop and searches in England and Wales have drugs as the ground for suspicion (Release 2013).

In sum it is unclear whether, as a general proposition, a proportional increase in the use of stop and search will lead to a proportional increase in the total number of arrests made, crime solved, offenders deterred (or vice versa), and so on. Not only are experimental studies of these questions almost non-existent, but other research designs, such as times series analysis, are beset with problems and there have not be enough of them for any firm conclusions to be drawn.

As part of a package

However, some experimental studies, which have not focused specifically on stop and search (or stop and frisk) but which nevertheless contain reference to this type of activity, suggest that as part of a broader set of directed police activities, stop and search may have a significant impact on crime, particularly, perhaps, violent crime in 'hot-spot' areas (Braga *et al.* 1999, 2012; Ratcliffe *et al.* 2011). When correctly targeted and considered as part of the tool-kit of order maintenance or Problem Oriented Policing (POP), stop and search can make a contribution to the success of such strategies. Existing studies do not however indicate the extent of this contribution, nor have they often considered the counterfactual (for example, what would have happened if hotspot approaches were implemented that excluded some or all stop and search activity). Some recent experimental studies have evaluated whether, for example, it might be increased foot patrol, POP or 'offender-focused' policing that has the most or best effects when focused on crime hotspot areas (Groff *et al.* 2014; see also Taylor *et al.* 2011), but even here stop and search/frisk tactics appear likely to feature in more than one condition, meaning the contribution of this particular tactic to any overall reduction in crime remains unclear.

Total utility

Finally, there is some evidence, admittedly rather weak, to suggest that if police suspended stop and search altogether crime might increase as a result (Boydston 1975). There may be an initial deterrence effect created by the mere existence of the power to stop and search, the removal of which would encourage crime. There is an interesting correspondence here between stop and search and the broader activity of policing as this is carried out by uniformed, professional, officers. It is difficult to ascertain whether stop and search has any concrete effect on marginal rates of offending or deterrence at the aggregate level; yet, concentrated 'applications' of stop and search may produce useful results in specific areas, particularly those most prone to crime (Ratcliffe *et al.* 2011) and, conversely, a complete cessation of stop and search activity may result in an increase in crime. Similarly, it is often remarked that it is hard to find a link between the mere presence of police in an area, or the number of officers, and overall levels of crime (Sherman and Eck 2002), although there is *some* evidence of a link between numbers of police officers and crime rates (Bradford 2011). There is much more evidence, however, that concentrated 'applications' of policing, whether under Hot Spot, POP or Pulling Levers paradigms, can have a positive effect on crime rates, in the short to medium term at least (Telep and Weisburd 2012); and, finally, police strikes and other 'removals' of police from specific areas have been linked with increases in crime (Sherman and Eck 2002). Stop and search, much like the presence or number of police, may have an initial deterrence effect; but subsequent marginal deterrence may rely on specific targeting and be unlikely to result from simply increasing the number of stops in a general sense (McCandless *et al.* 2016).

Intelligence led stop and search?

The discussion thus far has focused on the returns stop/searches might bring in terms of immediate arrests and/or deterrence. Yet the collection of intelligence is often cited as a key outcome of stop and search – albeit one that in most cases is not explicitly sanctioned by the legislation in question. Stops may be an important tool in gathering intelligence that is put to use in some other way; although, as this is not the stated purpose for stop and search, it can at best be seen as 'added value'. Equally, intelligence is frequently cited as an important driver of stop and search: the relationship between the two is a bi-directional process. On this account because searches under PACE and the Misuse of Drugs Act – by far the most common form of the power – require reasonable suspicion (i.e. they cannot be random) stop and search activity, perhaps particularly in relation to the extent it is concentrated in particular areas, should be based to at least some extent on intelligence. There should be some basis for deciding on where and whom to stop, that is, and it seems reasonable to suggest that previously gathered intelligence should play a role in this process.

However while police officers may feel that they target stop and search activity (Chainey and Macdonald 2012; Fitzgerald 1999) and utilize intelligence in their practice, there is only weak evidence that the distribution of stop and search matches the distribution of crime, in as much as this is known to police (Chainey and Macdonald 2012). Indeed, Chainey and Macdonald conclude that the geographical clustering of stop and search they identified in their study could not be explained by recourse to underlying levels of crime, nor could they identify a link between developments in crime rates and change in levels of stop and search over time. They also found that officers' ability to act on intelligence was impeded by a perceived prioritization by managers of the quantity of stops over quality. Miller *et al.* (2000), by contrast, note that stop and search can, at least in some circumstances, contribute to intelligence gathering

More broadly, there is little evidence relating to how officers decide on whom to stop and search, although what research there is suggests that decisions are made more on the basis of generalizations and stereotypes than objective suspicion of the type that might be formed in response to previously gathered intelligence (Quinton 2011). There is however some evidence relating to the idea that if intelligence could be better used this might make stop and search more effective. Miller *et al.* (2000) suggest that searches based on stronger grounds for suspicion, and on intelligence, are more likely to be successful (i.e. result in an arrest). They also found that searches appeared to be less effective the more frequently they were conducted (at the force level, they found a negative correlation between the number of searches and the hit-rate). Similarly, research into POP and similar police strategies, as noted, suggests that stop and search can be effective when it is used in a targeted fashion (Braga *et al.* 1999; Ratcliffe *et al.* 2011).

Police stops and social order

To summarize the above, police stops, defined as contacts between police and public occurring in public or quasi-public space, instigated by police, wherein the officer(s) concerned stop people going about their business and direct, question and/or search them, are one of the most commonly used powers of police in England and Wales. The extent of the use of stop and search and the wider power to 'stop' raises some important questions, particularly in light of the uncertain evidence concerning its effectiveness. Why do police conduct so many stops each year? Towards what end or ends is this power directed? Which social groups or types of person are most likely to be affected – and why? In the remainder of this chapter I sketch out a framework for answering these questions these questions, which are then covered in more depth as the book progresses.

Drawing on ideas well established in the police studies literature (Bayley 1994; Bittner 1990; Brodeur 2010; Ericson 1982; Manning 1978), I start from the premise that the police are involved in the production and reproduction of social order – in enforcing 'various types of rules and customs that promote a defined order in society' Brodeur (2010: 130). Three axes of interest provide for a conceptual map for thinking about the aims of policing and what contribution police stops might make to the police function(s). The first concerns the nature of social order, or more precisely, what is meant by social order when we are talking about policing, and how we envisage the role of the police in generating and maintaining this order. The second axis concerns the actual contribution police make to this order – how important, and successful, they are as agents of social control. The third and in some senses subsidiary axis concerns the extent to which police are engaged in 'fighting crime' compared with a different, more diffuse range of activities and responsibilities.

A preliminary issue is definition of the terms 'police' and 'policing'. It is common now to delineate these terms widely, to include not just the organizations and activity of 'traditional' uniformed state police but also those of other state actors, private police and other security providers (Brodeur 2010). At the extreme, all those engaged in social control activities – attempts to assure the norm-conforming behaviour of others (Chriss 2013) – can be said to be 'doing' policing. Furthermore, social control has itself tended to be 'defined up' to include 'everything that contributes to the reproduction of social order' (Reiner 2010: 4). This general approach has significant appeal, since it recognizes that anyone (and/or everyone) may, at some point in time, be engaged in 'policing' activity: by, for example, enforcing normative behaviour on children, resolving disputes between friends, neighbours or colleagues, or summoning the 'real' police to deal with an issue of crime or disorder. As this last example suggests there are moreover forms of social control that cross the boundaries of informal and formal mechanisms (Hunter 1995), and upon witnessing behaviours they consider wrong or inappropriate people will often make decisions to act by intervening themselves or invoking formal agents of social control. Often these agents will be the uniformed state police (Carr 2003), but others, such as local councils and other service providers, may also be invoked. It is hard not to label such acts as 'policing', since they are so definitively aimed at the maintenance and reproduction of particular forms of social order.

For current purposes, however, narrower definitions of social control and policing (or at least police) are perhaps more useful. Reiner (2010) notes Cohen's (1985) critique of the tendency to overdraw the boundaries of social control processes, risking, in both their views, its transmutation into a 'Mickey Mouse' concept with little real meaning or content. While this argument may be over-stated, the core insight is useful, since it positions social control as a particular set of activities set apart from other forms of social interaction (notwithstanding that all might contribute to social order). While almost any human behaviour might serve to generate and reproduce social order, social control is envisaged as the effort to prevent or address *threats* to this order and thus as a more limited set of behaviours. Social control can thus be considered as activity that does not stem merely or most importantly from the aggregate of social interaction but rather as involving the presence and activity of specialist organizations and collaborative attempts to address perceived or actual threats. According to Cohen, social control should be envisaged as 'the organized ways in which society responds to behavior and people it regards as deviant, problematic, worrying, threatening, troublesome or undesirable' (1985: 1–2; quoted in Reiner

2010: 4). It is this definition that guides the discussion below, which rests on the idea that police activity is an important component of social control processes.

Similarly, while it is recognized that many organizations are engaged in policing, the term police will be used in relation only the 'modern' police described by Reiner, a 'state agency with the omnibus mandate of order maintenance' that is engaged in 'regular uniform patrol of public space coupled with *post hoc* investigation of reported or discovered crime or disorder' (2010: 5–6). It is not coincidental that this definition of 'police' corresponds closely with lay conceptions of what or who police are. As discussed in Chapters 7 and 8 the way people react to being stopped by police – or indeed to any other interaction with officers – is heavily influenced by the association of 'the police' with the state, and the extent to which police officers, unlike for example private security guards, represent and indeed embody notions of nation, state and community.

What is social order?

Definitions suitably fixed, we can move on to discuss the first axis of interest – the meaning of 'social order' and the place of police within it. There are two dominant conceptualizations here. On the one hand, social order can be seen as something quite specific: as relating to structures of power and domination within a given society. When talking of social order, that is, a particular *form* or *type* of order is envisaged, most often one that rests on hierarchies of gender, race, ethnicity, class and/or wealth. This order functions to protect the interests of those with social, economic, political and other forms of capital, and is structured to ensure that those toward the bottom of such hierarchies do not pose too great a threat to those toward the top. The police serve as defenders of this order, and their function is first and foremost to maintain the existing relational structures of society.

Naturally there are many other ways of envisaging what a specific social order might look like, even among those subject in an objective sense to the same order. The version just outlined is far from the only one imaginable. Yet, when the discussion turns to the contribution of police to social order, it often revolves around 'class repression' (Marenin 1982) or the role of the police in 'keeping people in their place' (Waddington 1999), and such conceptualizations implicitly or explicitly rely on a vision of social order that is hierarchical and premised on an unequal distribution of power, wealth and influence.

On the other hand, social order can be seen as something much more general – as merely a state distinct from disorder, as the existence of stability in a given social context or, more concretely, as a state of affairs dependent on a set of social structures and processes that serve to regularize human behaviour and which are based on the shared norms and values of those living in a particular social context. Here, the police are 'professional order maintainers', specialists in a job that all members of a society engage in to some extent. Police activity enables other actors to go about their lives, for example by providing protection from crime and anti-social behaviour or, more broadly, creating the space for various forms of civil society to flourish. While some might find this understanding of social order and the role of police naïve, it is important to note that it likely underpins many lay understandings of the police, which position them as defenders of the general order and protectors of the citizenry (cf. Skogan 1996). Yet it also has significant explanatory power – police do provide protection from crime and disorder, both in a general sense and in specific times and places, and this protection does enable people to engage in economic, social and political activity.

These are of course ideal types. In reality police in England and Wales are engaged in maintaining existing social hierarchies *and* reproducing a general form of order upon which civil society is constructed – in parking tickets *and* class repression, as Marenin (1982) famously put it. These two different aspects of policing are, moreover, always and inevitably in tension, and one of the most interesting aspects of the theory and empirical study of policing is exploring how this tension plays out in police practice. The way political protest is policed provides just one example: are the police present at marches and demonstrations to enable peaceable political discourse and debate, and thus to serve as a prop to a general form of order upon which civil society can be built via (agonistic) political processes? Are police there to protect property owners from the depredations of the disenfranchised, and the machinery of the state from those who would wish to bypass or uproot it? Or are they, in fact, there to fulfil both these roles, with their exact function in any context modulating and shifting in response to the situations they confront? The ways in which public order tactics switch from one pole to another, over the short, medium and long term serves as an illustration of just how difficult police organizations can find it to reconcile the tension implicit in this process.

Be that as it may, the history of public order policing suggests, as do many other examples, that it is preservation of the specific, already existing, social order that it is the over-riding aim of police. As Brodeur (2010: 130) notes in his definition of 'policing agents' (by which he means a wider range of actors than the state or public police that are the main interest here), they are concerned with enforcing 'a *defined order* in society' (emphasis added). The order police are protecting, that is, already exists, and if that order is based on various forms of social hierarchy then the role of the police is in some definitional sense to maintain these hierarchies. Moreover, since what constitutes order is already 'defined', it is positioned as exogenous to the practice of policing rather than immanent within it. On this account the police operate in a space within which order has already been defined (which is not to claim that policing is not also generative of social inequalities). And, crucially, they do so at the behest of the political system that governs that space. In the final analysis police are a component of the 'political machinery' (Manning 1978: 112) that serves to protect the established order, rather than acting simply to ensure a general absence of disorder.

The contribution of police to social order

The second axis that can serve to orient understanding of the police function concerns the contribution of policing to social order. How successful and important are the social control activities of police? There are, again, two distinct conceptualizations here, which can be envisioned as forming a continuum anchored by two ideal types.

On one account *police are integral to the reproduction of social order*. In relation to specific forms of order, police are the foot soldiers of the elite, heavily involved in the reproduction of existing power relations and a vital crutch to the system. Police activity serves systematically to repress and exclude those at the bottom of the social hierarchy, and absent such activity the possibility for reforming or over-throwing it would be very much greater. This account is of course useful in understanding policing in some autocracies and dictatorships – but there is also much to suggest that these functions and outcomes can also be ascribed to police in liberal democracies, as the policing of protests again demonstrates.

Turning to the general notion of social order, police are positioned here as the effective enablers of social commerce (a notion that harks back to pre-nineteenth century conceptions of police) and a vital mediator between the state and citizens (Jacobs 2016). Police activity serves to reproduce widely supported norms of behaviour, and, in the most positive understandings, ethical values. This account forms the bedrock of normative liberal theories of police, and may have some explanatory power when considering the way in which liberal democracies are actually policed at the present point in time. The crucial idea here is that police not only create and defend *conditions for the creation* of specific forms of order, rather than creating and defending specific order directly, but also that they are necessary for, and efficacious in relation to, this effort. Social control activity conducted and coordinated by police provides a base upon which the superstructure of specific orders can be constructed.

According to the second understanding of the contribution of police to social order, however, *police activity is only tangentially connected with the reproduction of order*, and indeed can be seen as epiphenomenal to it. The argument here is, essentially, that police are not that important. In the case of specific forms of order other forms and processes of domination – such as political ideologies – ensure the reproduction of existing power relations. While police may indeed be repressive they are not an essential ‘prop’ to the system. This understanding of policing may be applicable when considering the policing of highly unequal developing countries with underfunded, often corrupt, police organizations (another claim might therefore be that corrupt, ineffective political systems produce bad police, rather than the other way round).

Equally, it is perfectly plausible to suggest that general social order is maintained with little – perhaps very little – input from police. Here, factors such as trust between citizens, and between citizens and state, are far more important than the activity of the police, who exist primarily as a mechanism for dealing with situations that fall through the cracks of other larger, more important and more efficacious systems of ordering and control (see Reiner 2007). One might characterize this is a classic social democratic view of police, which would envisage, for example, advanced welfare systems to be far more important enablers of normatively desirable forms of human interaction than police could ever be. And of course, from a historical perspective the vast majority of human societies have maintained some form of general social order in the absence of anything that remotely looks like 'police' as we currently understand the term – although all have had systems of 'policing'.

As before, it is important to underline that these are ideal types, and that in reality the contribution of the police to social order (whether specific or general) falls somewhere along the continuum just outlined rather than at one pole or another. My own position leans toward the idea that the social control activity engaged in by police is only one factor, and in all likelihood not the most important one, contributing to the reproduction of social order. There are so many other variables involved, at multiple political, social, cultural and economic levels, that the argument police are the 'thin blue line' between order and chaos, to provide just one example of the types of claims that, not least, police make about themselves, cannot stand up to sustained scrutiny. That said, it is undoubtedly true that police activity does provide effective social control at some times and in some places, whether this be through crime reduction at 'hotspot' locations or through the suppression, and indeed repression, of political dissent.

Policing and crime

The third axis concerns the relationship between police and, specifically, crime, and the extent to which the social control activity of police can be conceived as primarily concerned with dealing with crime and offending. This axis can again be envisaged as a continuum anchored by two ideal types. At one end lies the notion that police are primarily and most importantly crime fighters, and spend – or should spend – most of their time in this function. This is the image of police held by many politicians, the press, and arguably large sections of the public and the police themselves, and this view of policing tends to correlate or overlap with the idea that police are effective defenders of the general social order – maintaining a social space is that is relatively free from crime and the fear of crime is the key contribution police make to society, and this freedom provides the basis upon which specific forms of order can be constructed.

Yet, the notion that police are primarily crime fighters does not stand up to empirical scrutiny. As Brodeur (2010: chapter 5) has demonstrated, research consistently finds that public police spend less than half their time dealing with directly crime-related issues – with many studies converging on a figure of around one-third. Other police activities that often seem at least as important as dealing with crime, at least in terms of time commitment, include answering calls for service, order maintenance and problem-solving activities not directly related to crime. An important proviso here is of course that while an activity such as order maintenance might not be directly related to crime there are likely to be many important indirect links and patterns of association. Overall, though, it is clear that despite continued suggestions to the contrary by politicians and others the police do much more than simply 'fight crime'.

At the other end of the continuum lies the idea that police are *primarily* engaged in 'order maintenance activity' of a very broad and varied nature. Here, police are 'peace-keepers, not thief takers' (cf. Bittner 1990), and an over-emphasis on crime fighting in much social and political discourse serves to obscure the true role of the police. There is more evidence to support this idea, again as Brodeur (2010) shows – the police do spend much time dealing with non-criminal disputes, accidents, missing persons and so on – although he rightly cautions against exaggerating any claims that police are the 'secret social service' (Punch 1979) and an omnibus social care/response provider, and notes that in addition to the tasks already outlined they spend a lot of time on traffic duty, guardianship functions (and paperwork) that cannot be neatly fitted into a crime/order maintenance dichotomy.

Broadly speaking, though, it seems almost trivially true that (a) police engage a much wider range of activities than simply addressing and preventing crime, and (b) the aim of these activities can be corralled under the heading order maintenance and conceived of as the attempt to reproduce normative social order in a wide-ranging sense. While they do 'fight crime' in some important ways police also engage in a set of activities that are concerned with normative social order and restoring 'normality'. Police deal with threats to the status quo, disruptive events or individuals that threaten established social norms in criminal *or* non-criminal ways.

The function of police and the role of police stops

Recall that the discussion above was informed by a definition of police that referred to 'a state agency with the omnibus mandate of order maintenance' (Reiner 2010). To summarize the argument, the police can best be seen as a specialist social control institution engaged, in the final analysis, in protecting the established (i.e. specific) social order by means much wider than simply 'fighting crime'. While the extent of the contribution police make towards this end is unclear, there is no doubt that police organizations do play some role in the reproduction of 'order' conceptualized in such terms. Without police, crime would be higher and security more tenuous; and the established order would be less well protected and more subject to challenge – which is one reason why it is almost impossible to imagine a modern state without a police service.

However while is plain that police work to preserve a particular social and indeed *political* order – established in England and Wales, one might argue, by the three intertwined institutions of 'state', 'liberal democracy' and 'free market capitalism' – this does not exhaust the content or meaning of order in this or any other context. Social order also rests on a particular set of hierarchies imbricated within these institutions, which implicates, in turn, notions of class, race and gender, on the one hand, and processes of inclusion and exclusion, on the other. Stated thus, 'reproducing order' becomes not just the task of keeping established subaltern groups in their place – a role filled by the criminal justice system for writers as diverse as Alexander (2012), Gilroy (1987) and Wacquant (2008) – but also, as these and other authors would stress, of creating or at least demarcating these groups and of reproducing the broader inequalities upon which free market capitalism depends. While it would be wrong to claim that crime and crime-related issues do not take up a significant proportion of police time, it cannot be ignored that police do many other things as well. And the claim I want to explore in the chapters that follow is that police attention is concentrated disproportionately not only upon particular ethnic minority groups, but also upon the working class (and particularly young working-class men) and others who for one reason or another are considered marginal, different or surplus to requirements.

Iris Marion Young (2011: 53) defines 'marginals' as 'people the system of labor cannot or will not use', and characterizes marginalization as 'perhaps the most dangerous form of oppression'. Seen in these terms marginality is related to (although not synonymous with) social exclusion, when the latter is defined as a set of processes that result in groups and individuals being excluded 'from participation in ordinary social activities' (Seddon 2006: 682; Levitas 2000). It is these groups and individuals who are the particular object of policing. They are, no doubt, oppressed in Young's sense. They are also thought to be in need of disciplining and control (Bradford and Loader 2016) – an interesting distinction, since it points to the fact that policing aims not only to 'keep people in their place' (control them) but also to influence the way they think about their place and direct them toward more 'beneficial' behaviours (discipline them). As described above, seen over the *longue durée*, police activity aimed at marginal population groups was as often intended to bring them back into the fold of productive labour as it was meant to demonstrate that they had strayed from their proper position in society (Neocleous 2000).

Street and traffic stops are one way, and I think one important way, in which this discipline and control is exerted and made real – visible, tangible and an aspect of lived experience – in the lives of those subject to the police. This is the message, precisely, that becomes clear once one locates police stops in their contemporary and historical context, a point I will expand upon in Chapters 4 and 5. Such activity has something to do with crime, but it also has other functions; it is directed often at marginal individuals, groups and communities. This form of police activity therefore reveals much about which groups in society are seen as threats to the established order and who are, therefore, the special objects of police attention.

Note

1 This looks set to change. The Home Secretary announced in March 2016 that in the future police would be required to record stops made under the Road Traffic Act, although no time scale was provided in the announcement (see Chapter 9).

References

Alexander, M. (2012). *The New Jim Crow. Mass Incarceration in the Age of Colorblindness*. New York: The New Press.

Apel, R. (2016). On the deterrent effect of stop, question and frisk. *Criminology and Public Policy* 15(1): 57–66.

Ariza, J.J.M. (2014). Police-initiated contacts: young people, ethnicity, and the 'usual suspects'. *Policing and Society* 24(2): 208–223.

Bayley, D. (1994). *Police for the Future*. New York, NY: Oxford University Press. Bayley.

Bittner, E. (1990). *Aspects of Police Work*. Boston, MA: Boston University Press.

Borooah, V.K. (2011). Racial disparity in police stop and searches in England and Wales. *Journal of Quantitative Criminology*, 27(4), 453–473.

Bowling, B. and Phillips, C. (2002). *Racism, Crime and Justice*. Harlow: Pearson Education.

Bowling, B. and Phillips, C. (2007). Disproportionate and discriminatory: Reviewing the evidence on police stop and search. *The Modern Law Review* 70(6): 936–961.

Boydston, J. (1975). *San Diego Field Interrogation: Final Report*. Washington: Police Foundation.

Bradford, B. (2011). *Police Numbers and Crime: A Rapid Evidence Review*. London: HMIC.

Bradford, B. (2015). Assessing the impact of stop and search powers on individuals and communities, in Delsol, R. and Shiner, M. (eds) *Stop and Search*. Basingstoke: Palgrave Macmillan.

Bradford, B. and Loader, I. (2016). Police, crime and order: The case of stop and search, in Bradford, B., Jauregui, B., Loader, I. and Steinberg, J. (eds) *The SAGE Handbook of Global Policing*. London: SAGE.

Braga, A.A., Papachristos, A. and Hureau, D. (2012). *The Effect of Hot Spots Policing Efforts on Crime*. Oslo: The Campbell Collaboration.

Braga, A.A., Wesiburd, D.L., Waring, E.J., Mazerolle, L.G., Spelman, W. and Gajewski, F. (1999). Problem-oriented policing in violent crime places: A randomized controlled experiment. *Criminology* 37(3): 541–579.

Bridges, L. (2015). The legal powers and their limits, in Delsol, R. and Shiner, M. (eds) *Stop and Search*. Basingstoke: Palgrave Macmillan.

Brodeur, J.-P. (2010). *The Policing Web*. Oxford: Oxford University Press.

Carr, P.J. (2003). The new parochialism: The implications of the Beltway case for arguments concerning informal social control. *The American Journal of Sociology* 108(6): 1249–1291.

Chainey, S. and Macdonald, I. (2012). *Stop and Search, the Use of Intelligence and Geographic Targeting: Findings from Case Study Research*. London: NPIA.

Chriss, J.J. (2013). *Social Control: An Introduction* (2nd ed.). Cambridge: Polity Press.

Cohen, S. (1985). *Visions of Social Control: Crime, Punishment and Classification*. Cambridge: Polity Press.

Delsol, R. (2015). Effectiveness, in Delsol, R. and Shiner, M. (eds) *Stop and Search*. Basingstoke: Palgrave Macmillan.
Delsol, R. and Shiner, M. (2006). Regulating stop and search: A challenge for police and community relations in England and Wales. *Critical Criminology*, 14: 241–263.
Delsol, R. and Shiner, M. (eds) (2015). *Stop and Search*. Basingstoke: Palgrave Macmillan.
Dixon, D. (1997). *Law in Policing*. Oxford: Oxford University Press.
Dubber, M.D. (2005). *The Police Power. Patriarchy and the Foundations of American Government*. New York: Columbia University Press.
EHRC (2010). *Stop and think – A Critical Review of the Use of Stop and Search Powers in England and Wales*. London: Equalities and Human Rights Commission.
Emsley, C. (2010). *Crime and Society in England 1750–1900*. London: Taylor and Francis.
Ericson, R.V. (1982). *Reproducing Order: A Study of Police Patrol Work*. Toronto: University of Toronto Press.
Fitzgerald, M. (1999). *Final Report into Stop and Search*. Prepared for the Metropolitan Police Authority. London: MPA.
Fitzgerald, M., Hough, M., Joseph, I. and Qureshi, T. (2002). *Policing for London*, Cullompton: Willan Publishing.
Geller, A.B. and Fagan, J. (2010). Pot as pretext: Marijuana, race and the new disorder in New York City street policing. *Journal of Empirical Legal Studies* 7: 591.
Gilroy, P. (1987). *There Ain't no Black in the Union Jack*. London: Routledge.
Groff, E.R., Ratcliffe, J.H., Haberman, C.P., Sorg, E.T., Joyce, N.M. and Taylor, R.B. (2014). Does what police do at hot spots matter? The Philadelphia policing tactics experiment. *Criminology* 53(1): 23–53.
Hall, S., Critcher, C., Jefferson, T., Clarke, J. and Roberts, B. (1978). *Policing the Crisis*. London: Macmillan.
HMIC (2013). *Stop and Search Powers: Are the Police Using Them Effectively and Fairly?* London: Her Majesty's Inspectorate of Constabulary.
Home Office (2010). Theresa May's speech to the National Policing Conference, 29th June. Available at: www.gov.uk/government/speeches/police-reform-theresa-mays-speech-to-the-national-policing-conference. Accessed December 2015.
Home Office (2011). *Code A*. London: Home Office.
Home Office (2012). *Police Powers and Procedures England and Wales: 2010 to 2011* (2nd edn). London: Home Office.
Home Office (2013). *Drug Misuse: Findings from the 2012 to 2013 Crime Survey of England and Wales*. London: Home Office.
Home Office (2015a). *Code A Revised*. London: Home Office.
Home Office (2015b). *Police Powers and Procedures England and Wales, Year Ending 31 March 2015*. London: Home Office.
Hunter, A. (1995). Private, parochial and public social orders: The problem of crime and incivility in urban communities, in Kasinitz, P. (ed.) *Metropolis: Center and Symbol of Our Times*. New York: New York University Press.
Jacobs, J. (2016). Police, the rule of law and civil society: A philosophical perspective, in Bradford, B., Jauregui, B., Loader, I. and Steinberg, J. (eds) *The SAGE Handbook of Global Policing*. London: SAGE.
Kerr, T., Small, W. and Wood, E. (2005). The public health and social impacts of drug market enforcement: A review of the evidence. *International Journal of Drug Policy* 16: 210–220.
Levitas, R. (2000). What is social exclusion? In Gordon, D. and Townsend, P. (eds) *Breadline Europe: The Measurement of Poverty*. Bristol: Policy Press.

McCandless, R., Feist, A., Allan, J. and Morgan, N. (2016). *Do Initiatives Involving Substantial Increases in Stop and Search Reduce Crime? Assessing the Impact of Operation BLUNT 2.* London: Home Office.

Macpherson, Sir W. (1999). *The Stephen Lawrence Inquiry, Report of an Inquiry by Sir William Macpherson of Cluny CM 4262–1.* London: HMSO.

Manning, P.K. (1978). *Policing, A View from the Street.* Santa Monica: Goodyear Publishing.

Marenin, O. (1982). Parking tickets and class repression: The concept of policing in critical theories of criminal justice. *Contemporary Crises* 6: 241–266.

Miller, J. (2010). Stop and search in England: A reformed tactic or business as usual? *British Journal of Criminology* 50(5), 954–974.

Miller, J., Bland, N. and Quinton, P. (2000). *The Impact of Stops and Searches on Crime and the Community.* Police Research Series Paper 127. London: Home Office.

MoJ (2011). *Statistics on Race in the Criminal Justice System 2009/10.* London: Ministry of Justice.

Moon, D., Flatley, J., Parfrement-Hopkins, J., Hall, P., Hoare, P., Lau, I. and Innes, J. (2011). *Perceptions of Crime, Engagement with the Police, Authorities Dealing with Antisocial Behaviour and Community Payback: Findings from the 2010/11 British Crime Survey.* London: Home Office.

MOPAC (2015). Intrusive Tactics Dashboard. Available at: www.london.gov.uk/what-we-do/mayors-office-policing-and-crime-mopac. Accessed December 2015.

Murray, K. (2014). *Non-statutory stop and search in Scotland.* SCCJR Briefing Paper 6/2014.

MVA and Miller, J. (2000). *Profiling Populations Available for Stops and Searches.* London: Home Office.

Neocleous, M. (2000). *The fabrication of social order.* London: Pluto Press.

Openshaw, S. and Taylor, P. (1979). A million of so correlation coefficients: three experiments on the modifiable areal unit problem, in Wrigley, N. (ed.) *Statistical Applications in the Spatial Sciences.* London: Pion.

Punch, M. (1979). The secret social service, in Holdaway, S. (ed.) *The British Police.* London: Edward Arnold.

Quinlan, T.L. and Derfoufi, Z. (2015). Counter-terrorism policing, in Delsol, R. and Shiner, M. (eds) *Stop and Search.* Basingstoke: Palgrave Macmillan.

Quinton, P. (2011). The formation of suspicion: police stop and search in England and Wales. *Policing and Society* 21(4): 357–368.

Quinton, P. (2015). Race disproportionality and officer decision-making, in Delsol, R. and Shiner, M. (eds) *Stop and Search.* Basingstoke: Palgrave Macmillan.

Ratcliffe, J.H., Taniguchi, T., Groff, E.R. and Wood, J.D. (2011). The Philadelphia foot patrol experiment: A randomized controlled trial of police patrol effectiveness in violent crime hotspots. *Criminology* 49(3): 795–831.

Rawlings, P. (2002). *Policing – a Short History.* Cullompton: Willan Publishing.

Ream, G.L., Johnson, B.D., Dunlap, E. and Benoit, E. (2010). The role of marijuana use etiquette in avoiding targeted police enforcement. *Drugs: Education, Prevention and Policy* 17(6): 689–706.

Reiner, R. (2007). *Law and Order: An Honest Citizen's Guide to Crime and Control.* Cambridge: Polity Press.

Reiner, R. (2010). *The Politics of the Police* (4th edn). Oxford: Oxford University Press.

Release (2013). *The Numbers in Black and White: Ethnic Disparities in the Policing and Prosecution of Drug Offences in England and Wales.* London: Release.

Rosenfeld, R. and Fornango, R. (2014). The impact of police stops on precinct robbery and burglary rates in New York City, 2003–2010. *Justice Quarterly* 31(1): 6–122.

Sanders, A., Young, R. and Buron, A. (2010). *Criminal Justice* (4th edn). Oxford: Oxford University Press.

Scarman, L.G. (1981). *The Scarman Report: The Brixton Disorders*. London: HM Stationary Office.

Seddon, T. (2006). Drugs, crime and social exclusion. Social context and social theory in British drugs-crime research. *British Journal of Criminology* 46: 680–703.

Sherman, L.W. and Eck, J.E. (2002). Policing for crime prevention. In Sherman, L.W., Farrington, D.P., Welsh, B.C. and MacKenzie, D.L. (eds) *Evidence-based crime prevention*. New York: Routledge.

Shiner, M. and Delsol, R. (2015). The politics of the powers, in Delsol, R. and Shiner, M. (eds) *Stop and Search*. Basingstoke: Palgrave Macmillan.

Silver, A. (1967). The demand for order in civil society, in Bordua, D.J. (ed.) *The Police: Six Sociological Essays*. New York: Wiley.

Skogan, W.G. (1996). The police and public opinion in Britain. *American Behavioral Scientist* 39(4): 421–432.

Stopwatch (2011). *'Carry on Recording': Why Police Stops Should Still Be Recorded*. London: Stopwatch.

Taylor, B., Koper, C.S. and Woods, D.J. (2011). A randomized controlled trial of different policing strategies at hot spots of violent crime. *Journal of Experimental Criminology* 7: 149–181.

Telep, C.W. and Weisburd, D. (2012). What is known about the effectiveness of police practices in reducing crime and disorder? *Police Quarterly* 15(4): 331–357.

Wacquant, L. (2008). *Urban Outcasts: A Comparative Sociology of Advanced Marginality*. Cambridge: Polity Press.

Waddington, P.A.J. (1999). *Policing Citizens: Authority and Rights*. London: University College Press.

Waddington, P.A.J., Stenson, K. and Don, D. (2004). In proportion: Race and police stop and search. *British Journal of Criminology* 44: 889–914.

Ward, L., Nicholas, S. and Willoughby, M. (2011). *An assessment of the Tackling Knives and Serious Youth Violence Action Programme (TKAP) – phase ll*. Research Report 53. London: Home Office.

Weber, L. and Bowling, B. (2008). Valiant beggars and global vagabonds: Select, eject, immobilize. *Theoretical Criminology* 12(3): 355–375.

Werb, D., Kerr, T., Wood, E., Small, W., Strathdee, S. and Montaner, J. (2008). Effects of police confiscation of illicit drugs and syringes among injection drug users in Vancouver. *International Journal of Drug Policy* 19(4): 332–338.

Weisburd, D., Wooditch, A., Weisburd, T. and Yang, S.-M. (2015). Do stop, question and frisk practices deter crime? Evidence from microunits of space and time. *Criminology and Public Policy* 15(1): 31–56.

Whitfield, J. (2009). Stop and search: what can we learn from history? *BBC History Magazine*. Available at: www.historyextra.com/feature/stop-and-search-what-can-we-learn-history. Accessed May 2016.

Young, I.M. (2011). *Justice and the Politics of Difference*. Princeton: Princeton University Press.

3 Police stops and the problem of legitimacy[1]

It is entirely uncontroversial, writing in the spring of 2016, to state that stop and search as currently practiced in England and Wales presents challenges for public trust in the police and the legitimacy the service can command. Whether one thinks about recent events, such as the Mark Duggan case and the 2011 riots, or on a much longer time frame stretching back to the 'sus' laws and the 1981 Brixton riots (Scarman 1981) and beyond (Hall *et al.* 1978), the idea that stop and search can undermine the legitimacy of the police is well-evidenced, indeed almost self-evident.

I certainly do not wish to resile from such a position here. As described in Chapter 7, and in many other places besides (e.g. Bradford *et al.* 2009; Brunson and Miller 2006; Carr *et al.* 2007; Delsol and Shiner 2006; Fitzgerald *et al.* 2002; Miller *et al.* 2000; Sharp and Atherton 2007), stop/search activity *does* undermine public trust and police legitimacy, at least among those who experience such encounters and possibly more widely, as vicarious experience of police activity (Rosenbaum *et al.* 2005) spreads out among families, friendship networks and communities. What has often been missing from discussions of these issues, however, is elucidation of a detailed understanding of how police stops affect and are affected by legitimacy and processes of legitimation at both the conceptual level and at the level of beliefs and practices embedded in everyday life. Too often overly simplistic formulae (such as more stop and search equals less legitimacy) have obscured important questions concerning why, for example, police continue to use the tactic in the face of the problems it seems to create (Bradford and Loader 2016), or why public support for stop and search, at least in a general sense, remains relatively high (Fitzgerald 1999, although see also Stone and Pettigrew 2000). Moreover, few studies have used a robust definition of legitimacy (see Jackson *et al.* 2012, Mazerolle *et al.* 2012 and Van Damme 2015 for exceptions), or considered the importance of countercurrents in public opinion which express rather different views on this element of police practice. Some members of the public, for example, are likely to respond positively to evidence of 'aggressive' policing aimed at 'criminals' and the socially undesirable (Harkin 2014). The importance of a broad level of public support for visible, proactive policing that engages in 'the fight against crime' should not be underestimated.

In this chapter I want to begin the process of developing such understandings by, first, exploring why legitimacy is such an important aspect of the relationship between police and public. I aim to achieve this via a discussion of the types of influence police might reasonably expect to exert on people's offending and other crime-related behaviour. Contrasting instrumental understandings of both the influence of police on crime-related behaviours and the likely sources of police legitimacy with lessons drawn from procedural justice theory, I go on to outline a working, empirical notion of legitimacy that draws on recent criminological thinking on this topic, and describe some of the ways police legitimacy might itself influence offending and related behaviours (see Tyler *et al.* 2015 for a similar, although more wide-ranging, effort). Finally, the discussion will open up to consider how stop and search and cognate practices might be linked to processes of legitimation, both from the perspective of observers of police activity (and not just those immediately caught up in it) and police officers themselves.

To anticipate the main points, a key aspect of the 'wicked issue' of stop and search is that it can be seen, not least from the perspective of many police officers, as a practice closely linked to the establishment and reproduction of police legitimacy. Stop and search and related practices constitute a visible, apprehendable, effort towards achieving goals of crime prevention/reduction and order maintenance, and therefore demonstration of the usefulness and effectiveness of the police. Such activity can furthermore be taken as a demonstration that police are responding to public and policy imperatives to address problems of crime and disorder, which are of course seen by many within the police as central to their role (Jonathan-Zamir and Harpaz 2014; Reiner 2010; Way and Patten 2013; Nix 2015). But, and at the same time, stop/search can undermine legitimacy among the individuals and communities who experience it, often, arguably, those located in social and physical spaces where such legitimacy is both already in short supply and also most needed. Proper consideration of legitimacy and the processes that sustain or undermine should provide both a clear-sighted view of this apparent conundrum and, potentially, a way of circumventing it or at least attenuating its effects.

The social influence of policing

Police stops are nothing if not an attempt to influence the behaviour of the people stopped, whether in terms of what they are doing at that particular point in time or what they might wish to do in the immediate or more distant future. Consideration of this aspect and application of police power therefore turns almost inevitably to the question of how best police can exert influence on those they police. In particular, given the crime reduction and/or prevention role most commonly envisaged for proactive policing in general, and stop and search in particular, how can police best prevent crime and promote order in the communities they serve? This question looms large in any discussion concerning the nature and structure of police organizations, when considering their activity, what makes them legitimate and the potential benefits legitimacy may bring to them.

One current of thinking around both the basis of police legitimacy and the type of influence police can bring to bear on the policed is that both are founded on the demonstration of effective deterrent threat to offenders, potential offenders, and indeed the population at large. The continued relevance of this notion, despite significant evidence that it is, in important aspects, fundamentally mistaken, is related in important senses to the fact that deterrence remains the dominant policy model for the exercise of police authority (Nagin 2013; Tyler *et al.* 2014.

A deterrence or 'command and control' model of policing suggests that potential offenders will be dissuaded from committing a crime when, and if, they are convinced that the potential costs of detection and sanction are higher than the potential gains presented by its commission. Two important implications (or perhaps more correctly hypotheses) follow from the deterrence model of criminal justice in its more general form (Wright 2010). First, potential offenders will be deterred by the certainty of punishment: the higher the perceived probability of being caught, the lower the propensity to commit a crime. Second, potential offenders will be deterred when the severity of punishment is such that it outweighs the perceived gain involved. Police are only rarely positioned as having any influence on the second of these aspects of deterrence (despite the existence of sanctions such as fixed penalty notices), implying that any deterrent effect of policing must come primarily from the first.

Recognizing that the certainty/severity dyad is almost certainly an overly reductive view of human motivation, deterrence-based and associated models have also built in notions of the celerity of punishment – in essence, the idea that swifter punishments deter more. The importance of non-legal sanctions has also been stressed, particularly as these relate to the concept of cost. Factors such as shame in front of peers, commitment to moral rules, and the long-term loss of social and other forms of capital have all been cited as costs that would-be offenders might weigh up in their decision-making processes (Gottfredson 2011; Kennedy 2009; Rebellon *et al.* 2010; Morris and Piquero 2013). Notwithstanding these extensions, deterrence-based models retain a rational-choice understanding of human behaviour premised on neoclassical economics (Nagin 1998). When confronted with the possibility of a criminal act people draw on the information available to them in order to arrive at a decision to act in a way that maximizes their utility. They are, on this account, willing and able to think through the choices open to them, at least in some overall sense, and are cognisant of the potential consequences arising from each choice. The benefits of a crime, whether financial, emotional (Katz 1988) or calibrated in some other way, are therefore weighed against the potential dis-benefits: a crime occurs when the result of this calculation appears favourable to the individual concerned (Clarke and Cornish 1985).

On this account, the police 'fight against crime' is pursued by providing a credible threat of sanction, and order is maintained via the threat or application of police power and presence on the streets. Moreover, it follows that public support for police activity is purchased by the demonstration of effectiveness in the execution of these activities. As rational choice calculators, non-offenders as much as offenders assess the success of police against avowed crime prevention and order maintenance goals, and grant legitimacy to the extent they perceive effectiveness in achieving these goals. When police organizations provide a material return on the various forms of capital (social and cultural as well as financial) that are invested in them, then the policed grant them legitimacy.

The policy implications of deterrence-based models of crime control are clear. Police organizations should act in ways that demonstrably increase the risk of detection, the certainty of sanction, and, where applicable, the severity of punishment. Both the creation of greater sanction threat *and* communication of this to the policed are important, since people will only be deterred from crime if they recognize there is a chance of being caught if they engage in illegal activity. The policy dominance of deterrence-based theories is reflected in much criminological thinking concerning the role of institutions in controlling crime, which focuses primarily on instrumental motivations and material incentives: where and when might deterrence policies be effective? How can those who are already predisposed to commit crime be prevented from actually doing so? Policies or practices such as 'hot-spot' policing, and the academic literature that surrounds them, can be seen precisely in this light.

The relevance of this model to the specific issue of stop/search and cognate practices is also clear. Police stops may have both specific and general deterrent effects, apprehending and/or dissuading interdicted individuals from carrying out a crime either in the immediate or more distant future, and suggesting to onlookers that police represent a credible threat in terms of detection and sanction. As discussed in Chapter 2 police stop activity is also often an important component of policy innovations such as hot-spot policing (Weisburd and Telep 2014) or 'pulling levers' strategies (Kennedy 2009), composing a key aspect of officers' activity in areas singled out for concentrated 'doses' of policing or in relation to individuals targeted by police for particular attention. Finally, such activities may serve to indicate to the public that the police are 'doing something', exerting their power in a visible effort to deal with crime and disorder and actively asserting order in neighbourhoods and communities. If it is nothing else, stopping and perhaps searching someone in the street is a highly visible instantiation of police power.

Yet, the current weight of research evidence casts doubt on the strength of the association between the certainty and/or severity of punishment and the level of crime. In their review of the research evidence concerning deterrence theory, Pratt *et al.* (2006) report that associations between crime and deviance response variables and explanatory variables specified by deterrence theory – certainty, severity and non-legal sanctions – tend to be 'modest to negligible'. Even on the most optimistic reading (e.g. including simple bivariate associations) effect sizes in relevant studies are typically lower than those found in research, for example, into peer effects and self-control (ibid.: 383). Factors outwith the control of the criminal justice system, that is, they seem to have a much greater influence on crime and offending. As discussed in Chapter 2, again, there is also little direct evidence that stop and search exerts any deterrent threat whatsoever, either immediately on those stopped or in a general sense.

It would be wrong to suggest that deterrence-related factors have *no* effect on crime. This is likely to be true in a general sense – the mere existence of a more or less functioning criminal justice system is probably sufficient to deter some acts of crime (Kennedy 2009; Sherman and Eck 2002) – but more importantly, deterrence may work in specific and contextualized cases. People's behaviour *can* be influenced by their estimate of the probability of being caught if they break the law, and moving away from simplistic assumptions that the behaviour of large numbers of individuals can be predicted as if all behave as rational choice calculators, recent approaches have stressed the subjective and situationally embedded nature of individuals' decisions about crime (Piqeuro *et al.* 2011). Context and framing are important factors mediating how people see potential acts of crime – the possibility of offending and the extent of the risk of getting caught will present differently to different people. Moreover, the threat of informal sanctions – ranging from loss of employment to loss of respect – appears to be a more consistent predictor of criminal behaviour than formal sanctions, albeit that for some people, in some situations, the latter may still be more pertinent (see *inter alia* Kleiman 2009). Finally, there is evidence that strategies such as hotspot policing can reduce crime in local areas, at least in the short to medium term.

In sum, there is evidence that the perceived certainty of punishment does affect *some* people's compliance with the law (Paternoster 1987; Piquero *et al.* 2011; Nagin and Pogarsky 2001; cf. Jacobs, 2010). The police can, in certain circumstances at least, hope to contribute to this perceived risk, and street and traffic stops may contribute something to this effort (Weisburd *et al.* 2015). By contrast, Pratt *et al.* (2006) demonstrate that the severity of potential punishment appears to have very little association at all with levels of crime (see also Doob and Webster 2003). Faced with a mass of weak and sometimes contradictory evidence, Pratt *et al.* (2006) have argued that if it is to survive deterrence theory must be integrated with other, more expansive, theories of crime causation. Most pertinently for current purposes, research both within and outside the deterrence paradigm has begun to point to the importance of the subjective nature of judgement formation in relation to potential criminal acts and, in particular, the focus has turned to the ways individuals' relationships with legal authorities might influence their orientations toward, and motivations concerning, crime.

Procedural justice theory

The most important alternate account of the relationship between police and public – and of the types of influence the former can hope to exert on the latter – is currently provided by procedural justice theory (Bradford and Jackson 2016: 228–229). Originally developed by Tom Tyler and colleagues in the United States (Lind and Tyler 1988; Tyler 2006; Tyler and Blader 2000; Tyler and Huo 2002) and subsequently applied in many contexts across the world (e.g. Akinlabi

2015; Hasisi and Weisburd, 2011; Hinds and Murphy 2007; Murphy *et al.* 2008; Tankebe 2009; Van Damme *et al.* 2013), procedural justice theory stresses the social connection between police and policed. In particular, it suggests that trust and legitimacy in the relationship between police and public are powerful influences on peoples' propensities to comply with the law and cooperate with police officers working in their communities. If we are to understand the influence police might have on citizen's law-related behaviours there is a need to integrate understandings of officers' instrumental activity – their ability to deter in the strict meaning of the word – with insight into the effects of the more expressive aspects of police behaviour, particularly as these relate to actions that promote (or undermine) legitimacy.

Studies of the general population have found that the experience or perception of procedural justice is a strong predictor of legitimacy. Across many different contexts there is a marked tendency for people to regard the police as legitimate when, and to the extent that, they believe officers exercise their authority through fair and impartial means; that is, when they behave in a procedurally just manner (Tyler 2006; Tyler and Huo 2002). Procedurally just policing comprises officer (and organizational) activity and decision making processes that are experienced as transparent, fair, equitable and respectful by citizens, which follow correct procedure and do not exhibit bias, and which provide those with whom police interact a sense of control over, or at least input into, the process concerned. When interacting with police people value *voice* (Hirschman 1970) during the encounter, *neutrality* on the part of the authority, treatment with *respect and dignity*, and a sense of *trust*.

It is important to note that the term 'procedural justice' used in this literature refers neither to procedure in a technical/legal sense – for example in terms of police regulations or protocols – nor to justice in a normative or philosophical sense. It concerns, instead, the judgements people make about the behaviour of police during interactions with offices and in terms of the wider policing processes that affect them. Treatment that is *experienced* as fair, decent and respectful encourages people to trust the officers involved. A general perception that police behave in a fair way, garnered perhaps through vicarious experience or media stories, similarly promotes public trust. People's trust in the police, which has consistently been found to be linked with legitimacy, is premised by definition on incomplete knowledge of actual police behaviour (if people had such knowledge they would not need to trust – see Bradford *et al.* 2016). Procedural justice theory is thus concerned primarily with the ways people read, interpret and understand police activity. This is not to claim that the 'reality' of police behaviour – for example, the extent to which it conforms, or not, to legal standards – is unimportant or immaterial, but merely that reality is filtered through the subjective experiences of those exposed to police activity.

In contrast to the well-established 'procedural justice effect', research has failed to find any consistent association between perceptions of the instrumental effectiveness of police and legitimacy. While in some contexts, such as developing countries (see for example Tankebe 2009) efficacy and efficiency seem to be strongly linked to legitimacy, studies conducted in developed countries typically find only weak associations between measures of police effectiveness, for example in dealing with crimes or maintaining order, and measures of legitimacy (for an overview of the European context see Hough *et al.* 2013). Just as it seems that deterrence – via the practice and demonstration of effective modes of policing – has relatively little direct influence on offending (although it can have some), the association between police effectiveness and the legitimacy granted to the organization by those it polices is inconsistent and often relatively weak.

While perceptions of procedural fairness have consistently been linked with legitimacy, and perceptions of instrumental effectiveness only inconsistently, the place of judgements about distributive justice within procedural justice theory is less clear. Distributive and procedural justice are clearly conceptually different – at the simplest level the former relates to the fairness of outcomes while the latter relates to the fairness of the processes that lead to those outcomes. Further, on some accounts perceptions of the fairness of processes can be used as a way through which people judge the fairness of outcomes (e.g. Lind and Tyler 1988). Fairness heuristic theory (van den Bos *et al.* 1997), for example, proposes that people often do not have sufficient knowledge to judge whether an outcome provided to them by an authority was fair, since they do not know the outcomes received by others. In such circumstance their judgements about the process through which they were dealt with by that authority – something they do know about – can be used as a heuristic for making assessments about the likely fairness of the outcome they receive. Yet, outside experimental research paradigms it can often be difficult to disentangle distributive and procedural justice. At that level of individual experience these two factors often seem to be intimately related to each other and, in a sense, mutually constitutive. People may find it hard to imagine that an unfair outcome resulted from a fair procedure; symmetrically, it can be hard to believe that unfair processes produce fair outcomes.

These issues are plainly pertinent in the context of police stops, and particularly so given the historical context of stop and search in England and Wales. On the one hand a key factor driving debate around the power is its apparent distributive unfairness. People from different ethnic groups receive different outcomes from police, in terms of their chances of being stopped and the end results of those stops; and the outcomes they experience are distinct from the way the stops were handled by the officers involved. On the other hand, many individuals experiencing stops believe the decision to stop them in the first place, a procedural decision that should be based on unbiased, neutral decision-making, was, precisely, biased and partial. Equally, the judgement that in a general sense the outcomes provided by police in relation to stop/searches are unfair may influence the way people read the behaviours of individual officers during specific encounters. If an individual with a black ethnicity believes that police disproportionately stop black people, then they may well believe that the decision to stop *them* stems not from reasonable suspicion but from biased, stereotyping or prejudiced policing.

In this book I take a pragmatic stance to these issues. Since (a) I am concerned primarily with the way people experience police power as and when it is applied to them; (b) the majority of police stops do not result in any further outcome; and (c) available survey sources cover procedural justice far better than distributive justice, I concentrate primarily on people's concerns about the process through which police deal with them and the effects their experiences of police stops have on their legitimacy judgements. Questions of distributive justice, by contrast, come into play in those sections of the text where I am concerned with identifying who is more or less likely to experience this type of police contact, and therefore sit somewhat aside from the subjective experiences of those affected.

What is legitimacy?

Although an empirical or subjective notion of legitimacy (Hinsch 2008) is a central component of procedural justice theory it remains a contested, uncertain and rather fuzzy concept. In this section I will outline a working concept of legitimacy that will be used in the analyses presented in later chapters. The discussion is not intended to provide a detailed account of the concept, its development and application (for much fuller treatments see Jackson *et al.* 2012; Jackson and Gau 2015; Tankebe and Liebling 2013; Tyler and Jackson 2013). The emphasis will be, in particular, on how legitimacy has been conceptualized and measured in the procedural justice and associated literatures.

In this literature legitimacy been usually been measured, first, by assessing individuals' sense that they have a duty to obey and defer to authority figures such as police officers. Seen in these terms legitimacy is a property of an authority that leads those subject to it to believe they should obey its directives because such obedience is the right thing to do *in and of itself* (Sunshine and Tyler 2003). People may not feel such a sense of duty, of course, in which case one would conclude that from their perspective the legitimacy of the authority is in question. This is a concept of legitimacy that therefore harks back to Weber and the notion that legitimacy inheres in 'acceptance of the validity of an order of rules' (Lassman 2000: 87) or, perhaps more appositely, a belief among those governed by an organization or institution that the position of the governing party is valid (Whimster 2004) and therefore worthy of deference. Belief in or acceptance of the validity of a set of social arrangements motivates behaviour that is in accord with the set of principles governing those arrangements and, in the case of legal authority, with the set of rules that both constitutes the authority of and is mandated by the organization or institution concerned. In the case of police, specifically, this *recognition* of power translates into a sense of duty toward a valid power-holder – i.e. the police officer – and a feeling that obeying the instructions or orders of that power-holder is *the right thing to do*.

A second important aspect of this notion of legitimacy is that the actions engendered by a sense of duty toward an authority – deference, obedience, compliance, cooperation – are themselves partly constitutive of the legitimacy of that authority. These are 'actions which express recognition or acknowledgement of an authority on the part of relevant agents, and hence *contribute* to its legitimacy' (Beetham 2013: 26, emphasis in original). While the types of survey research commonly used in procedural justice studies have only been able to approximate these effects, since people are asked only about their sense of duty, how right it is to obey police officer, or their self-assessed propensity to cooperate or comply, the measures used may nevertheless tap into the discursive (Beetham 2013) or dialogic (Bottoms and Tankebe 2012) nature of legitimacy and, in particular, the extent to which police legitimacy is an emergent property of the *relationship between* police and citizens. On this account, and from an empirical, sociological, perspective, the legitimacy of the police is instantiated, made real and reproduced in those moments when citizens willingly defer to and cooperate with officers. Asking people about their sense of duty toward police is a necessarily imperfect way of assessing the probability that such legitimacy generating, and affirming, interactions will take place.

More recent approaches have begun to stress a second element of legitimacy – individuals' assessments of the moral behaviour of authorities (Bottoms and Tankebe 2012; Gilley 2009; Jackson *et al.* 2012). In a sense these have built on a second aspect of legitimacy ever-present (although often underplayed) in the procedural justice literature; namely, the idea legitimacy also comprises a sense of trust and, in particular, a sense of trust in the motives of power-holders (Tyler 2006; Tyler and Huo 2002). A considerable body of theoretical and empirical work has attempted to better tease out what such a sense of trust represents – specifically, a judgement that the trustee has the right intentions toward the trustor – and separate as clearly as possible the two concepts of trust and legitimacy (Jackson and Gau 2015). One key idea, for example, has been that individuals (officers) are trusted, while the role (police officer) or institution (police) is legitimate (Tyler and Jackson 2013). Trust therefore flows into legitimacy, and most likely vice versa, but the two are conceptually distinct.

Based primarily on the work of David Beetham (1991), these more recent accounts stress that the legitimacy of the police is established in part by citizen's judgements about the behaviour and moral character of police officers and organization. When thinking about police, people ask: do they share the same sense of right and wrong as me? Do they operate according to a moral framework I myself share? Do they follow the rules intended to govern their activity, and are these the right rules? The argument is that one way police officers – and organizations – can demonstrate to citizens that they do indeed share their values is by treating them fairly and with dignity, and by engaging in meaningful dialogue with them. An important implication of this idea is thus that people's sense of 'moral' or 'normative' alignment (Jackson *et al.* 2012) with police is not based on direct concurrence or agreement with, for example, the laws the police enforce, but rather on a broader sense that the actions of officers generally adhere to and reproduce a normatively justifiable set of relationships between police and citizen (Tyler and Jackson 2013). What is at stake in such judgements is not the relationship between a citizen and an individual officer but that between a citizen and '*the police*'. While the latter may be represented by an individual officer in any given instance, it also has a corporate or institutional existence that transcends the individual yet which is also something with which citizens can (imagine that they) have a relationship. People can, and do, make judgements about the moral character of 'the police' that are not necessarily reducible to their judgements about individual officers. Furthermore, perceptions of the extent to which police adhere to a general set of shared moral values may condition the way people react to the behaviour of individual officers, which is the same as saying, to reiterate, that there are likely to be potentially important feedback loops between legitimacy and trust.

How does legitimacy affect behaviour?

How then might the legitimacy of an authority influence the behaviour of those subject to it, and how might this close the circle opened by the relative paucity of evidence for deterrent effects of policing on individuals' 'crime-related behaviours'?

Procedural justice theory – as a model of social regulation – posits that fair treatment at the hands of criminal justice agents (and more generally a perception that they act in a fair manner) promotes the legitimacy of the agency and perhaps of the criminal justice 'system' as a whole. This idea is in turn linked to a wider set of claims about the likely influence of a legitimate, or conversely illegitimate, police force on those it polices. The key idea is that when people grant legitimacy to legal authorities they are less likely to transgress the laws those authorities represent (Tyler 2006; Jackson *et al.* 2012). Institutional configurations can influence individuals' decision-making processes in ways other than merely providing a credible risk of sanction (or not). People's orientation toward the law contains a significant normative dimension, and this dimension is constituted, in part, by the legitimacy of legal authorities, and, in particular, by the legitimacy of the police as the most visible representation of 'the law'.

On this account, legal authorities generate public compliance, cooperation and voluntary deference by encouraging processes of identification and legitimation among those they govern. Indeed, social identity and notions of shared group membership comprise, in procedural justice theory, an important 'bridge' linking procedural fairness, legitimacy, cooperation and compliance. When people feel fairly treated by important group representatives such as police officers this generates, encourages and/or enhances a sense of inclusion and value within the group the office represents, and promotes identification with the authority figure concerned and with the values it represents (Bradford 2014; Bradford *et al.* 2014; Blader and Tyler 2003, 2009). Chapter 8 deals with these questions in much more depth, but most important at this stage is the idea that when people identify with an authority – when they feel that it represents a social group they belong to, is a valid repository of power within this group, and acts in ways aligned with their own sense of right and wrong – they grant it legitimacy and, contingently, the right to define proper behaviour. Legitimacy activates self-regulatory mechanisms: people defer to, and cooperate with, legitimate authorities because they feel it is right to do so. Such normative compliance is based moral or ethical obligations or commitments, and, in a distinct and important contrast to the situation imagined by deterrence theory, not on instrumental factors related to risk and reward (Tyler 2008). The key claim here is that people comply with police and the laws police represent not only when, or because, they perceive a threat of sanction, but also when they hold police to be legitimate – and this legitimacy is itself premised on procedural justice and closely associated with a sense of inclusion and belonging.

It seems therefore that legitimate authorities can affect an individual's behaviour in a number of distinct ways (Kelman and Hamilton 1989). One route is via *identification*. The ways authorities act – particularly in relation to the procedural fairness of their behaviour – can activate individuals' roles within important self-satisfying (and often self-defining) social relationships. When people feel fairly treated by authorities they will identify more with them and the group(s) they represent: indeed, this sense of identification is one reason for holding the authority to be legitimate. The police (and the British police in particular) powerfully represent nation, state and community (Reiner 2010; Loader and Mulcahy 2003), and roles people have within such groups may include that of 'citizen' (in the Aristotelian sense of being a full member of society with a set of duties as well as rights). A feeling of inclusion and recognition activates attendant expectations for behaviour and, all else equal, we may expect abiding by the law to be one of these expectations (since being a 'citizen' involves adhering to properly established norms of conduct). To do otherwise – to act contrary to role expectation – risks undermining self-image and damaging the relationship between individual and group. Naturally, there is the real possibility of a reverse process: an illegitimate police force may activate different roles that do not discourage, and may even promote, law-breaking behaviour. Put simply, people who feel excluded from the group the police represent are less likely to believe they should behave in ways that support it, or at least that they should do no damage. This refers again to the idea that legitimacy, as discussed here at least, is a discursive, processual and fungible phenomena generated by and through the shifting relationships between, in this case, police and policed.

The idea that procedural fairness may activate individuals' sense of inclusion in the group the police represent, and strengthen identification with group aims and objectives, runs alongside and interacts with the notion of legitimacy proposed in the procedural justice literature, and there is likely to be a complex interplay between these two aspects of people's relationships with police. Identification may in and of itself influence law-related behaviour, as people are motivated to follow the rules of groups they belong to and are more likely to cooperate with group representatives. Procedural fairness can thus be thought of as having both affective and evaluative aspects. It *communicates* status and inclusion within the group the police represent, and it *demonstrates* that the police are acting in normatively justifiable ways and are therefore legitimate holders of the powers vested in them. A more phenomenological way of stating this might be that people experience police fairness (or unfairness) in a quite visceral manner, yet they also judge the fairness (or unfairness) of the police against more or less consciously expresses norms of justice and probity.

Legitimate authorities can also influence people via *internalization* (Kelman and Hamilton 1989). This may be a complex, iterative social process somewhat akin to the civilizing process envisaged by Norbert Elias (1994). Individuals' value systems are shaped in large part by the institutional context into which they are born and socialized (Berger and Luckmann 1966), and legal authorities such as the police will form part of that context. Processes of legal socialization lead many people to internalize the idea that it is right and proper follow the dictates of legal authorities. But, more immediately, legitimate authorities can exert influence by creating situations wherein certain actions are encouraged or precluded in order that individuals maintain congruence with their own internal value-systems. The sense that crime is wrong is very widely shared (Robinson and Darley 2007), but people are more likely to act in accordance with their personal moral judgements concerning criminal acts if they feel the social context they inhabit is integrated and in accordance with their own values. A legitimate police force may provide one element of a strong normative framework toward which people orient themselves and through which they experience and understand the social world (cf. Wikström *et al.* 2012).

Affective or instrumental influences?

Current evidence suggests, although by no means definitively proves, that procedural justice, and the legitimacy and sense of inclusion it generates, may be both a more stable and a more powerful driver of people's crime-related behaviour than the promise of reward or risk of punishment. Internal motivations – to do the right thing, to support legitimate authority – are also likely to exert a more enduring influence on behaviour than external or environmental factors such as the presence and actions of formal agents of social control which, often by definition, are likely to be only fleetingly present. Discussions of the influence police may be able to exert on compliance with the law and public cooperation need therefore to attend not only to their instrumental activities but also to the way in which they treat those citizens they encounter and to wider vicarious or mediated experiences of their behaviour. Deterrence is not the only way that police activity affects peoples' views on crime, and the fairness of officer's actions may exert a deeper and more long-lasting influence on potential offenders than the proximate threat of being caught and sanctioned.

It is worth noting that this is also a normatively more desirable way in which to reproduce social order. Modes of governance that rely on legitimacy, premised on fair process, would appear *prima facie* to be preferable to those that rely to a greater extent on the threat or use of force. Which is not to claim that the threat of force is or could ever be absent from police behaviour, but simply that it can be more or less salient in the relationship between police and policed and more or less constrained at the point of application – and the less salient and more constrained the better. Moreover, a clearer understanding of what motivates people to comply or cooperate with police has a number of additional potential benefits. Legal authorities that command widespread legitimacy are 'freed up' to concentrate their efforts on the minority of committed or dangerous offenders, since legitimacy, once established, encourages compliance among the majority of the population. Equally, those who grant the police and criminal justice system legitimacy may be more 'deterrable', more open to influence by the more instrumental aspects of police behaviour. So, for example, when temptation or other factors suggest the possibility of crime, individuals who grant police *more* legitimacy may be *less* likely to commit an offence as they are more attuned to the presence or behaviours of police and other authorities. There is also evidence that the trust engendered by procedural justice is linked to more favourable assessments of the effectiveness of criminal justice agencies (Bradford 2011), thus enhancing the perceived risk of sanction. While the effect of police fairness and legitimacy on compliance and cooperation is consistently found to be more important than that of effectiveness, there will still be some circumstances in which a belief that the police are effective deters crime and encourages cooperation.

Police activity as legitimation process

Thus far the discussion has been framed positively: procedural fairness encourages a sense of belonging, legitimacy, cooperation and compliance. This, however, a bi-directional relationship, and if we reverse the narrative pursued above extant research suggests that police activity experienced as unfair may actually *encourage* offending, something which directs our attention once more to the fact that police stops are quite often judged unfair by those who experience them. While there is little direct evidence concerning *causal* processes here, the weight of current research is strongly in favour of the idea that police stops damages police legitimacy overall (see Jackson *et al.* 2013 and Chapter 7 for more on this issue), and the associative (or correlational) links between police legitimacy and self-reported offending are well known (e.g. Tyler 2006; Jackson *et al.* 2012). Moreover, a number of studies have provided evidence of the deleterious effect of 'police contact' on offending behaviour (see Chapter 8), and Bradford *et al.* (2014) suggest one reason for this may be a decline in police legitimacy among those affected. Being stopped by the police might promote offending; and it is quite likely to undermine trust and legitimacy.

It is with some sense of irony, therefore, that many commentators have noted the continued dominance of deterrence models in the policing field, both in terms of the ways police activity is envisaged to affect crime and the factors thought to shape police legitimacy (Hough *et al.* 2010). Despite the evidence summarized above, procedural fairness is often thought to be 'nice to do but not essential' (Foster and Jones 2010), and it has seemed difficult for policy makers, and many police officers, to consider that particular types of police activity might have unintended consequences and result in perverse outcomes. Nowhere has this been more obvious in the debates that rage around stop and search. Why, given (a) the problems the use of this power may cause in terms of legitimacy (some of which are described in Chapter 7 and which form a mainstay of academic studies of stop and search as well as many popular accounts) and (b) doubts about the extent to which this form of police activity deters people from preventing crime, do police continue to seemingly use – or overuse – it with such regularity?

The answer to this question may be provided by a change of perspective. The discussion above, in keeping with the spirit of the volume as a whole, confined its attention primarily to public experiences of police. Yet, as described by Bottoms and Tankebe (2012, 2013), police perspectives are a central aspect of the dialogic construction of legitimacy within a given context. Police are continuously making, in various ways, claims to legitimacy; furthermore, police officers have a sense of their own legitimacy that is premised on such claims (Barker 2001), as well as on other factors such as their experiences of public cooperation and support (Bradford and Quinton 2014). This sense of 'self-legitimacy' may itself be influential in enabling or conditioning the types of wider legitimacy claims the organization is able to make, as well as their likelihood of success. To put it bluntly, a police service which did not believe it its own legitimacy would seem unlikely to be able to convince or persuade citizens otherwise (although it is entirely possible for a police service that did perceive itself legitimate to be perceived as illegitimate by those it policed), and it is likely to draw on those aspects of its practice which it feels grant or generate legitimacy to it when it is seeking to convince others that it is, indeed, legitimate.

Given the continued broad dominance of the deterrence model of policing described above, police stops, more or less proactive policing aimed at solving or preventing crimes and asserting order on the streets, may be an important element in both officer's sense of their own legitimacy and a variety of legitimation claims made by police in England and Wales. Most importantly, despite the problematic history of stop and search, this is a power that can nevertheless represent in an important sense the activity of policing, its chance for success, and indeed the place of police in wider society (that is, the types of problems police should address and the types of solutions police can offer). Stop activity may therefore serve as a mechanism or tool through which legitimacy is claimed; the need to make such claims, and the types of benefits they might bring for police if successful, may provide one set of reasons for the continued use of stop and search in the face of the level of dispute it provokes. There are a number of reasons for suggesting why this might be the case, all of which may be important in terms of both officers' sense of their own legitimacy and for the types of legitimating claims they make.

First, many police officers believe they are the thin blue line separating order from chaos. Such a belief, along with other aspects of 'cop culture' such as action-orientation, suspiciousness and the need for efficacy in practice (Reiner 2010: Chapter 4), seems highly likely to promote a sense that proactive 'stop' activity – whether it is stop and search, stop and account or some other modality – is both a useful tool of policing and an important aspect of the process of legitimation. If police believe they are legitimate because they protect the public, and that they can protect the public by instigating stop/search activity, then doing so becomes a way of demonstrating legitimate policing in action.

Second, police officers believe that stop and search and related activity 'works'. I have often been engaged in conversations with serving officers during which they strongly evince a belief that stop and search produces useful returns and, at the very least, keeps 'bad guys' either under control or off the streets (although, as ever, it is important to note significant variation of opinion within the service; some officers take a more sceptical stance to the usefulness of stop and search as a policing tool, and many are alive to the troubling aspects of current practice).

Third, developments in 'evidence-based' policing seem likely to be pushing police toward targeted applications of stop and search/account during hotspot and similar activities. Leaving aside the effectiveness of such policies, evidence-based policing is nothing if not a claim to legitimate authority over the realm of crime control (Loader 2010). When – or rather if – police stops are conducted on the basis that they contribute to effective policing, where what is effective is closely defined and measured with the appearance of precision, reliability and validity, the practice becomes intimately linked to a set of claims about the rectitude and propriety of police activity. As one London borough commander put it in a blog entry:

> So does stop and search reduce crime?… If I'm honest the scientific evidence isn't as compelling as the evidence you might expect before the National Institute of Clinical Excellence sanction the use of a new drug. This is where 'Evidenced Based Policing' comes in and where the Met and the College of Policing see the future heavily routed. If it's legal, ethical and the evidence says it works *then we should be doing it.*
>
> (http://hackneyboroughcommander.tumblr.com/post/56899353859/stop-and-search-in-hackney, emphasis added. Last accessed 1 February 2015, now deleted)

In other words, if 'scientific' evidence is adduced that stop and search reduces crime then it becomes the *duty* of police to use the power; at the very least it becomes, as a police tactic, part of a particular discourse concerned with demonstrating the validity of police claims to knowledge and influence within its specific area of competence.

Finally, it is undoubtedly the case that there is significant support for police stop activity among the general public, certainly in a general sense and, on occasion, in specific instances (Fitzgerald *et al.* 2002). Proactive, and sometimes aggressive, policing is popular among significant sections of the population (Girling *et al.* 2000), at least as long as it is not aimed at them (ibid.), and it is not *entirely* unreasonable for police managers to respond to such preferences by encouraging officers to use stop and search/account. In other words, as well as pressure from within the service, both cultural and managerial, there are external factors that may encourage police to believe increased, or at least continued, use of stop and search is not only acceptable but desirable and supported by the communities they serve. Responding to community priorities is, of course, central to legitimation processes, at least in as much as these embedded in discursive or dialogical forms of legitimacy, and we should not imagine that such community priorities revolve only around procedural justice.

None of the above should be taken to mean that a particular level of police stop activity is an inevitable aspect of policing; indeed, the prevalence of this type of activity varies significantly over time and space. As described in Chapter 2, and discussed at length by Shiner and Delsol (2015), Murray and Harkin (2016) and others, the extent to which police use stop and search powers can be strongly influenced by a range of external social, political and economic pressures. Most notably, political pressure on police can trigger change in the use of stop/search powers. Such pressure has been heaped on stop and search in England and Wales since the 2010 general election (Shiner and Delsol 2015), often led by a Conservative Home Secretary who has used a critique of the unfairness of current stop/search practice as something of a stick with which to beat police. In Scotland similar pressure eventually followed revelations of extremely high levels of stop and search across the country (and in all likelihood directed at marginalized population groups – Murray 2014; Murray and Harkin 2016). Such pressure seems to have resulted in a significant reduction in the use of stop and search in both contexts, albeit that other factors, such as reductions in the number of police in England and Wales, may also have an effect.

These fluctuations serve however to underline the association between police stops and legitimacy, and particularly the idea that this is a bi-directional relationship. Stop activity may be one way police seek to promote a sense of legitimate action; yet they can be sensitive to the legitimacy-undermining claim that use of the power to stop and/or search people is unfair or excessive and reduce its use accordingly.

Summary

To return to a point raised in the introductory chapter, police stop activity is located at an important locus of tension within the broader field of policing. Much of this tension plays out in processes that generate, or undermine, legitimacy. In as much as it is believed that policing is about providing a deterrent threat and retaining an aggressive form of control over the street, and that the police garner legitimacy when seemingly successful in achieving these ends, stopping, questioning and perhaps searching people appears to be the right thing to do. A range of pressures within and outwith the service encourages continued, and even increased, use of powers to do so, something that may help explain their continued use in the face of all the attendant, and well known, problems.

Yet police effectiveness, in a country such as England and Wales at least, is not particularly highly correlated with legitimacy, and, moreover, deterrence has relatively little to do with crime. Procedural fairness *is* associated with legitimacy, however, and legitimacy with offending (and conversely, perceived unfairness is linked with lower legitimacy, and through this higher offending). It is this latter fact that may offer a partial solution to the problem at hand. Far from making policing more effective, stop activity, in as much as it considered unfair, may reduce effectiveness, because it serves to encourage, not discourage offending. Police stops may therefore be problematic not only in terms of issues of fairness and legitimacy but in relation to issues directly pertinent to the instrumental effectiveness of police. Shifting the terms of the debate, then, may contextualize and problematize the kind of pressures promoting the use of police stops, and open up a space for more holistic, and nuanced appraisal of the utility of this form of practice.

The present chapter closes with three important caveats. First, just as deterrence can work in some times and places, and for some individuals, so can stop and search/account, particularly when it is included in targeted 'packets' of police activity. The argument is not for abolition but for parsimony or minimalism (Marks and Wood 2010) in the use of the power, based on a more realistic and accurate appraisal of its usefulness and externalities.

Second, while the circumstantial evidence for an association between police legitimacy and offending is strong, direct, robust, empirical evidence is at the current time rather lacking. While it certainly seems that low police legitimacy is linked to higher *propensities* to offend, there is relatively little evidence of a direct causal link between legitimacy judgements and offending. Much more research on this issue is needed, and the kinds of links drawn above are at this stage tentative, at best.

Third, care should be taken to avoid framing the debate purely in terms of effectiveness. While it is important to note that this kind of police practice can have significant, and negative, unintended consequences in terms of crime and offending, absence of such would not necessarily imply that continued use of the power at the levels seen in recent years is acceptable. Police stop activity, if it is not as fairly distributed across the population as is possible, and/or not experienced as procedurally just by those affected by it, is problematic even if it cannot be shown that, as a consequence of this unfairness, more crime results. Not only do people deserve, and have the right, to be governed by a police service they find legitimate, various forms of unfairness in the application of police power have been linked to negative outcomes that go beyond increased propensities for crime, such as alienation (Bradford 2014), stigmatization (McAra and McVie 2005), and a reduction in life chances, for example by becoming 'known to' the police. These points are picked up in the chapters that follow – all, however serve to emphasize the importance of understanding the effect being stopped can have on the individuals concerned, and the importance of this effect is in many respects independent of any consideration of whether the stop 'worked' or not.

Note

1 Elements of this chapter are closely based on a paper given at Renmin University, Beijing, China in the summer of 2011.

References

Akinlabi, O.M. (2015). Young people, procedural justice and police legitimacy in Nigeria. *Policing and Society* Advance Access.

Barker, R. (2001). *Legitimating Identities*. Cambridge: Cambridge University Press.

Beetham, D. (1991). *The Legitimation of Power*. London: Macmillan.

Beetham, D. (2013). Revisiting legitimacy, twenty years on, in Tankebe, J. and Liebling, A. (eds) *Legitimacy and Criminal Justice: An International Perspective*. Oxford: Oxford University Press.

Berger, P.L. and Luckmann, T. (1966). *The Social Construction of Reality: A Treatise in the Sociology of Knowledge*. Harmondsworth: Penguin.

Blader, S.L. and Tyler, T.R. (2003). A four-component model of procedural justice: Defining the meaning of a "fair" process. *Personality and Social Psychology Bulletin* 29: 747–758

Blader, S. and Tyler, T.R. (2009). Testing and expanding the group engagement model, *Journal of Applied Psychology*, 94: 445–464.

Bottoms, A. and Tankebe, J. (2012). Beyond procedural justice: A dialogic approach to legitimacy in criminal justice. *Journal of Criminal Law and Criminology* 102(1): 119–170.

Bottoms, A. and Tankebe, J. (2013). 'A voice within': Power-holders perspectives in authority and legitimacy, in Tankebe, J. and Liebling, A. (eds) (2013). *Legitimacy and Criminal Justice: An International Perspective*. Oxford: Oxford University Press.

Bradford, B. (2011). Voice, neutrality and respect: Use of Victim Support services, procedural fairness and confidence in the criminal justice system. *Criminology and Criminal Justice* 11(4): 345–366.

Bradford, B. (2014). Policing and social identity: Procedural justice, inclusion, and cooperation between police and public. *Policing and Society*, 24(1): 22–43.

Bradford, B. and Jackson, J. (2016) Enabling and constraining police power, in Jacobs, J. and Jackson, J. (eds) *The Routledge Handbook of Criminal Justice Ethics*. Abingdon: Routledge.

Bradford, B. and Loader, I. (2016). Police, crime and order: The case of stop and search, in Bradford, B., Jauregui, B., Loader, I. and Steinberg, J. (eds) *The SAGE Handbook of Global Policing*. London: SAGE.

Bradford, B. and Quinton, P. (2014). Self-legitimacy, police culture and support for democratic policing in an English Constabulary. *British Journal of Criminology* 54(6): 1023–1046.

Bradford, B., Jackson, J. and Hough, M. (2013). Police futures and legitimacy: Redefining 'good policing', in Brown, J. (ed.) *The Future of Policing*. Oxford: Routledge, pp. 79–99.

Bradford B., Jackson J. and Stanko, E.B. (2009). Contact and confidence. Revisiting the impact of public encounters with the police. *Policing and Society* 19: 20–46.

Bradford, B., Murphy, K. and Jackson, J. (2014). Officers as mirrors: Policing, procedural justice and the (re)production of social identity. *British Journal of Criminology* 54(4): 527–550.

Bradford, B., Sargeant, E., Murphy, T. and Jackson, J. (2016). A leap of faith? Trust in the police among immigrants in England and Wales. *British Journal of Criminology* Online First.

Brunson, R.K. and Miller, J. (2006). Young black men and urban policing in the United States. *British Journal of Criminology* 46: 613–640.

Carr, P.J., Napolitano, L. and Keating, J. (2007). We never call the cops and here is why: A qualitative examination of legal cynicism in three Philadelphia neighbourhoods. *Criminology* 45(2): 445–480.

Clarke, R. and Cornish, D.B. (1985). Modeling offenders' decisions: A framework for research and policy. *Crime and Justice* 6: 147–185.

Delsol, R. and Shiner, M. (2006). Regulating stop and search: A challenge for police and community relations in England and Wales. *Critical Criminology* 14: 241–263.

Delsol, R. and Shiner, M. (eds) (2015). *Stop and Search.* Basingstoke: Palgrave Macmillan.

Doob, A.N. and Webster, C.N. (2003). Sentence severity and crime: Accepting the null hypothesis. *Crime and Justice* 30: 143–195.

Elias, N. (1994). *The Civilising process.* Oxford: Blackwell.

ESS (2011). *Trust in Justice: Topline Results from Round 5 of the European Social Survey.* European Social Survey.

Fitzgerald, M. (1999). *Final Report into Stop and Search.* Prepared for the Metropolitan Police Authority. London: MPA.

Fitzgerald, M., Hough, M., Joseph, I. and Qureshi, T. (2002). *Policing for London.* Cullompton: Willan Publishing.

Foster, J. and Jones, C. (2010). 'Nice to do' and essential: improving neighbourhood policing in an English police force. *Policing: a Journal of Policy and Practice* 4(4): 395–402.

Gilley, B. (2009). *The Right to Rule: How States Win and Lose Legitimacy.* New York: Columbia University Press.

Girling, E. Loader, I. and Sparks, R. (2000). *Crime and Social Change in Middle England.* London: Routledge.

Gottfredson, M.R. (2011). Sanctions, situations and agency in control theories of crime. *European Journal of Criminology* 8(2): 128–143.

Hall, S., Critcher, C., Jefferson, T., Clarke, J. and Roberts, B. (1978). *Policing the Crisis.* London: Macmillan.

Harkin, D. (2014). The police and punishment: Understanding the pains of policing. *Theoretical Criminology* 19(1): 43–58.

Hasisi, B. and Weisburd, D. (2011). Going beyond ascribed identities: the importance of procedural justice in airport security screening in Israel. *Law and Society Review,* 45(4): 867–892.

Hinds, L. and Murphy, K. (2007). Public satisfaction with police: Using procedural justice to improve police legitimacy. *The Australian and New Zealand Journal of Criminology,* 40(1): 27–42.

Hinsch, W. (2010). Justice, legitimacy and constitutional rights. *Critical Review of International Social and Political Philosophy* 13(1): 39–54.

Hirschman, A.O. (1970). *Exit, Voice, and Loyalty: Responses to Decline in Firms, Organizations, and States.* Cambridge, MA: Harvard University Press.

Home Affairs Select Committee (2007). *Young Black People and the Criminal Justice System.* London: Houses of Parliament.

Hough, M., Jackson, J. and Bradford, B. (2013). The drivers of police legitimacy: Some European research. *Journal of Policing, Intelligence and Counter Terrorism* 8(2): 144–165.

Hough, M., Jackson, J., Bradford, B., Myhill, A. and Quinton, P. (2010). Procedural Justice, Trust, and Institutional Legitimacy. *Policing: A Journal of Policy and Practice* 4(3): 203–210.

Jackson, J. and Gau, J.M. (2015) Carving up concepts? Differentiating between trust and legitimacy in public attitudes towards legal authority, in Shockley, E., Neal, T.M.S., PytlikZillig, L. and Bornstein, B. (eds) *Interdisciplinary Perspectives on Trust: Towards Theoretical and Methodological Integration.* Springer: New York.

Jackson, J., Bradford, B., Hough, M., Kuha, J., Stares, S., Widdop, S., Fitzgerald, R., Yordanova, M. and Galev, T. (2011). Developing European indicators of trust in justice. *European Journal of Criminology* 8(4): 267–285.

Jackson, J., Bradford, B., Hough, M., Quinton, P., Myhill, A. and Tyler, T.R. (2012). Why do people comply with the law? Legitimacy and the influence of legal institutions. *British Journal of Criminology* 52(6): 1051–1071.

Jackson, J., Bradford, B., Stanko, E.A. and Hohl, K. (2013). *Just Authority? Public Trust and Police Legitimacy.* London: Routledge.

Jacobs, B.A. (2010). Deterrence and deterrability. *Criminology* 48: 417–441.

Jonathan-Zamir, T. and Harpaz, A. (2014). Police understanding of the foundations of their legitimacy in the eyes of the public: The case of commanding officers in the Israel national police. *British Journal of Criminology* 54(3): 469–489.

Katz, J. (1987). *The Seductions of Crime.* Basic Books.

Kelman, H.C. and Hamilton, V.L. (1989). *Crimes of Obedience.* New Haven, CT: Yale University Press.

Kennedy, D.M. (2009). *Deterrence and Crime Prevention: Reconsidering the Prospect of Sanction.* New York: Routledge.

Kleiman, M.A.R. (2009). *When Brute Force Fails: How to Have Less Crime and Less Punishment.* Princeton: Princeton University Press.

Lassman, P. (2000). The rule of man over man: Politics, power and legitimation, in Turner, S. (ed.) *Cambridge Companion to Weber.* Cambridge: Cambridge University Press.

Lind, A.E. and Tyler, T.R. (1988). *The Social Psychology of Procedural Justice.* New York: Plenum Press.

Loader, I. (2010). Is it NICE? The appeal, limits and promise of translating a health innovation into criminal justice. *Current Legal Problems* 72: 63.

Loader, I, and Mulcahy, A. (2003). *Policing and the Condition of England.* Oxford: Oxford University Press.

McAra, L. and McVie, S. (2005). The usual suspects? Street-life, young people and the police. *Criminology and Criminal Justice* 5(1): 5–36.

Marks M. and Wood, J. (2010). South African policing at a crossroads: The case for a 'Minimal' and 'Minimalist' public police. *Theoretical Criminology* 14: 311–329.

Mazerolle, L., Bennett, S., Antrobus, E. and Eggins, E. (2012). Procedural justice, routine encounters and citizen perceptions of the police: Main findings from the Queensland Community Engagement Trial (QCET). *Journal of Experimental Criminology* 8(4): 343–366.

Miller, J., Bland, N. and Quinton, P. (2000). *The Impact of Stops and Searches on Crime and the Community.* Police Research Series Paper 127. London: Home Office.

Morris, R.G. and Piquero, A.R. (2013). For whom do sanctions deter and label? *Justice Quarterly* 30: 837–868.

Murphy, K., Hinds, L. and Fleming, J. (2008). Encouraging public cooperation and support for the police. *Policing and Society* 18(2): 136–155.

Murray, K. (2014). *Non-statutory stop and search in Scotland.* SCCJR Briefing Paper 6/2014.

Murray, K. and Harkin, D. (2016). Policing in cool and hot climates: Legitimacy, power and the rise and fall of mass stop and search in Scotland. *British Journal of Criminology* Advance Access.

Nagin D.S. (1998). Criminal deterrence research at the outset of the twenty-first century. *Crime Justice* 23: 1–42.

Nagin, D.S. (2013). Deterrence: A review of the evidence by a criminologist for economists. *Annual Review of Economics* 5: 83–105.

Nagin, D.S. and Pogarsky, G. (2001). Integrating celerity, impulsivity, and extralegal sanction threats into a model of general deterrence: Theory and evidence. *Criminology* 39(4): 865–892.

Nix, J. (2015). Do the police believe that legitimacy promotes cooperation from the public? *Crime and Delinquency* online before print.

Paternoster, R. (1987). The deterrent effect of the perceived certainty and severity of punishment: a review of the evidence and issues. *Justice Quarterly* 4:173–218.

Paternoster, R., Brame, R., Bachman, R. and Sherman, L.W. (1997). Do fair procedures matter? The effect of procedural justice on spouse assault. *Law and Society Review* 31: 163–204.

Piquero, A.P., Paternoster, R., Pogarsky, G. and Loughran, T. (2011). Elaborating the individual difference component in deterrence theory. *Annual Review of Law and Social Science* 7: 335–360.

Pratt, T.C., Cullen, F.T., Blevins, K.R., Daigle, L.E. and Madensen, T.D. (2006). The empirical status of deterrence theory: A meta-analysis. *Taking Stock: The Status of Criminological Theory* 15: 367–396.

Rebellon, C.J., Piquero, N.L., Piquero, A.R. and Tibbetts, S.G. (2010). Anticipated shaming and criminal offending. *Journal of Criminal Justice* 38(5): 988–997.

Reiner, R. (2010). *The Politics of the Police* (4th ed.). Oxford: Oxford University Press.

Robinson, P.H. and Darley, J.M. (2007). Intuitions of justice: Implications for criminal law and justice policy. *Southern California Law Review* 81: 1.

Rosenbaum, D., Schuck, A., Costello, S., Hawkins, D. and Ring, M. (2005). Attitudes toward the police: The effects of direct and vicarious experience. *Police Quarterly* 83: 343–365.

Scarman, L.G. (1981). *The Scarman Report: The Brixton Disorders.* London: HM Stationary Office.

Sharp, D. and Atherton, S. (2007). To serve and protect? The experiences of policing in the community of young people from Black and other ethnic minority groups. *British Journal of Criminology* 47(5): 746–763.

Sherman, L.W. and Eck, J.E. (2002). Policing for crime prevention, in Sherman, L.W., Farrington, D.P., Welsh, B.C. and MacKenzie, D.L. (eds) *Evidence-Based Crime Prevention.* New York: Routledge.

Shiner, M. and Delsol, R. (2015). The politics of the powers, in Delsol, R. and Shiner, M. (eds) *Stop and Search.* Basingstoke: Palgrave Macmillan.

Stone, V. and Pettigrew, N. (2000). *The Views of the Public on Stops and Searches.* London: Home Office.

Sunshine, J. and Tyler, T.R. (2003). The role of procedural justice and legitimacy in shaping public support for policing. *Law and Society Review* 37: 513–548.

Tankebe, J. (2008). Police effectiveness and police trustworthiness in Ghana: an empirical appraisal. *Criminology and Criminal Justice* 8(2): 185–202.

Tankebe, J. (2009). Self-help, policing, and procedural justice: Ghanaian vigilantism and the rule of law. *Law and Society Review* 43(2): 245–270.

Tankebe, J. and Liebling, A. (eds) (2013). *Legitimacy and Criminal Justice: An International Perspective*. Oxford: Oxford University Press.

Tyler, T.R. (2006). *Why People Obey the Law* (2nd ed.). New Haven: Yale University Press.

Tyler, T.R. (2008). Psychology and institutional design. *Review of Law & Economics* 4(3): 801–887.

Tyler, T.R. (2011). Trust and legitimacy: Policing in the USA and Europe. *European Journal of Criminology* 8: 254–266.

Tyler T.R. and Blader, S. (2000). *Cooperation in Groups: Procedural Justice, Social Identity, and Behavioral Engagement.* Philadelphia, PA.: Psychology Press.

Tyler, T.R. and Fagan, J. (2008). Legitimacy and cooperation: Why do people help the police fight crime in their communities? *Ohio State Journal of Criminal Law* 6(1): 231–275.

Tyler, T.R. and Huo, Y.J. (2002) *Trust in the Law: Encouraging Public Cooperation with the Police and Courts.* New York: Russell Sage Foundation.

Tyler, T.R. and Jackson, J. (2013). Future challenges in the study of legitimacy and criminal justice, in Tankebe, J. and Liebling, A. (eds) *Legitimacy and Criminal Justice: An International Perspective*. Oxford: Oxford University Press.

Tyler, T.R. and Wakslak, C.J. (2004). Profiling and police legitimacy: procedural justice, attributions of motive, and acceptance of police authority. *Criminology* 42(2): 253–281.

Tyler, T.R., Goff, P.A. and MacCoun, R.J. (2015) The impact of psychological science on policing in the United States: Procedural justice, legitimacy and effective law enforcement. *Psychological Science in the Public Interest* 16(3): 74–109.

Tyler, T.R., Jackson, J. and Bradford, B. (2014). Psychology of procedural justice and cooperation, in Bruinsma, G. and Weisburd, D. (eds) *Encyclopedia of Criminology and Criminal Justice*. New York: Springer.

Van Damme, A. (2015). The impact of police contact on trust and police legitimacy in Belgium. *Policing and Society* Online First.

Van Damme, A., Pauwels, L.J.R. and Svensson, R. (2013). Why do Swedes cooperate with the police? A SEM analysis of Tyler's procedural justice model. *European Journal on Criminal Policy and Research* 21(1): 15–33.

van de Bos, K., Vermunt, R. and Wilke, H. (1997). Procedural and distributive justice: What is fair depends more on what comes first than on what comes next. *Journal of Personality and Social Psychology* 72(1): 95–104

Way, L.B. and Patten, R. (2013). *Hunting for Dirtbags*. Boston: Northeastern University Press.

Weisburd, D. and Telep, C. (2014). Hot spots policing: What we know and what we need to know. *Journal of Contemporary Criminal Justice* 30(2): 200–220.

Weisburd, D., Wooditch, A., Weisburd, T. and Yang, S.-M. (2015). Do stop, question and frisk practices deter crime? Evidence from microunits of space and time. *Criminology and Public Policy* 15(1): 31–56.

Whimster, S. (ed.). (2004). *The Essential Max Weber*. Abingdon: Routledge.

Wikström, P.-O., Oberwittler, D. Treiber, K. and Hardie, B. (2012), *Breaking Rules. The Social and Situational Dynamics of Young People's Urban Crime*. Oxford: Oxford University Press.

Wright, V. (2010). *Deterrence in Criminal Justice. Evaluating Certainty vs. Severity of Punishment*. Washington, DC: The Sentencing Project.

4 The social and geographic distribution of police stops (in theory)

There were, on average, about one million stop/searches under PACE and associated legislation per year in England and Wales over the period 2001/2002 to 2014/2015. However this figure represents only a fraction of the total number of people who experience some sort of police stop in a given year. Not only are there those that occur under other pieces of legislation – most notably traffic stops – but there are other forms of contact between police and public that might be said to be police stops in a sociological but not a legal sense.

This chapter and the next are concerned with the question of who experiences these stops (and searches): what is the social and geographic distribution of experiences of this aspect of policing, and how might this distribution be explained? Answers to these questions have tended to rely on the police recorded data, meaning they are limited to both stop and search and the data recorded in the stop forms, and by definition they miss the broader context (for exceptions see Bradford and Loader 2016; Fitzgerald *et al.* 2002; Ariza 2014). Data from the Crime Survey of England and Wales (CSEW, previously the British Crime Survey) are therefore used in order to widen the angle of view to take in the whole range of police stops. This survey data also brings some additional benefits. First, it allows consideration of some of the factors beyond race and ethnicity that may predict experiencing this type of contact with the police. Second, it provides the opportunity to investigate how the interplay between different variables affects the distribution of police stop activity across geographical and social space.

The CSEW data are presented, described and explored in Chapter 5 below. The purpose of the current discussion is to develop a theoretical account of the social and spatial distribution of police stop activity. This is achieved first by examining the issue of ethnic disproportionality in stop and search activity, and second by expanding the discussion to consider other forms of stop activity and other possible predictors the odds of being stopped. At the threshold it is worth reiterating that the experience of being stopped by the police is relatively common, or at least more common that the police recorded stop and search statistics would seem to suggest. Around 10 per cent of the population experience some form of police stop each year. To be sure, many of the stops reported in the CSEW would not necessarily be considered as such by the police officers involved, in a legal sense, or even from the subjective viewpoint of others watching the encounters. Yet this might often mean little to the individuals concerned, who must, in most cases, experience them as the application of the power of the police to impinge on their freedom – to literally stop them – otherwise they would not feel they had been 'stopped' and responded accordingly when prompted by, in this case, the CSEW survey instrument. When considering this type of police activity it is important to bear in mind that it is relatively common and, in some ways, widespread.

Disproportionality and distribution of police stops

Much of the research on stop and search (or its non-British equivalents, such as stop and frisk) has concentrated on the issue of ethnic disproportionality – that is, on the extent to which people from some ethnic groups are more likely to be the targets of this type of police activity than others. This work has provided a rich seam of empirical and theoretical research stretching back over 30 years. Consideration of one of its central concerns, explanation of the gross fact of ethnic disproportionality, provides an obvious route into thinking about the practice of police stops in a wider sense. Much research has asked whether the disproportionality observed in the police recorded data, which is broadly uncontested (black people simply *are* more likely to be stopped and searched than white people), is the result of police bias, discrimination and/or racism, or whether it is rather the product of some factor or set of factors external to the behaviour of the police, or at least connected in a complex way with police activity, which taken together explain and/or excuse the bias disproportionality seems to represent? For example, research has attempted to 'explain away' disproportionality by introducing other factors into the equation that, once present, break the link between ethnicity and stop and search, such as offending (Borooah 2010), or the use of public space and consequent 'availability' to police (Waddington *et al.* 2004).

A common research strategy is to start from the idea that the socio-demographic characteristics of minority ethnic groups could have a major effect on the disproportionality identified in the official police data. In England and Wales, as elsewhere, ethnic minority populations tend to have a younger age profile than the general population, have lower incomes, and are more concentrated in urban areas (Office for National Statistics 2003) – all of which are factors that powerfully predict increased contact with the police (Bowling and Phillips 2003; Jefferson 1992; Smith 1997). On this account it is not surprising that people from ethnic minority groups are more likely to be stopped by the police; and the importance of police discrimination as an explanatory factor would therefore appear diminished – although this would not in and of itself negate issues of distributive fairness (even if black people are more likely to be stopped and searched because they are younger, they are still more likely to be stopped and searched).

By contrast, many have started with the premise that disproportionality is a result of discriminatory police practice. What, though, does discrimination mean in this context, and how might it find expression in police practice? Reiner (2010) provides a cumulative schema for exploring the evidence for and against discrimination in policing, where discrimination is defined as 'a pattern of exercise of police powers which results in some social categories being over-represented as targets of police action, even when legally relevant variables (especially patterns of offending) are held constant' (ibid.: 160). This typology provides a useful way of exploring the issues at hand (see Norris *et al.* 1992 for a similar, earlier, effort).

Discrimination in policing

To be clear, Reiner (2010: 164) stresses that there *is* a clear pattern of 'differentiation' in police practice, which disproportionately concentrates on young men, and particularly those who are unemployed and/or economically marginal and/or from an ethnic or other minority group. These characteristics are 'associated with a higher probability of being stopped, searched, arrested, detained in custody, charged, making complaints against the police … and failing to have these complaints substantiated' (p. 165). The question is, of course, whether this differentiation is justified in terms of 'legally relevant variables'. In the case of being young and male this is indeed likely to be the case. While the slope of the age–crime curve is not constant (McAra and McVie 2012), and there may have been some convergence between male and female offending rates over recent years (Heidensohn and Silvestri 2012), there seems little doubt that the behaviour of young men really does systematically vary on legally relevant variables in ways that would suggest they are more likely to come to the attention of the police. Differential policing is in this case therefore justified, to some degree at least.

Drawing on the left realist approach of Lea and Young (1984), Reiner goes on to argue that, to an extent, the same is true in relation to people from some ethnic minority groups, although this argument is immediately qualified by the suggestion that much, if not all, of the ethnic variation in offending is likely to be due to different age structures, rates of employment and similar patterns within minority populations. The idea here is that the socio-economic position of people from many ethnic minority groups is such that it would be hardly surprising if they committed more crime, and, for this reason, they are more likely to 'come to the attention of' the police. This is also, of course, the mainstay of 'common sense' media portrayals of stop and search – black people, in particular, are thought to have a higher offending rate than white people, which in turn is thought to explain why they are more likely to be stopped and searched – although here the left realist emphasis on structural preconditions tends to be ditched and arguments about personal responsibility and 'criminal propensity' come to the fore.

The argument that levels of offending are higher among (some) ethnic minority groups is heavily reliant on police recorded data. For example Reiner (2010: 168) notes that the arrest imbalance (the proportion of black people arrested compared with the proportion of white people arrested) is so strong that it cannot possibly be explained by 'mistaken' arrests – black people arrested when they should not have been – and that therefore levels offending probably are higher within the black community. It is arguable, however, that the realist position grants too much credence to arrest data, which many have claimed should be seen primarily if not entirely as an artefact of police practice with no necessary connection to the underlying 'reality' of crime (Coleman and Moynihan 1996). One problem with the approach taken by Reiner, for example, is that it concentrates on arrests that actually occurred, whereas those that *did not occur* may be equally important. Incidents where white people should or could have been arrested, but were not, may also have an effect on differentiation in arrest rates and therefore on the apparent variation in offending across majority and minority groups.

Indeed, moving away from police recorded data a quite different pattern of ethnic variation in offending begins to emerge, and while people from some minority ethnic groups are undoubtedly over-represented within the criminal justice in England and Wales (May *et al.* 2010; Phillips and Bowling 2012), there is relatively little evidence that such over-representation reflects differential levels of underlying offending (Phillips and Bowling 2012). Self-report offending surveys, for example, regularly find either little difference between minority and majority populations in terms offending, or that people from ethnic minority groups are in fact significantly *less* likely to offend (Sharp and Budd 2005). Notably, self-reported drug consumption (recall that drug offences are a key premise for many stop/searches) is lower in most ethnic minority groups than in the white population (Smith and Flatley 2011). In sum, differential levels of offending seem unlikely to be a significant factor 'driving' disproportionality at a population/aggregate level, although this does not discount the possibility that some forms of offending may be higher in local areas and/or among specific socio-cultural groups.

Despite the left realist stance outlined above, Reiner (2010: 170–172) does not disavow the importance of police discrimination in creating disproportionalities within the criminal justice system. He elucidates five forms of discrimination which are in turn divided into two groups – 'transmitted', 'interactional' or 'institutionalised', on the one hand, and 'statistical' or 'categorical', on the other. All are relevant to the issues at hand.

The first three forms of discrimination refer to situated practices that arise from the form and nature of police relations with other actors and the way police activity is patterned across social and geographical space. *Transmitted discrimination* occurs when police act as a conduit for the discriminatory urges of others, whether in terms of the identification of suspects (Henry 2007; Quinton 2015) or victim's preferences in terms of arrests or charges. In other words, victims may be more likely to identify offenders as black, and therefore direct police toward black suspects, with such identification based not on actual experiences but bias or discrimination. This would predict ethnic disproportionality in police stops because police will tend to be directed toward particular ethnic groups by victims and witnesses.

Interactional discrimination occurs when police officers themselves react differentially to the actions of those with whom they interact – classically, via variable enforcement of unwritten 'contempt of cop' rules. On this account police respond differently to challenges from people conditional on the characteristics of the person involved – one suggestion therefore being that when challenged they are more aggressive or punitive toward people from some groups compared with others (Glaser 2015; Trinkner and Goff 2016). Relatedly, Norris *et al.* (1992) suggested that citizen behaviour toward police may vary on a systematic basis and, specifically, that black people may be disproportionately disrespectful to officers, thus triggering a more stringent use of officer's discretionary powers. There appears to be very little hard evidence of this phenomenon in the UK, however, and Norris *et al.*'s own work suggests no significant differences in attitudes to the police among black and white people stopped (ibid.: 216). In the US, by contrast, some research has suggested that African Americans may be more likely than others to show disrespect to police during encounters (see for example Reisig *et al.* 2004)

Finally, *institutionalized discrimination* occurs when police policies and practices enacted for other reasons – for example the devotion of extra resources to high crime areas – result in disproportionate experiences or outcomes for particular groups. A key example here may be 'hotspot' and similar policing strategies, and, indeed,

> as police agencies continue to promote and advance practices that have demonstrated effectiveness [such as hotspots], it is likely that racial ethnic disparities in stops and stop outcomes will continue or perhaps even increase based on … saturation patrols on minority areas.
>
> (Engel and Cohen 2014: 401)

While these forms of discrimination may all be important at some times and in some places they are, in the final analysis, epiphenomenal, having little independent explanatory power but rather serving to mediate the effect of other factors or processes. They assume blindness to issues of race and equality within the police service, as when police target activities at certain areas without considering, or discounting, the impact on those living there, raising immediate questions as to (a) whether such an assumption is justified and (b) even if police are 'race blind' what might explain this myopia. They are also often dependent for explanatory mechanisms on *prior* bias or stereotypes, as when an officer reacts to 'disrespect' differently when it comes from a black as compared to a white youth. In such cases the discrimination displayed must have some exogenous source, such as bias or prejudice on the part of the officer. Interactional discrimination cannot simply be generated at the moment disrespect is experienced.

Reiner's second group of factors relate more clearly to prejudice and active discrimination within police ranks. *Statistical discrimination* occurs when police make assumptions about the nature and prevalence of offending within particular population groups: Reiner characterizes this type of discrimination as a form of noble cause corruption, deriving from an honestly held, if misguided, belief that it constitutes a justifiable method for targeting scarce police resources. Research on police attitudes and culture has found that stereotypes are indeed used by officers to classify people on the basis of their ethnic origin and appearance in ways that would appear to increase the probability of those stereotyped in a particular way being stopped/search (Quinton 2011; Loftus 2009; Way and Patten 2013). Others have suggested that Asians tend 'to be regarded as devious, liars and potential illegal immigrants', while black people are seen as 'incomprehensible, suspicious, hard to handle, naturally excitable, aggressive, lacking brainpower, troublesome and tooled up' (Bowling and Phillips 2003: 529). Yet, racist constructions of different groups are of course unlikely to be unidirectional (Jefferson 1992). While stereotyping of black men, in particular, as criminal may well result in people who 'fit the description' experiencing more stops than population proportions would suggest they should, there are stereotypes of Asians as being law abiding and family centred which may work in the opposite direction, although Webster (2004) noted a decade ago evidence of a shift in perceptions of British Asians, particularly Muslims, for example through media reports of drug dealing and abuse and 'gang culture' among young Pakistani and Bangladeshi men, and via the wider post-9/11 context (see also Pantazis and Pemberton 2009). Others, by contrast, have cast doubt on the extent to which police officers *act* on the basis of statistical discrimination, as opposed to simply holding stereotyped views about certain groups that have little or effect on their behaviour (e.g. Waddington *et al.* 2004).

Finally, *categorical discrimination* stems, essentially, from ethnic bias and out-and-out racism. This issue goes to the heart of much of the debate around stop and search. There is no doubt that racism exists in the police service, as it does in any other walk of life, and many studies have found 'negative views of people from ethnic minorities and support for extreme right political parties (to be) widespread' within police organizations (Bowling and Phillips 2003: 529; see also Loftus 2009). Furthermore, discrimination (as the acting out of racist prejudice) is most likely when, among other things

> decisions depend on subjective judgements rather than (or in addition to) objective criteria ... where there is considerable scope for exercise of individual discretion; where there is no requirement to record or monitor decisions or decision-making process; and where local or organisational cultural norms ... strongly influence decision making.
>
> (Bowling and Phillips 2003: 42)

It is hard to think of a better description of the way in which police stops, in their totality, operate. Street and traffic stops, as is most street level police activity, is of intrinsically low visibility to regulating authorities (Sanders and Young 2008), which would appear to only exacerbate the problem. Indeed, it may be that the very nature of police work and the structure of police organizations encourages – if not insists – on racialized thinking, in that police officers are continuously placed in situations within which they must make very rapid assessments of the threat posed by and/or likely behaviour of a person, based largely on appearance and demeanour but with no prior knowledge of them as an individual (Holdaway 1997). Under such conditions, decisions based on stereotypes, if not outright prejudice, seem almost inevitable. The 'thin blue line' ideology (Reiner 2010), according to which officers perceive themselves to be involved in a Manichean 'battle' to 'save' the streets and which retains significant purchase in police cultures would, moreover, seem to be a belief system that 'readily lends itself to negative labelling of people and places … and unquestioned racist stereotyping' (Foster 2003: 207), as individuals and groups are identified as the opposing forces in the 'fight against crime'.

Yet it is not at all clear that racism per se – which the Institute of Race Relations defines as 'the belief or ideology that "races" have distinctive characteristics which gives some superiority over others … (and) discriminatory and abusive behaviour based on such a belief or ideology'[1] – informs conscious decision-making among officers in any widespread manner. It is moreover not clear that individuals from minority ethnic groups tend to be treated in a less fair or respectful manner than others once stops have been initiated. This apparent disconnect has been a consistent theme in police research for many years. A Policy Studies Institute study produced many years ago (quoted by Norris *et al.* 1992) concluded that in routine policing 'there was no widespread tendency for black or Asian people to be given greatly inferior treatment'. Working around the same time, Jefferson *et al.* (1992) highlighted the disparity between the mass of quantitative evidence for disproportionality with the lack of observational or qualitative evidence for police racism being its cause; a conundrum which persists to this day. More recently, based on extensive observation of stop and search encounters Quinton (2015: 77) concluded that while stereotyping is 'the' primary way in which police develop their suspicions, 'the effect of categorical discrimination on racial disparities is likely to be fairly small … [and] encounters with people from BME groups were generally well-handled and on a par with those involving white people'. On these and other accounts the discrimination that produces ethnic disproportionality in stop and search stems from forms of implicit bias, stereotyping and 'structural factors' (ibid.), not overt or active racism.

Allport's (1958: 187–188) definition still guides much thinking on stereotypes, which he defined as 'an exaggerated belief associated with a category' of person that are generally inaccurate and which often evoke negative reactions toward target groups (Katz 1991: 150). Stereotypes are a 'natural' result of group formation processes (particularly those involving constructs like race and ethnicity), adhering to outgroups against which the ingroup is defined. While the existence of stereotypes is generally positioned as a negative, stereotyping is of value to individuals because such beliefs 'can provide mental shortcuts, providing rapid and efficient access to knowledge stored in memory whenever a social category is detected' (Martin *et al.* 2014: 1777). Stereotypes serve as heuristics to guide behaviour, particularly in low information or uncertain contexts. The concept of implicit bias, on the other hand, 'posits the importance of unconscious mental processing that can lead even the most egalitarian of individuals to engage in racially disparate behavior' (Trinkner and Goff 2016: 66). Bias arises when there are errors in the processes of implicit cognition ('Type I' thinking – Kahneman 2011) all human beings use to navigate their daily lives. Such biases can arise, notably, where there exist stereotypes about particular groups – and it is entirely possible the individual concerned is unaware that their behaviour is being guided by stereotyped thinking. On this account police officers, as does everyone else, operate according to a set of implicit categorizations that affect their decision-making processes. The almost inevitable result, it seems, those from socially marginalized groups, about whom there are widespread stereotypes, are the most likely to receive police attention (Glaser 2015; Quinton 2011; Smith and Alpert 2007).

The causes of ethnic disproportionality

Institutional and statistical forms of discrimination, and the implicit bias and unthinking stereotypes they assume, seem then on an a priori basis to be the most likely explanans of disproportionality. On this account police activity is governed to a significant degree by a set of assumptions about the offending behaviour of different social groups which, while not necessarily racist in inception is certainly racist in effect (which is to claim that individual officers do not consciously set out to stop and search black people more than others but, for a number of reasons, they end up doing precisely this). Yet, it has to be said that that there is actually rather little evidence on this issue one way or the other: while it is *believed* that police can and do act in discriminatory ways the extent to which this explains the disproportionality observed in the police recorded stop and search data, for example, is unclear. We are also far from being able to explain the sheer magnitude of this disproportionality. While stereotyping, bias and discrimination within the police would seem to be important factors, current evidence of the scale of such problems within the service does not seem to match the extent of ethnic disproportionality in the recorded stop and search data. In particular, evidence that significant numbers of police officers are explicitly racist in thought and deed is notably lacking – yet collectively they manage to produce outcomes that appear profoundly troubling.

In part to address these issues, recent research has suggested a set of factors influencing the distribution of stop activity, and in particular disproportionality, that go beyond police stereotyping, bias and discrimination. These revolve around a nexus of individual characteristics, geographical, social, and economic environments, and, importantly, police reactions to this set of factors and the relationships between them. Building on an approach initiated by Young (1994) and developed by Fitzgerald (1999) and others, MVA and Miller (2000) examined disproportionality in terms of the population *available* to be stopped by the police. While the concept of disproportionality has historically been based on comparing the proportion of a group stopped with their proportion in the general population, the inevitable targeting of police activity both temporally and spatially means that even fine-grained Census data on the population composition of local areas may not accurately reflect who is actually present on the streets and therefore 'available' to be stopped and searched by police operating in those areas. For example, higher rates of both school exclusion and unemployment among black youths may mean that a higher proportion are available during the day than would otherwise be the case, while different patterns of socializing may have an effect during the evening or at weekends. Waddington *et al.* (2004) take this point further and develop the idea that by looking at ethnicity as opposed to race it is possible to explore ways in which wider cultural practices and behaviour may affect who is available to the police to be stopped (in essence, people from different ethnic groups use public space in different ways that do not necessarily correlate with other social or economic factors). The ethnic composition of the 'available' population may therefore be very different than that of the resident population that is captured by the Census, and against which stop and search data are compared. This is, essentially, a version of routine activity theory (Felson 2002): from the perspective of the citizen, whose circumstance and socialization predisposes her (or more likely him) to be in particular places at particular times; and from the perspective of the police, who are provided with a very particular 'menu' of individuals from which to choose whom to stop.

By defining 'stop zones' where most police stops and searches occurred, and comparing the ethnic breakdown of those stopped with a measurement of the 'available' population derived by observation, MVA and Miller claimed to demonstrate that there was no general pattern of bias against ethnic minorities in the five police divisions they examined. Indeed, in many cases white people tended to be more likely to be stopped than their presence in the available population suggested (2000: 53). Asian people tended to be under-represented, while the picture for black people was mixed. Waddington *et al.* (2004), using different research sites, report broadly similar findings.

This argument seems, on the face of it, sensible, particularly in its emphasis on a version of routine activity theory. Yet, there is a danger in using it to 'explain away' the problem. Most immediately, the fact that there are more people from ethnic minorities available to be stopped by the police does not erase the fact that people from such groups are more likely to be exposed to this type of police behaviour, and, quite apart from issues of individual equity and fairness this can have profound effects on police community relations (Bowling and Phillips 2002; Bradford 2015 Jackson *et al.* 2013 and see Chapter 7). There are also methodological issues with the research – the areas chosen by MVA and Miller, for example, were those targeted by the police as areas of high crime, and areas of high crime may be poorer and more ethnically diverse, leading to a conflation of factors which may – or may not – be linked by complex casual pathways. Furthermore, the very presence of individuals from minority ethnic groups on the streets may be one thing that attracts police to an area, especially if statistical discrimination is occurring and/or there is racialization of specific types of crime under which the presence of specific groups in a particular is seen as an indicator of the presence of crime (Holdaway 1997; Solomos 2003). Indeed, MVA and Miller note that in some of their research areas, stop and search operations were targeted at locations where there were large numbers of people from minority ethnic groups but with crime rates which did not apparently warrant such attention.

Waddington *et al.* (2004) further contended that the issue of racism in police stop and search practice should be addressed at the institutional level (in the sense put forward by the Lawrence Enquiry report, Macpherson 1999) rather than at the level of specific police/citizen interactions or the practice of individual police officers. They suggested that disproportionality, while not 'created' by officer racism, may result from the interaction of police culture, the spatial patterning of socio-economic inequalities, and societal level structures and discourses that both racialize certain types of crime and ascribe certain types of criminal behaviours to certain geographical locations. Choongh (1997, 1998) summarized what such a process might mean in an article and book both entitled 'Policing the dross'. On this account the police concentrate their efforts on (racially inflected) socially 'problematic' categories of person. The existence of these categories is both prior to and re-created by the actions of police officers, whose reaction to, and ways of thinking and dealing with, such problem categories is deeply inscribed within police operational culture. This is a process that transcends individual proclivities and is not necessarily reducible to them. Police, even when operating with the *best* of (race-related) intentions, may produce distributively unfair, disproportionate outcomes – engage, that is, in differential policing – due to a confluence of factors revolving around the characterizations of places and individuals, which are driven in turn by the subjectivities of 'cop culture' as well as more widespread stereotypes *and* the 'objective' reality of the distributions of crimes and populations in the areas that they patrol.

Naturally, factors other than race or ethnicity may place people in the category of 'dross': social class is the obvious example. Police scholars have always emphasized the extent to which the police, traditionally drawn from the 'respectable' working class, have as a primary function the protection of the respectable classes in general, and what was once called the ruling class, in particular, from the disrespectable, *lumpenproletariat*, working class (see Reiner 2010 for a discussion). Criminological and sociological work continues to find that police work is shot through with the issue of class, broadly understood, whether this be conceptualized and assessed at the individual level (e.g. Loader 1996; McAra and McVie 2005) or, perhaps now more commonly, at the area level (e.g. Sampson 2012). People identifiable as members of certain sections of the working class, or who are from or encountered in 'disadvantaged' areas, are more likely than others to be classified by officers as potentially problematic and policed accordingly (Brogden 1981). As a result, moreover, such individuals are more likely to become labelled as the 'usual suspects' (McAra and McVie 2005) who because they become 'known' to the police register more strongly in officers' operational consciousness and are thus more likely to be stopped again the future (see also Ariza 2014). As McAra and McVie (2005: 28) argue

> The impact of police working rules, in particular the rules relating to previous form and suspiciousness (keeping the wrong company), serve to construct a population of young people viewed by the police as innately criminal and who become the objects of continual scrutiny.

There are also likely to be important interactions between the individual- and area-level variables. How police behave once attracted/directed to an area – or in a more general sense whenever they encounter some they assign to a particular social category – may be less straightforward than a simple search for the usual suspects. Looking at police stops, specifically, there is evidence that within a specific area the police are more likely to stop those who 'stand out' by not being from the 'right' ethnic group. Jefferson *et al.* (1992) found that white people were more likely to be stopped in areas with large ethnic minority populations, while in areas with only a few ethnic minority residents the converse was true. MVA and Miller (2000) also found that black people were more likely to be stopped in the two areas with the lowest 'available' black population (see also Release 2013).

Lessons from the United States?

The notion of 'race out of place' is a key theme in US research on these issues. Corresponding directly to ideas developed in the UK, in the US context this broadly translates to the idea that black people are more likely to be stopped if they are in a predominantly white neighbourhood, while white people are more likely to be stopped if they are in a predominantly black neighbourhood (Novak and Chamlin 2012; Carroll and Gonzalez 2014). Race out of place therefore correlates closely with the idea that police operate according to implicit bias and stereotyping; specifically, in relation to who 'should', and 'should not' be in a particular area (perhaps at a particular time).

Further aspects of the UK-based research described above – and certainly the more convincing aspects of it – correspond with a significant US literature on the distribution of 'stop and frisk', traffic stops and related practices, that revolves around a number of key organizing concepts (Bradford and Loader 2016: 244–245). These include conflict theory; consensus theory; group threat; race out of place; and the nexus of disorder, disadvantage and zero tolerance policing. This US work provides different, and sometimes contrasting, perspectives on the ways in which police activity may be initiated and directed, and subsequent implications for the social and geographic distribution of police stops. A key organizing theme has been that of racial profiling:

> the use by the police of generalizations based on race, ethnicity, religion or national origin, rather than individual behaviour, specific suspect descriptions or accumulated intelligence, as the basis for suspicion in directing discriminatory law enforcements actions such as stops, identity checks, questioning or searches
>
> (Delsol 2009: 263)

This clearly chimes with Reiner's (2010) statistical discrimination, although as commonly used the term racial profiling also frequently implies categorical discrimination as well (Engel and Cohen 2014).

Conflict theory (Chambliss and Seidman 1971; see Petrocelli *et al.* 2003 for a useful summary) proposes that the police, as a bureaucratic agency, will like all other such organizations tend to gravitate toward policies and practices that minimize strains and maximize rewards. Because police agencies are dependent on political organizations, structures and processes for funds and legitimacy, there are many incentives that motivate them to engage in behaviours that minimize friction with the politically powerful while at the same time focusing on those who, first, lack such power. Police are motivated to take the path of least resistance when deciding who and what to police, and will consequently focus disproportionately on those who have the least ability to seek redress. Second, the structural position of the police is such that attention will also be focused on those who pose a threat, whether social, economic, or indeed criminal, to the interests of those who *do* wield political influence. Under such conditions, so the argument goes, it is hardly surprising that police stop activity is directed disproportionality towards marginalized and excluded groups, and particularly those who are *visibly* so, since these constitute an apprehendable 'threat' to those on whom the police rely for political and economic support. Perhaps not coincidentally, they are also often those least able to 'kick back' against the over-policing they experience.

Conflict theory both contrasts with and complements *consensus* theory, which has been described as a structural functionalist approach (Renauer 2013). Here, a general agreement over society's aims and objectives is assumed, as is concord around the need for police to direct activity toward dealing with issues of crime and disorder and about what *constitutes* crime and/or disorder. Police will therefore be drawn to areas with high levels of crime, both because this is unproblematically seen to be their job and because they will be summoned there by residents who wish for crime to be dealt with and prevented. It thus follows that irrespective of their race, ethnicity or other characteristics, people living in these areas will be more likely to experience tactics such as stop and search (Gaines 2006; Novak and Chamlin 2012; Withrow 2004). While this seems less a theory of police activity than an operationalization of naïve common sense, it nonetheless seems relatively uncontroversial to suggest that all else equal police activity might well be concentrated in areas with higher levels of crime and that this will have an impact on those living in those areas. A further twist to this argument might be provided by noting that people with less economic and social capital – and particularly those living in deprived areas alongside many others in a similar situation – may all else equal be more likely to *need* to call the police, since they may lack resources to deal with problems in other ways.

Conflict and, in a counterfactual sense, consensus theories directly implicate the third organizing concept in the US literature, group (or racial) threat (Liska 1992; Petrocelli *et al.* 2003; cf. Bobo and Tuan 2006). Here, the idea is that minority populations pose a threat – symbolic, economic, or both – to the interests of existing or dominant social groups, triggering a response from agents of social control – i.e. police – who represent the interests of those dominant groups. On this account, street and traffic stops are part of the disciplinary architecture of policing, utilized along with a number of other techniques to circumscribe the activities of, and hence control, subordinate social groups considered threatening by superordinate groups.

The focus on a particular version of order maintenance policing in the US – encapsulated by the phrase 'zero tolerance' – provides yet another lens through which to view police stop activity. In some senses sitting within the conflict, consensus *and* group threat models (Renauer 2013), this understanding of the way police activity is directed suggests that police stops are more likely to occur in poorer and, in particular, more disorderly areas. There are a number of reasons to suggest why this might be case, related both to policies such as zero-tolerance, which focus police attention on incivilities and low-level disorder (Fagan *et al.* 2010) and, perhaps, the extent to which police officers as much as members of the public (Innes 2004; Jackson and Bradford 2009) use disorder as a visual cue indicating the possible presence of more serious crime, thus altering the way they behave in more disorderly, compared with less disorderly, areas. Alternatively, if one accepts the (broken windows) thesis that disorder is causally linked to both crime and a breakdown in informal social control (an idea that is open to significant doubt – Harcourt 2001), the presence of disorder may indicate the need for greater intervention from agents of formal social control as a corrective. In short, the idea here is that policing aims toward not only 'fighting crime' but exerting discipline in a wider sense, by for example attempting to restore order to areas perceived to be in some way disorderly.

Despite the intuitive appeal of many of these ideas Renauer (2013: 7) reports that studies have found only weak or inconsistent support for an association between disorder, disadvantage and police stops: evidence in support of consensus *or* conflict theories is inconclusive. Yet there is some evidence to suggest such associations may be identified in some times and places. Most notably, Fagan et al's (2010) research in New York found some relationship between measures of disorder and disadvantage, on the one hand, and police stop (and arrest) rates, on the other. This may not be a surprise, given the focus on so-called 'zero tolerance' policing in that context over a number of years, but it does suggest that police activity can be distributed in ways that do not match the crime rate, as such, but are rather influenced by the wider nexus of disorder and/or poverty.

A last noteworthy finding from US research is that black and Hispanic people are more likely than whites to be frisked or searched once they have been stopped (Carroll and Gonzalez 2014; Rojek *et al.* 2012; Tillyer *et al.* 2012). Rojek *et al.* (2012) interpret this finding in the light of Black's (1976) notion of law as quantifiable social control. Since a frisk or search amounts to the application of 'more' law than a simple stop these more invasive behaviours will be more frequently used against those positioned further down social hierarchies that, in the United States, are so often racially defined (since the less status accorded to an individual the more law it is appropriate to use against them). Those who are more in need of 'controlling' will be more likely to experience more coercive interventions. Equally, of course, the implicit bias or stereotyping that might guide the decision to stop may also guide the decision to search (Carrol and Gonzalez 2014).

Drugs and stop and search

Finally, there is the role of drug policing/prevention in stimulating stop and search practice. This is an important issue, since drugs are cited as the grounds for approximately half of all searches conducted under PACE and associated legislation. Research conducted by the charity Release and the London School of Economics (Release 2013) concluded that the policing of drug crime was a primary driver of the ethnic disproportionality in stop and search and, consequently, of the entry of ethnic minority individuals into the criminal justice system. Using publicly available police recorded data for the year 2009/2010, the researchers concluded (p. 12) that while stop rates for drugs over the population as a whole was 10 per 1,000 people, for the white population this figure was 7 per 1,000 people: for mixed race it was 14 per 1,000; for Asian, 18 per 1,000; and for black, 45 per 1,000. It is worth reiterating here that there is no evidence that drug use is any higher among ethnic minority populations (Sangster *et al.* 2002; Stevens 2011); indeed, based on the CSEW self-report data, drug use appears to be lower among most ethnic minorities than among the white majority (Home Office 2013). Moreover, the arrest rate from drug searches is low, around 7 per cent in 2009/2010, and is similar across ethnic groups (Release 2013).

Drugs, then, constitute what is by some margin the most common grounds for stopping and searching someone, and drug searches appear to be a significant factor driving ethnic disproportionality. So is the story here really about the counterproductive nature of 'the war on drugs' and its perverse outcomes? In a sense the answer to this question must be yes – the numbers quoted above are compelling – and it certainly seems that to understand stop and search one needs an understanding of the policing of drugs. However some caution is also required. Most obviously, while drugs were the *grounds* for many searches the arrest rate suggests they were not often found. The arrest rate is a highly imperfect measure of success, both because it does not cover other disposals such as fixed penalty notices and because any arrest may have been caused by the stop, for example because the person stopped became angry, rather than by the alleged behaviour that triggered it (HMIC 2013). Yet arrests seem a good enough proxy to suggest that actual drug *use* may not be the only, or indeed the main, factor behind the numbers outlined above. It is possible that in many cases drugs are given as the grounds for searches that are conducted for other reasons, whether specifically crime related or to do with the need for police to establish and maintain control in a particular situation. This is not to claim that police are lying when they record drugs as the grounds for searches (although some may be). Nor is it to claim that drug use is not crime (because it clearly, and unfortunately, is). Rather, it is to note that the policing of drugs may act as a symbol for and be part of some other, arguably more deep-seated, set of processes and concerns. Most pertinently drug use and the characteristics ascribed to those believed to use drugs have consistently be positioned as pose a threat to 'the security of social order' (Dubber 2005: xi). More prosaically, however, it might be noted that an ostensible search for drugs can provide an omnibus justification for stop/searches conducted for other reasons.

Taking a wider view

When it comes to explaining ethnic variation in the distribution of police stops a wide range of factors have thus been suggested. The extent to which out-and-out racism influences officer decision-making is unclear in all but a small minority of cases. By contrast, the evidence concerning implicit bias and stereotyping as 'drivers' of police behaviour seems much more certain (Glaser 2015; Trinkner and Goff 2016; Quinton 2015), and it seems highly likely that disproportionality is caused at least in part by police officers acting not out of direct racial prejudice but on the basis of unexamined, implicit and sub-conscious stereotypes, biases and cultural assumptions.

Moreover, there may be an association between policing and the targeting and/or control of marginal populations that does deeper than the proclivities of individual officers. This might well be characterized as institutional racism, the product of either the wider social environment within which police operate and/or carelessly applied or deliberately unexamined aspects of policy and practice that produce ethnically based variation in experiences of policing as a by-product of other activities. Ethnic disproportionality is therefore predicted not only by bias and stereotyping but also by the fact that people from minority groups are affected by much wider processes of exclusion and are therefore more likely to be placed into marginal social categories that draw attention from police.

All that being said, the extent of ethnic disproportionalities can seem excessively large given what is known about the level of racism within the police service, on the one hand, and known levels of offending among the minority groups concerned, on the other. The size of the problem seems too big for the answers for it that are most commonly offered. If we conceive of the practice of policing as fundamentally concerned with the control of marginal groups, however, then the extent of such disproportionality is rendered less of a puzzle.

It may indeed stem from a foundational principle of policing: the identification, marking and control of social groups that are different from and therefore potentially threatening to the 'mainstream'. While differential policing is in these terms prior to categories of race and ethnicity – the history of the police power can be traced back to well before modern understandings of these terms came into existence (Dubber 2005; Neocleous 2000; Zedner 2006), and policing has always been unequally distributed social and spatially – it is now heavily bound to them. Physical markers of ethnic difference provide, for example, a ready heuristic for police looking for those who do not 'fit' in a particular social situation, signify a higher risk of offending according to occupational and wider cultural stereotypes, or, at the extreme, simply indicate demonstrable, troubling, difference. On this account black people are not only stopped because stereotyping suggests to officers they are more likely to offend, but also because they are a category of person who have come to be defined as suitable as objects of police attention (by implication, there are also likely to be categories of person not suitable as objects of such attention, which is one reason why police might react differently two dissimilar individuals behaving in otherwise similar ways).

According to Dubber (2005) the police power – of which the uniformed police are just one particular instantiation – is oriented most importantly towards maintaining a specific notion of social order concerned with established notions of propriety and the reproduction of extant social hierarchies. Under this understanding it would be surprising if police attention was *not* disproportionality directed at the marginal, the excluded and those who seem to provide a threat to established order, precisely because, for example, they are 'in the wrong place at the wrong time'. Indeed, since their existence is inherently troubling members of marginalized groups may find it hard *not* to be in the wrong place at the wrong time. Disproportionate or differential policing can therefore also be characterized as stemming from the fundamental premise of (or urge to) *police*, where this is characterized as the basic effort the state to use whatever means are necessary to maintain normative social order (Bradford and Loader 2016). Such order is by definition predicated on particular hierarchies, and police power is required to maintain and reproduce these relationships.

Factors influencing disproportionality that are in the first instance external to the police organization, its culture and practice may tap into similar processes. Particularly pertinent may be the extent to which police activity is, for a variety of reasons, directed *by other actors* toward the disorderly, the threatening and the out-of-place. Most police activity occurs because it is stimulated by another actor (Brodeur 2010) – for example via a call for service, through the volunteering of information, or because police action is triggered in some way by another authority – and the role of others in drawing police toward particular people must be relevant in terms of explaining disproportionality, at least at some times and in some places. The behaviour of those invoking police may equally be shaped by a concern to address perceived threats to the established social order. The extent to which police activity is directed towards more deprived areas, for similar reasons and with similar consequences, may also be relevant. Here, the external actors may range from 'concerned citizens' living in those areas to high level policy makers concerned with what they see as social breakdown and decay.

It is clear that many of the factors described above suggest disproportionalities in the experience of police stops that go beyond categories of race and/or ethnicity. Other groups and types of person experience discrimination, are stereotyped, marginalized and excluded, and are concentrated in particular parts of towns and cities. They, too, are more likely than others to experience invasive forms of policing. Indeed, the focus of the police gaze on such groups and individuals has a long historical pedigree. Dubber (2005) provides detailed lists of the social categories of most interest to police regulations, ordnances and practices, drawn up from legislation applied from the sixteenth century onwards across many jurisdictions. Taken together, and in the light of the discussion above, these invoke remarkable present-day parallels. For example, Blackstone, in his Commentaries on the Laws on England (1769 – see Dubber 2005: 54) provided the following list of individuals, groups and behaviours that were properly subject to the supervisory and disciplining oversight of police.

> haunting bawdy houses with women of bad fame; or of keeping such women in his own house; or for words tending to scandalize the government; or in abuse of the officers of justice … night-walkers; eaves droppers; such as keep suspicious company, or are reported to be pilferers or robbers; such as sleep in the day, and wake on the night; common drunkards; whoremasters; the putative father of bastards; cheats; idle vagabonds.

Police regulations drawn up by American legislatures in the eighteenth and nineteenth centuries have a similar feel. In New York State, for example, behaviours and individuals subject to police regulation – to the supervision of state structures of governance and control – included among many others: hawkers and idlers; beggars and disorderly persons; apprentices and servants; bastards; idiots and lunatics; those engaged in cursing and swearing; drunkenness; poor relief; and those using the highways (Dubber 2005: 88–89). It is no coincidence that these lists match many elements of the population groups and behaviours positioned by more recent authors as 'police property' and as social categories given over to the control of police by 'the dominant powers of society' (Lee 1981, quoted in Reiner 2010: 123):

> low status, powerless groups whom the dominant majority see as problematic or distasteful … vagrants, skid row alcoholics, drug addicts, the unemployed or casually employed residuum, youth adopting a deviant cultural style, ethnic minorities, gays, prostitutes, and radical political organizations.

In addition to this focus on the marginal and the problematic, it is also worth noting that what Colquhoun called the 'system of police' (Neocleous 2000: 51) was also centrally concerned with regulating movement within the metropolis and with promoting the 'comfort and convenience' of its inhabitants by ordering traffic and commerce. Maintaining the good order of society involved not only control of the poor but also regulation of movement and the encouragement of commerce and civility in public spaces (Hunt 2006).

Summary

While the emphasis in academic research on stop and search has for understandable reasons tended to focus on the issue of ethnic disproportionality, there is much to suggest that there will be other disproportionalities in the targeting of this type of police activity. Consideration of police power in historical perspective suggests that particular groups of people and types of behaviour are particularly likely to be subject to the regulatory power of police – as well as those using public space and, particularly, the highway.

Yet the importance of ethnic disproportionality in stop and search, in particular, is not diminished by positioning it as something that is immanent in the 'structure' of policing as an activity and the ways in which this find expression in an unequal society. Indeed, Dubber's concept of police power may provide a solution to some of the well-known problems with the concept of 'institutional racism', as proposed in the Macpherson report (Macpherson 1999) and often cited as a key reason for disproportionality in stop and search. These problems are summarized by Lea (2003: 51), who argues that Macpherson located 'the source of racism in the social and cultural life of police officers rather than in the dynamics of operational policing itself' (see also Souhami 2014: 4–5). Noting that low arrest rates problematize the argument that stop and search is primarily about crime, Lea goes on to argue that this form of practice needs to be seen in light of the 'historical necessity' for the police to monitor and control populations deemed as problematic or threatening:

> The indicators required by police as a basis for stops are therefore less those of explicit criminality then membership of the underclass. Race is used by the police in precisely this way as a trigger for general surveillance and control. It is not, of course, the only such sign. Being a skinhead or dressing in a certain way or being in the 'wrong place at the wrong time' will also function. Large numbers of Whites are stopped on the basis of such signs. These signs are reproduced as stereotypes of dangerousness, and they are reinforced in the practical street wisdom and occupational culture of police officers.
>
> (Lea 2003: 63)

On this account ethnic disproportionality is to a significant degree a product of the basic requirement for police to control populations defined as difficult, marginal, problematic or dangerous. It stems not so much from racism on the part of individual officers as from the fact that they operate within a society marked by a racialized vision of who or what constitutes a 'problem'. Constituting one element of the wider effort of the state to reproduce order, police attention will continuously be directed toward individuals and groups defined as threatening to that order. Race or ethnicity can mark a person out as potential problem, but as Lea notes, other signs can be equally as important.

Note

1 www.irr.org.uk/research/statistics/definitions/. Accessed May 2016.

References

Allport, G.W. (1958). *The Nature of Prejudice* (Abridged). Garden City, NY: Doubleday Anchor Books.

Ariza, J.J.M. (2014). Police-initiated contacts: young people, ethnicity, and the 'usual suspects'. *Policing and Society* 24(2): 208–223.

Black, D. (1976). *The Behavior of Law*. New York: Academic Press.

Bobo, L.D. and Tuan, M. (2006). *Prejudice in Politics*. Cambridge, MA: Harvard University Press.

Borooah, V.K. (2010). Racial Disparity in Police Stop and Searches in England and Wales. *Journal of Quantitative Criminology* 27(4): 453–473.

Bowling, B. and Phillips, C. (2003). Policing ethnic minority communities, in Newburn, T. (ed.) *The Handbook of Policing*, pp. 528–555. Cullompton: Willan Publishing.

Bradford, B. (2015). Assessing the impact of stop and search powers on individuals and communities, in Delsol, R. and Shiner, M. (eds) *Stop and Search*. Basingstoke: Palgrave Macmillan.

Bradford, B. and Loader, I. (2016). Police, crime and order: The case of stop and search, in Bradford, B., Jauregui, B., Loader, I. and Steinberg, J. (eds) *The SAGE Handbook of Global Policing*. London: SAGE.

Brodeur, J.-P. (2010). *The Policing Web*. Oxford: Oxford University Press.

Brogden, A. (1981). 'Sus' is dead: but what about 'Sas'? *New Community* 9(1): 44–52.

Carroll, L. and Gonzalez, M.L. (2014). Racial stereotypes and the ecology of frisks and searches following traffic stops. *Journal of Research in Crime and Delinquency* 51: 559–584.

Chambliss, W. and Seidman, R. (1971). *Law, Order and Power*. Philippines: Addison-Wesley Publishing Co.

Choongh, S. (1997). *Policing as Social Discipline*. Oxford: Clarendon Press.

Choongh, S. (1998). Policing the dross: a social disciplinary model of policing. *British Journal of Criminology* 38(4): 623–634.

Coleman, C. and Moynihan, J. (1996). *Understanding Crime Data: Haunted by the Dark Figure*. Buckingham: Open University Press.

Delsol, R. (2009). Racial profiling, in Wakefield, A. and Fleming, J. (eds) *The SAGE Dictionary of Policing*. London: SAGE.

Dubber, M.D. (2005). *The Police Power. Patriarchy and the Foundations of American Government*. New York: Columbia University Press.

Engel, R.S. and Cohen, D. (2014). Racial profiling, in Reisig, M. and Kane, R. (eds) *The Oxford Handbook on Police and Policing*. New York: Oxford University Press.

Fagan, J., Geller, A., Davies, G. and West, V. (2010). Street stops and broken windows revisited: The demography and logic of proactive policing in a safe and changing city, in Rice, S.K. and White, M.D. (eds) *Race, Ethnicity and Policing: New and Essential Readings*. New York: New York University Press.

Felson, M. (2002). *Crime and Everyday Life* (3rd edn). London: Sage.

Fitzgerald, M. (1999). *Searches in London under Section 1 of the Police and Criminal Evidence Act*. London: Metropolitan Police.

Fitzgerald, M., Hough, M., Joseph, I. and Qureshi, T. (2002). *Policing for London*. Cullompton: Willan Publishing.

Foster, J. (2003). Police cultures, in Newburn T (ed.) *The Handbook of Policing*, pp. 196–227. Cullompton: Willan Publishing.

Gaines, L. (2006). An analysis of traffic stop data in Riverside, California. *Police Quarterly*, 9(2): 210–233.

Glaser, J. (2015). *Suspect Race*. New York: Oxford University Press.

Harcourt, B. (2001) *Illusion of Order: The False Promise of Broken Windows Policing*. Cambridge, MA: Harvard University Press.

Heidensohn, F. and Silvestri, M. (2012). Gender and Crime, in Maguire, M., Morgan R. and Reiner, R. (eds) *The Oxford Handbook of Criminology* (5th edn), pp. 337–369. Oxford: Oxford University Press.

Henry, A. (2007). Policing and ethnic minorities, in Henry, A. and Smith, D.J. (eds) *Transformations of Policing*, pp. 79–112. Aldershot: Ashgate.

HMIC (2013). *Stop and Search Powers: Are the Police Using Them Effectively and Fairly?* London: Her Majesty's Inspectorate of Constabulary.

Holdaway, S. (1997). Constructing and sustaining race in the police work force. *The British Journal of Sociology*, 48(1): 19–34.

Home Office (2013). *Drug misuse: Findings from the 2012 to 2013 Crime Survey of England and Wales*. London: Home Office.

Hunt, A. (2006). Police and the regulation of traffic: Policing as a civilizing process?, in Dubber, M.D. and Valverde, M. (eds) *The New Police Science: The Police Power in Domestic and International Governance*. Stanford: Stanford University Press.

Innes, M. (2004). Signal crimes and signal disorders: Notes on deviance as communicative action. *British Journal of Sociology* 55(3): 335–355.

Jackson, J. and Bradford, B. (2009). Crime, policing and the moral order: On the expressive nature of public confidence in policing. *British Journal of Sociology* 60(3): 493–522.

Jackson, J., Bradford, B., Stanko, B. and Hohl, K. (2013). *Just Authority? Trust in the Police in England and Wales*. London: Routledge.

Jefferson, T. (1992). The racism of criminalization: Policing and the reproduction of the criminal other, in Gelsthorpe LR (ed.) *Minority ethnic groups in the criminal justice system*, pp. 26–48. Cambridge: University of Cambridge Press.

Jefferson, T., Walker, M. and Seneviratne, M. (1992). Ethnic minorities, crime and criminal justice: A study in a provincial city, in Downes, D (ed.) *Unravelling Criminal Justice*. Basingstoke: Macmillan Press.

Kahneman, D. (2011). *Thinking Fast and Slow*. New York, NY: Farrar, Straus and Giroux.

Katz, I. (1991). Gordon Allport's "The Nature of Prejudice." *Political Psychology* 12(1): 125–157.

Lea, J. (2003). Institutional racism in policing: The Macpherson report and its consequences, in Matthews, R. and Young, J. (eds) *The New Politics of Crime and Punishment*. Cullompton: Willan.

Lea, J. and Young, J. (1984). *What Is To Be Done About Law and Order?* Harmondsworth: Penguin.

Lee, J.A. (1981). Some structural aspects of police deviance in relations with minority groups, in Shearing, C. (ed.) *Organized Police Deviance*. Toronto: Butterworth.

Liska, A.E. (ed.) (1992). *Threat and Social Control*. Albany: SUNY Press.

Loader, I. (1996). *Youth, Policing and Democracy*. London: MacMillan.

Loftus, B. (2009). Police occupational culture: Classic themes, altered times. *Policing and Society*, 20(1): 1–20.

McAra, L. and McVie, S. (2005). The usual suspects: Street-life, young people and the police. *Criminal Justice* 5: 3–36.

McAra, L. and McVie, S. (2012). Critical debates in developmental and life-course criminology, in Maguire, M., Morgan, R. and Reiner, R. (eds) *The Oxford Handbook of Criminology* (5th edn), pp. 531–560. Oxford: Oxford University Press.

Macpherson, Sir W. (1999). *The Stephen Lawrence Inquiry, Report of an Inquiry by Sir William Macpherson of Cluny CM 4262–1*. London: HMSO.

Martin, D., Hutchinson, J., Slessor, G., Urquhart, J., Cunningham, S.J. and Smith, K. (2014). The spontaneous formation of stereotypes via cumulative cultural evolution. *Psychological Science* 25(9): 1777–1786.

May, T., Gyateng, T. and Hough, M. with the assistance of Bhardwa, B., Boyce, I. and Oyanedel, J.C. (2010). *Differential Treatment in the Youth Justice System*. London: Equalities and Human Rights Commission.

MVA and Miller, J. (2000). *Profiling Populations Available for Stops and Searches*. Police Research Series Paper 131. London: Home Office.

Neocleous, M. (2000). *The Fabrication of Social Order*. London: Pluto Press.

Norris, C., Fielding, N., Kemp, C. and Fielding, J. (1992). Black and blue: an analysis of the influence of race on being stopped by the police. *The British Journal of Sociology* 43(2): 207–224.

Novak, K.J. and Chamlin, M.B. (2012). Racial threat, suspicion, and police behaviour: The impact of race and place in traffic enforcement. *Crime and Delinquency* 58(2): 275–300.

Office for National Statistics (2003). *Social Focus in Brief: Ethnicity*. Internet only.

Office for National Statistics (2010). *Standard Occupational Classification 2010*. Basingstoke: Palgrave Macmillan.

Pantazis, C. and Pemberton, S. (2009). From the 'old' to the 'new' suspect community: Examining the impacts of recent UK counter-terrorist legislation. *British Journal of Criminology* 49(5): 646–666.

Petrocelli, M., Piquero, A.R. and Smith, M.R. (2003). Conflict theory and racial profiling: An empirical analysis of police traffic stop data. *Journal of Criminal Justice* 31: 1–11.

Phillips, C. and Bowling, B. (2012). Ethnicities, racism, crime and criminal justice, in Maguire, M., Morgan, R. and Reiner, R. (eds) *The Oxford Handbook of Criminology* (5th edn). Oxford: Oxford University Press.

Quinton, P. (2011). The formation of suspicion: police stop and search in England and Wales. *Policing and Society* 21(4): 357–368.

Quinton, P. (2015). Race disproportionality and officer decision-making, in Delsol, R. and Shiner, M. (eds) *Stop and Search*. Basingstoke: Palgrave Macmillan.

Reiner, R. (2010). *The Politics of the Police (4th edn)*. Oxford: Oxford University Press.

Reisig, M., McCluskey, J.D., Mastrofski, S.D. and Terrill, W. (2004) Suspect disrespect toward the police. *Justice Quarterly* 21(2): 241–268.

Release (2013). *The Numbers in Black and White: Ethnic Disparities in the Policing and Prosecution of Drug Offences in England and Wales*. London: Release.

Renauer, B.C. (2013). Neighbourhood variation in police stops and searches: A test of consensus and conflict perspectives. *Police Quarterly* 15(3): 219–240.

Rojek, J., Rosenfeld, R. and Decker, S. (2012). Policing race: The racial stratification of searches in police traffic stops. *Criminology* 50: 993–1024.

Sampson, R. (2012). *Great American City*. Chicago: University of Chicago Press.

Sanders, A. and Young, R. (2008). Police powers, in Newburn, T. (ed) *Handbook of Policing* (2nd edn). London: Routledge.

Sangster, D., Shiner, M., Patel, K. and Sheikh, N. (2002). *Delivering Drug Services to Black and Minority Ethnic Communities*. London: Home Office.

Sharp, C. and Budd, T. (2005). *Minority Ethnic Groups and Crime: Findings from the Offending, Crime and Justice Survey 2003*. Home Office online report 33/05. London: Home Office.

Smith, D.J. (1997). Ethnic origins, crime and criminal justice, in Maguire, M., Moore, R. and Reiner, R. (eds) *The Oxford Handboook of Criminology*. Oxford: Oxford University Press.

Smith, K. and Flatley, J. (eds) (2011). *Drug Misuse Declared: Findings from the 2010/11 British Crime Survey*. HOSB 12/11. London: Home Office.

Smith, M. and Alpert, G. (2007). Explaining police bias: A theory of social conditioning and illusory correlation. *Criminal Justice and Behavior* 34: 1262–1283.

Solomos, J. (2003). *Race and Racism in Britain*. Basingstoke: Palgrave MacMillan.

Souhami, A. (2014). Institutional racism and police reform: an empirical critique. *Policing and Society* 24(1), 1–21.

Stevens, A. (2011). *Drugs, Crime and Public Health: The Political Economy of Drug Policy*. London: Routledge.

Tillyer, R., Klahm IV, C.F. and Engel, R.S. (2012). The discretion to search: A multilevel examination of driver demographics and officer characteristics. *Journal of Contemporary Criminal Justice* 28: 184–205.

Trinkner, R. and Goff, P.A. (2016). The colour of safety: The psychology of race and policing, in Bradford, B., Jauregui, B., Loader, I. and Steinberg, J. (eds) *The SAGE Handbook of Global Policing*. London: SAGE.

Waddington, P., Stenson, K. and Don, D. (2004). In proportion: race, and police stop and search. *British Journal of Criminology* 44: 889–914.

Way, L.B. and Patten, R. (2013). *Hunting for Dirtbags*. Boston: Northeastern University Press.

Webster, C. (2004). Policing British Asian communities, in Burke, R.H. (ed.) *Hard Cop, Soft Cop: Dilemmas and Debates in Contemporary Policing*, pp. 69–84. Cullompton: Willan publishing.

Withrow, B.L. (2004). Driving while different: A potential theoretical explanation for race-based policing. *Criminal Justice Policy Review* 15(3): 344–364.

Young, J (1994). *Policing the Streets: Stops and Searches in North London*. Centre for Criminology, Middlesex University.

Young, J. (1999). *The Exclusive Society*. London: Sage.

Zedner, L. (2006). Policing before and after the police. The historical antecedents of contemporary crime control. *British Journal of Criminology* 46(1): 78–96.

5 The social and geographic distribution of police stops (in practice)

The previous chapter catalogued some of the potential causes of ethnic disproportionality in the distribution and experience of police stops. Explanations ranged from the idea that police activity will be concentrated in areas with high levels of crime – which might also have larger ethnic minority populations – to the possible existence of various forms of discrimination within the police service. Discussion of ethnic disproportionality also opened up some of the wider issues that are likely to surround this particular application of police power. We can now turn to the immediate issue of the distribution of police stops experiences across England and Wales as they are recorded in the CSEW.

What, then, might we expect to find in this data? Drawing on the research described in Chapter 4, a number of hypotheses will guide the analysis. I expect that, first, people from some ethnic minority groups – particularly black ethnic groups – will be more likely to be stopped by police than those from a white ethnic group. Not only does the recorded data strongly suggest this will be the case but so do ideas about the nature of police discrimination and stereotyping, conflict theories, and group threat; as well, of course, as over 40 years of research into policing. Given this convergence of perspectives, it might be expected that the association between an individual's ethnicity and their probability of experiencing a police stops will be robust to any number of statistical controls. Even controlling for people's behaviours, it seems reasonable to hypothesize that people from ethnic minority groups will still be more likely to be stopped than their white counterparts.

Second, I expect that people from disadvantaged social categories will, for similar reasons, be more likely to be stopped by police. This effect, too, should be independent of statistical controls. This hypothesis relates to the idea, developed in the preceding chapters, that policing is concerned with controlling and regulating forms of marginality other than simply those relating to race/ethnicity. Following the 'usual suspects' argument, I also expect people who have been experienced one mode of stop are also more likely to have experienced the other.

Third, people's 'routine activities' (e.g. time spent out of home, visiting pubs and night clubs) will be associated with the probability that they experience police stops. This general hypothesis relates to the availability thesis – certain behaviours make people more visible or available to police, and they are, on that basis alone, more likely to be stopped. More specifically, I also expect that drug use will predict an individual's probability of being stopped/searched.

Fourth, it seems likely that police stop activity will be concentrated in areas with higher crime, hence, people living in those areas will be more likely to be stopped irrespective of their personal characteristics and behaviour. This hypothesis is really claiming little more than that all else equal police will use street stops, in particular, in areas where there is more crime as a response to that crime.

Fifth, independent of crime levels, police stop activity will be concentrated in more disadvantaged, disorderly areas; which is in part to claim that stop and search has a social disciplinary function that extends beyond 'fighting crime'. Sixth, police stop activity will be higher in areas with, in particular, larger black populations. The disproportionate targeting of police stop activity at ethnic minority groups should play out at the area as well as the individual level.

Seventh, in light of the well-established (in the United States) 'race out of place' thesis, I expect that people from visible ethnic minority groups will be more likely to be stopped by police if they live in areas with larger majority group populations.

Eighth, and finally, I expect that the same characteristics that predict a higher chance of being stopped will also predict a greater chance of being searched once stopped. In as much as police stops comprise 'general surveillance and control' (Lea 2003: 63) then a search following a stop indicates if nothing else a higher level of such attention. A search is a stronger intervention than a mere stop, and should therefore be directed more consistently toward those groups 'in need' of social control. Equally, implicit bias and stereotyping that affects the judgement of individual officers in terms of the decision on whom to stop should also affect their behaviour during the stop, particularly in regard to the need for a more intrusive search.

Police stops in the CSEW

A dataset derived from three years' worth of CSEW data (2008/2009, 2009/2010 and 2010/2011) was used to address these hypotheses. The annual CSEW has a very large sample size – over 40,000 in each of the three years in question; the full dataset created therefore included 137,677 respondents. However its complex design (TNS-BMRB 2010), which involves respondents answering a 'core' set of questions, 'victim forms' if they indicate they have been victims of one or more crimes, and then one of four modules (plus further additional items), means that only one-quarter were asked questions relevant to the issues at hand (and less in the 2010/2011 survey). Only those respondents randomly allocated to module A of the survey are asked questions about their experiences of police stop. Allowing for missing data, this meant that the basic effective sample size for analyses of stops and searches was around 28,300 individuals.

Respondents allocated to module A – which included questions about their experiences of police stops – were asked four questions relevant for current purposes. Two items probed experiences of foot stops. First, 'Have you EVER been stopped and asked questions by the police when you were on foot?' (Yes/no). Those who answered yes to this question were then asked 'Has this happened at all since the first of [date]?', where [date] is set to the first day of the month 12 months prior to the date of interview (so if the interview took place on 14 April 2010, respondents were asked to think back to 1 April 2009). Similarly, two items probed experiences of vehicle stops: 'Have you EVER been in a car or on a motorcycle which was approached or stopped by police officers?' (Yes/no); and if yes, 'Has this happened at all since [date]?' (Yes/no).

Two binary indictors were created from these variables for further analysis. The first recorded whether a respondent had been stopped on foot in the previous 12 months (3 per cent had experienced this form of police contact in the preceding 12 months), while the second recorded whether they had been stopped while in a car or driving a motorcycle (8 per cent had experienced this). Overall 10 per cent of people reported having been stopped by police in one or other mode in the year preceding interview. Given the over-16 population of England and Wales during the time of the surveys numbered over 45 million (ONS 2012) this amounts to millions of police stops, and far more encounters between police and public than are covered the police-recorded stop and search statistics. There was no significant change in the rate of stops over the four calendar years included in the dataset. Indeed, the stop rate as recorded by the CSEW seems to have remained relatively constant over the last decade or so – according to the 2003/04 survey, for example, 10 per cent of adults had been stopped by the police in a vehicle in the previous year, while 3 per cent had been stopped while on foot (Allen *et al.* 2005: 9) – and are corroborated by other sources. The Policing for London survey conducted in 2000, to name just one, reported almost identical proportions (11 per cent and 3 per cent, respectively). The extent of the similarity across the period is striking, given the fluctuation in the use of stop and search, specifically, over the same time scale (see Chapter 2). While the recorded 'headline' rate of stop and search varies considerably, that is, the underlying rate of police stops may be rather more stable, and points to around one in 10 people being experiencing some form of police stop each year.

Two further survey items are of immediate interest. Those who had been stopped in the past 12 months, in either mode, were asked whether they or anyone they were with had actually been searched by police. It was thus possible to observe whether someone who had been stopped was subsequently searched (albeit that in a small number of cases the respondent might not have been the person searched).

As an initial matter, around 1 per cent of people over the age of 16 had been stopped and searched in the previous year.[1] While the stop and search experiences recorded in this dataset have been explored in detail elsewhere (Bradford and Loader 2016), some brief consideration of this issue is warranted in the present context: not least because it provides an interesting counterpart to the police recorded data described in Chapter 2. Ethnic variation in the experience of stop and search is shown in Figures 5.1 and 5.2. The first figure replicates the

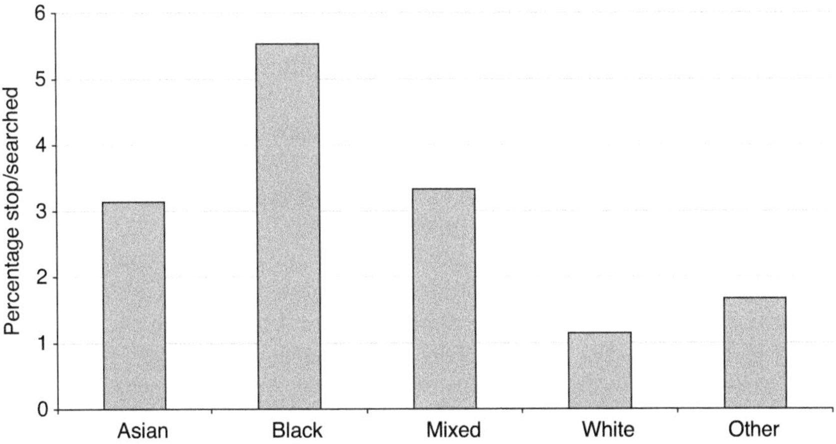

Figure 5.1 Disproportionality in stop and search.

Source: CSEW, 2008/2009 to 2010/2011.

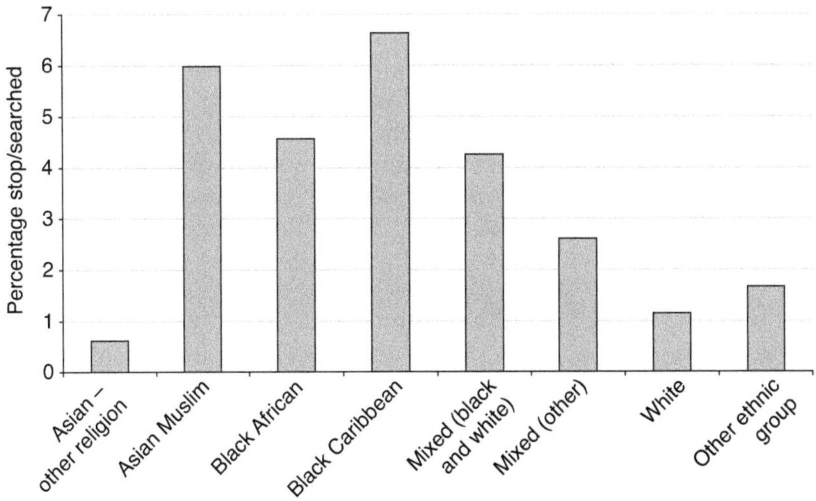

Figure 5.2 Disaggregating groups reveals significant variations in disproportionality.

Source: CSEW, 2008/2009 to 2010/2011.

'headline' ethnic categorization used in the recorded statistics, while the second uses a slightly more detailed categorization that, here, splits the Asian group into Muslims and non-Muslims, and the black group into black Africans and black Caribbeans. This analysis thus begins to move towards the idea of investigation ethnicity as well as race (Waddington *et al.* 2004), and breaks up to some small degree the broadly 'racial' categorizations commonly used in research in this area. The utility of doing so is immediately apparent. According to the CSEW data Asian Muslims were much more likely to have been stopped and searched than their non-Muslim counterparts (the difference between the two black groups was not statistically significant, although it is highly suggestive of variation of experience within the 'black' group, too). While it is of course dangerous to speculate on the basis of this simple analysis it is hard not to conclude that some form of religious profiling is in operation that may stem from statistical discrimination – that is, from police and wider societal perceptions that Muslims are more likely to be involved in terror-related activities.

What is also striking from the data displayed in Figures 5.1 and 5.2 is the similarity in the level of disproportionality suggested by the CSEW and the recorded statistics. According to the police recorded data collected over the same period as the CSEW data described here black people were around 7 times more likely to be stopped and searched than white people, with Asian people twice as likely and people with mixed ethnicities around 2.5 times as likely. *These figures are almost exactly reproduced in the CSEW data.* Around 1 per cent of white people reported a stop and search; for the mixed group this figure was 3 per cent, for black Africans, 5 per cent and for the black Caribbeans, 7 per cent (all white/BME differences were statistically significant at the 5 per cent level). The only divergence from the recorded statistics was the result of disaggregating Asians into Muslims and non-Muslims – less than 1 per cent of non-Muslim Asians reported a stop and search, compared with 6 per cent of their Muslim counterparts (again, the difference between the Asian Muslim and white groups was significant at the 5 per cent level). While these CSEW figures need to be treated with caution, and are not completely comparable with the recorded data, there seems to be a strong correspondence between the two sources, something that strengthens the face validity of both.

Police stops – people or places?

Implicit in the hypotheses laid out above is something of a distinction between area- and individual-level characteristics. An initial question is therefore whether it is people or places that are most important in attracting this type of police attention? To take account of the possible influence of area type and characteristics on the probability of being stopped by the police, geocoded CSEW datasets were obtained. These allow respondents to be grouped at many levels of geographical aggregation, from Police Force Area (PFA) right down to 'Lower Super Output Area' (LSOA) level. This latter is a Census-based area-level classification: there are over 30,000 LSOAs in England and Wales, each with a population of between 1,000 and 3,000 people. Because the CSEW uses a stratified sampling technique (TNS-BMRB 2010), respondents in each sweep are clustered in certain areas rather than spread evenly across England and Wales. In the analysis below a total of 14,031 LSOAs were represented, with an average of 1.9 respondents living in each. In the full CSEW sample there were 22,811 LSOAs, with a mean sample size of 6.

This clustering of respondents in small local areas makes multi-level modelling of the data a viable proposition. This technique allows the idea that an individual's probability of experiencing a police stop (for example) may be partly due to their personal characteristics (level 1 of a multi-level model) and partly due to the characteristics of the area in which they live (level 2) to be properly taken into account. It also allows 'partitioning' of the variance in the response variable (experience of stop encounters) between that which is explained at the area level (e.g. LSOA), and that explained at the individual level.

Multi-level (random effects) binary logistic regression modelling was therefore used to investigate the distribution of police stop experiences within the CSEW sample. First, two variance components models were estimated, predicting the probability of a respondent having experienced a foot stop and a car stop, respectively, in the 12 months prior to interview. Each included LSOA as the level 2 (or clustering) variable. Variance components models are empty models that simply provide insight into how much variation in the response variable is explained at the individual and area levels. These models suggested that around 21 per cent of the variance in experience of foot stops was explained at the LSOA level. Multi-level modelling in social science contexts rarely seems find more than 25 per cent of variance explained at the area level (see for example Hedges and Hedberg 2007), and values are very often far lower (Gulliford *et al.* 1999), so in this context 21 per cent is a significant number. It seems the characteristics of the areas in which people live might be an important predictor of their chances of experiencing foot stops.

By contrast only around 2 per cent of the variance in experience of car stops was explained at the LSOA level. Unsurprisingly, the characteristics of the areas in which people live seem to be much less important predictors of their chances of being stopped while in a car or other vehicle – car stops seem by definition to be more likely to occur away from people's local neighbourhoods. Since they are at face value and, it seems, in analytical terms two different phenomena, the analysis proceeds below by treating foot stops and car stops separately.

Foot stops

Concentrating first on foot stops, then, a pertinent question given the strong geographical clustering in experiences of this form of police stop is which characteristics of local areas are associated with higher or lower levels of stop and search. To investigate this issue, data from the 2011 Census[2] were added to the CSEW dataset. Use of 2011 data in this context is obviously not ideal – recall that the CSEW data run from 2008/2009 to 2010/2011, so area-level measures derived from the Census technically apply to the very end of the data collection period. However this approach is probably justified, not only because the characteristics of local areas are unlikely to change greatly over a three or four year period (and stability in area characteristics can last decades – Sampson 2012) but also because the 2011 Census data will provide a far more accurate picture of the characteristics of the local areas present in the CSEW dataset than available alternatives, including the 2001 Census and the 2010 Index of Multiple Deprivation (which does not allow identification of particular elements of interest, such as the ethnic composition of local areas, and which in any case generally used data relating to 2008).

A number of characteristics of local areas might be expected to be associated with a higher probability of experiencing foot stops among the people living there. To those available in the Censes data were added measures created directly from the CSEW itself, by using the full 137,677 respondent dataset (all measured at the LSOA level):

- Proportion of residents born in the UK as recorded by the Census (logged to remove a very heavy skew)
- Proportion of residents from a black and minority ethnic group (BME), as recorded by the Census
- Proportion of population aged 15–29 as recorded by the Census
- Proportion of CSEW respondents reporting victimization in the previous year
- Disorder, measured by an index created from items covering perceptions of low-level disorder as measured by the CSEW[3]
- Disadvantage, as measured by an index created from a number of Census measures[4]

Results from a series of multi-level binary logistic regression models predicting the probability of recent experience of a foot stop, including in turn each of the above variables as a single explanatory variable, are shown in Table 5.1 (note that the models also include the survey year in order to take into account any trend in the rate of foot stops over the period). All the area variables tested were, individually, significant predictors foot stop experiences at the individual level, and in very predictable directions. People who lived in areas with a higher proportion of BME residents were more likely to have been stopped, as where those living in areas with more young people; higher rates of victimization; more disorder; and higher levels of disadvantage. Foot stops appeared to be less common in areas with a greater proportion of UK-born residents.

When all explanatory variables were added together (Model 9) the percentage born in the UK, disadvantage, victimization and disorder emerged as significant 'unique' area-level predictors. In other words, absent individual-level factors, it was the level of crime, disorder and disadvantage that were the important predictors of the experience of police stops, along with the proportion of UK-born residents. Interesting in the light of many years of US research (which has found a consistent link between the racial/ethnic composition of local areas and police activity) is that this does not seem to be a particularly important factor in this British data. If we take two areas with the same level of deprivation, for example, individuals living in the area with the larger BME population were not more likely to have been stopped than those living in the area the smaller BME population.

Table 5.1 Do area-level characteristics predict experiences of foot stops?

Multi-level binary logistic regression models predicting experience of foot stop, LSOA level correlates only									
Betas	*Model 1*	*Model 2*	*Model 3*	*Model 4*	*Model 5*	*Model 6*	*Model 7*	*Model 8*	*Model 9*
Survey year (2008/2009)									
2009/2010		0.04	0.03	0.03	0.04	0.04	0.04	0.07	0.06
2010/2001		–0.11	–0.12	–0.12	–0.12	–0.12	–0.1	–0.09	–0.1
Percentage aged 15–29			0.03***						0
Percentage born in the UK				–1.34***					–0.85*
Percentage BME					0.19***				–0.04
Concentrated disadvantage						0.31***			0.15**
Victimization rate							1.23***		0.65**
Disorder								0.60***	0.35***
Constant	–4.22***	–4.21***	–4.70***	1.82=	–4.46***	–4.17***	–4.50***	–4.22***	–0.5
ICC	0.21	0.21	0.20	0.19	0.19	0.19	0.20	0.18	0.17
N	27,270	27,270	27,270	27,270	27,267	27,270	27,270	27,270	27,267

Source: CSEW, 2008/2009 to 2010/2011.

Notes

* $p<0.05$;

** $p<0.01$;

*** $p<0.001$.

Adding individual-level variables

The next step was to add individual-level variables to the analysis. Building on the discussion in Chapter 4 and the existing literature, these can grouped into four categories: demographic, geographic (in addition to those measured at the LSOA level), routine activities, and social class related. It is worth noting that there are significant conceptual slippage between many of the variables that might be included in these categories – for example, ethnicity and social class may be linked with routine activities, which themselves are likely to be imbricated with issues of disadvantage – and the categories below should be considered illustrative, not definitional.

Demographic factors

- Gender (coded 1 if the respondent was female and 0 if they were male)
- Age (entered as a continuous variable)
- Age squared (to allow for any non-linear effect of age)
- Ethnicity (as before)
- Country of birth (coded 1 if the respondent was born in the UK and 0 otherwise).

Geographic or area-based factors

As well as the characteristics of the LSOA in which they live (see Table 5.1 above), other geographic or area-based factors may affect people's exposure to police activity. Most notably, given the discussion above and in previous chapters, we might expect stop activity to be concentrated in 'inner city' areas, in areas with higher levels of social housing, and in London. Three additional variables considered in the analysis were therefore:

- Housing tenure (represented by two dummy variables, one coded 1 if the respondent lived in socially rented accommodation and the other coded 1 if they lived in privately rented accommodation, such that the reference category was 'owner-occupier' in each case). Since someone's housing tenure will not usually be 'visible' by police officers this variable will presumably, if significant, be acting as a proxy for some other factor, one possible candidate being the idea that police are particularly active in areas with high concentrations of social housing. Equally, however, housing tenure may act as a proxy for social class.
- A binary variable indicating whether the respondent lived in London or not.
- A second binary variable indicating whether the respondent lived in an 'inner city' area or not.

Routine activities

As argued by Waddington *et al.* (2004), Ashby and Tompson (2015) and others, the ways in which people organize their lives and utilize public space may influence their 'availability' to the police. Unemployed people or those working part time may be more available, for example, because they are out and about throughout the day and/or spend time simply walking or sitting in public areas. While no variable in a survey such as the CSEW can directly represent this availability, a large number may act as partial proxies:

- Marital status (1 = single, 0 otherwise)
- Time spent out of home on weekday (entered as a continuous variable)
- Trips to pub or bar in the past month (entered as a continuous variable)
- Visits to club in past month (entered as a dummy variable)
- Employment status (entered as three dummy variables, with full-time employment as the reference category: employed part time; unemployed; and economically inactive (including retired people and students))
- Self-reported health status (entered as two dummy variables, with 'good' as the reference category: 'fair health' and 'poor health')
- Victim of crime (1 = victim, 0 if not)
- Car access (1 = yes, 0 if not)

The final variable in this section is an important one, and requires a little more explanation. Each year the CSEW fields a 'self-report' module on drug use. Respondents to the survey aged 16–59 are asked whether they will consent to answering some questions on their personal consumption of drugs. Those who agree (most do so, over 90 per cent in 2010/2011 – see TNS-BMRB 2011) are then able to either answer the questions themselves on the interviewer's laptop (and out of their sight) or ask the interviewer to complete the questions for them. A large majority choose the first option (ibid.).

Given the strength of the links between stop and search and the policing of drugs described above this is a highly relevant variable in the analysis. It comes with a number of provisos, however. Most importantly, non-response is higher for some groups compared with others and, notably, respondents from black and Asian ethnic groups are more likely to refuse to answer these questions than their white counterparts (ibid.). Furthermore, while there seems no *a priori* reason to think people from one group may be more likely than those from another to lie or dissemble in their responses, this remains a possibility. The self-report drug use questions should be treated as indicative rather than definitive. That said this is the first attempt I know of to add drug-use – self-reported offending behaviour – to analysis of police stops in the CSEW (although see Ariza 2014), and is an important step to take. A dummy variable coded 1 if the respondent reported using any illegal drugs in the previous year was therefore added to the models.

Social class

All the factors above may be correlated with, and indeed confounded by, social class, and there are strong theoretical reasons to think that an individual's social class will influence their chances of experiencing police stops. A final set of variables therefore aim to measure CSEW respondent's social class:

- National Statistics Socio-Economic Classification (ONS 2010) – entered as five dummy variables with 'higher professional' as the reference category
- Education (entered as two dummy variables, with GCSE/A level/equivalent as the reference category: no qualifications; degree level and above)

The usual suspects

Finally, to take into account the usual suspects argument, also included as a covariate in each model was experience of a car stop in the past year (in the case of foot stops) and experience of foot stop model (in the case of car stops). This is of course a very rough measure, not least because the police conducting a foot stop of an individual would almost certainly be different to those who conducted a car stop. Nevertheless, there is much to suggest that having been stopped by police once makes a person more likely to be stopped again in the future (see also Chapter 8).

Bivariate analysis

Which groups and types of individual are most likely to experience this form of police contact? Tables 5.2 and 5.3 show the bivariate associations between the variables described above and the experience of foot stops (and car stops). The patterns in relation to foot stops are very clear. People from all the visible ethnic minority groups were more likely to have been stopped while on foot than those with white ethnicities; men were more likely than women, and young people were more likely to have been stopped than older people. Beyond these expected associations others also leap out. The unemployed and students were over four times more likely to have been stopped than those in employment. People with degrees were less likely to have been stopped than those with other qualifications or none, while single people were over four times more likely to have been stopped than those who were married or cohabiting.

Turning to the routine activity and other variables shown in Table 5.3, we find that people who went to pubs and clubs were more likely to have been stopped on foot than those who did not. Spending more time out of the home was associated with a higher probability of having been stopped. Notably, those who had used drugs in the past year were five times more likely to have been stopped than those who had not used drugs. Victims of crime were also more likely to have been stopped than non-victims, and owner-occupiers were less likely to have been stopped than those with other tenancies. Finally, those stopped in one mode were also more likely to have been stopped in the other – 7 per cent of people stopped

Table 5.2 Experience of police stops: by stop type and socio-demographic characteristics

Percentage stopped at least once in the previous 12 months

	Foot stop	*Car stop*	*Unweighted* n *(numbers)*
Age			
16–18	23	*16*	754
19–21	9	*21*	693
22–24	5	*18*	901
25–34	4	*11*	3,904
35–44	1	*9*	5,055
45–54	1	*8*	4,630
55–64	1	*6*	4,811
65–74	1	*4*	3,941
75 plus	–	*2*	3,605
Gender			
Female	*2*	*6*	15,571
Male	*5*	*12*	12,723
Ethnicity			
Asian Muslim	*7*	*14*	400
Asian – other religion	*1*	*9*	575
Black African	*4*	*11*	295
Black Caribbean	*7*	*12*	296
Mixed (Black and White)	*13*	*16*	105
Mixed (other)	*3*	*13*	112
White	*3*	*9*	26,144
Other ethnic group	3	*6*	353
Country of birth			
UK	3	*9*	25,236
Other	6	*9*	3,049

	Foot stop	*Car stop*	*Unweighted* n *(numbers)*
Economic activity status			
Employed	*3*	*11*	15,396
Unemployed	*14*	*13*	849
Student	*13*	*11*	686
Looking after family	*1*	*6*	1,483
Long term sick	*4*	*6*	1,300
Retired	*0*	*3*	8,167
Educational attainment			
First degree or higher	*1*	*9*	5,728
Below degree level	*4*	*11*	14,793
No qualifications	*2*	*6*	7,773
Social class (NS-SeC)			
Professional	*2*	*9*	9,384
Intermediate/self-employed	*2*	*9*	8,620
Routine and semi-rout	*3*	*8*	8,033
Never worked/long term unemployed	*7*	*6*	1,008
Not classified	*12*	*14*	1,249
Relationship status			
Single	*9*	*15*	3,265
Married/cohabiting	*2*	*8*	25,029
Health status			
Good/very good	*3*	*10*	21,248
Fair	*3*	*8*	5,249
Poor/very poor	*2*	*5*	1,782

Source: CSEW, 2008/2009 to 2010/2011.

Table 5.3 Experience of police stops: by stop type, routine activities and other characteristics

Proportion stopped at least once in the previous 12 months

	Foot stop	*Car stop*	*Unweighted* n *(numbers)*
Housing tenure			
Owner/occupier	2	8	19,453
Socially rented	5	9	4,640
Privately rented	6	12	4,201
Hours out of home average weekday			
None	1	5	660
Less than 1 hour	1	3	1,325
1 to 3	2	5	6,449
3 to 5	3	6	4,871
5 to 7	5	9	2,859
7 hours or more	4	12	12,072
Visits to clubs in last month			
None	2	8	25,703
At least 1	8	19	2,591
Victim of crime?			
No	2	8	21,676
Yes	5	13	6,618
Drug use in last year?			
No	3	10	16,305
Yes	15	22	1,414

	Foot stop	*Car stop*	*Unweighted* n *(numbers)*
Visits to pub/bars in last month			
None	3	6	14,531
1 to 3	3	9	7,799
4 to 8	4	13	4,407
9 to 12	6	16	884
More than 12	7	18	672
Lives in 'inner city' area?			
No	3	9	25,993
Yes	4	9	2,301
Lives in London?			
No	3	9	25,802
Yes	4	8	2,492
Access to a car/van?			
No	4	4	5,950
Yes	3	10	22,344
Stopped in car/on foot?			
No (car)	3		27,664
Yes (car)	7		624
No (foot)		9	26,047
Yes (foot)		22	2,115

Source: CSEW, 2008/2009 to 2010/2011.

in a car over in past year had, over the same period, also been stopped while in foot, compared with 3 per cent of those who had not been stopped while in a car.

At the bivariate level, then, many of the arguments presented in the previous chapter appear supported by the data. People from minority groups and other socially disadvantaged or marginal categories – such as the unemployed, victims of crime, or people living in rented accommodation – were all more likely to have been stopped by police. Equally, though, engaging in activities that making someone more 'available' to police, and using drugs, was also associated with a greater chance of being stopped on foot. Naturally these simply bivariate correlations do not allow the effect of potentially confounding factors to be taken into account, and regression modelling was therefore used to explore the data in more detail.

Modelling foot stops

All the potential explanatory variables described above were included in multilevel binary logistic regression models predicting the probability of having experienced a foot stop in the past year. Results are shown in Table 5.4, which displays four different models. The first was estimated using the full available sample. It was generated by a backwards selection process, in which all the variables shown in Tables 5.1, 5.2 and 5.3 were first included. Non-significant variables were then removed one by one until all those remaining in the model were significant at the 10 per cent level. Given the final model (Model 1 on Table 5.4) none of the other area or individual variables described above were significant at that level when added. The second model replicates the first, but includes only that proportion of the sample that answered the drug use module; and the third adds the drug use variable itself. First, this design allows development of a parsimonious model that identifies socio-demographic and other variables that have a 'unique' association with the probability of experiencing a foot stop. Second, it enables examination of the extent to which these associations may, in part, be down to differing levels of drug use among people from different social categories. Third, comparison of models 1 and 2 allows consideration of the extent to which use of the restricted sample (only those who responded to the self-report module) had an effect on the results. Finally, model 4 adds the car stop variable, and asks essentially whether the police concentration on 'the usual suspects' explains any of the other associations identified.

Perhaps what is most striking from these models is that once the other covariates are taken into account the association between ethnicity and the probability of experiencing a police foot stop is attenuated in important ways. Model 1 shows that controlling for the other covariates, only people with mixed black and white and black Caribbean ethnicities were significantly more likely than their white counterparts to have experienced a foot stop in the last year; conversely, however those with 'other' Asian ethnicities were *less* likely to have experienced such a stop. By model 3, only the other Asian coefficient retained significance. While people from many ethnic minority groups were, overall, more likely to be stopped on foot by police (as shown in Table 5.2 above), it

Table 5.4 What predicts experiences of foot stops?

Results from multi-level binary logistic regression models predicting experience of foot stop

	Model 1		*Model 2*		*Model 3*		*Model 4*	
	β	*se(β)*	β	*se(β)*	β	*se(β)*	β	*se(β)*
Survey year (ref: 2008/2009)								
2009/2010	0.05	0.1	0.04	0.11	0.07	0.11	0.07	0.11
2020/2011	–0.09	0.12	–0.07	0.14	–0.06	0.14	–0.07	0.14
Individual level measures								
Gender (ref: male)								
Female	–1.00***	0.1	–1.05***	0.11	–0.96***	0.11	–0.93***	0.11
Age	–0.11***	0.02	–0.22***	0.03	–0.22***	0.03	–0.21***	0.03
Age squared	0.00***	0	0.00***	0	0.00***	0	0.00***	0
Ethnicity (ref: White)								
Asian Muslim	–0.02	0.3	0.06	0.34	0.21	0.34	0.17	0.34
Asian other	–1.05*	0.45	–1.19*	0.5	–1.10*	0.5	–1.10*	0.5
Black African	–0.24	0.41	–0.19	0.43	–0.06	0.42	–0.07	0.42
Black Caribbean	0.52+	0.31	0.47	0.36	0.47	0.36	0.45	0.36
Mixed White and Black	0.76*	0.38	0.49	0.45	0.51	0.44	0.5	0.44
Mixed other	–0.74	0.63	–0.72	0.65	–0.62	0.64	–0.66	0.64
Other ethnic group	0.04	0.37	–0.47	0.47	–0.32	0.46	–0.32	0.46
Country of birth (ref: other)								
UK	0.34+	0.18	0.16	0.2	0.11	0.2	0.11	0.2
Educational attainment (ref: other)								
No qualifications	0.08	0.12	0.05	0.14	0.03	0.14	0.03	0.14
First degree or higher	–0.38**	0.14	–0.43**	0.16	–0.41**	0.16	–0.40*	0.16
Car access (ref: no)								
Yes	–0.58***	0.12	–0.65***	0.13	–0.62***	0.13	–0.65***	0.13

Marital status (ref: married/partnership)								
Single	0.68***	0.12	0.49***	0.14	0.45**	0.14	0.45**	0.14
Time spent out of home on weekdays (hours)	0.10*	0.05	0.08	0.05	0.07	0.05	0.07	0.05
Employment status (ref: full-time)								
Part-time	0.21	0.15	0.11	0.16	0.09	0.16	0.11	0.16
Unemployed	0.89***	0.17	0.80***	0.19	0.72***	0.19	0.75***	0.19
Economically inactive	0.27+	0.14	0.11	0.16	0.11	0.16	0.15	0.16
Health status (ref: good)								
Fair	0.35**	0.13	0.25+	0.15	0.19	0.15	0.18	0.15
Poor	0.42*	0.21	0.50+	0.26	0.46+	0.25	0.46+	0.25
Victim of crime (ref: no)								
Yes	0.38***	0.09	0.38***	0.1	0.30**	0.11	0.28**	0.11
Housing tenure (ref: owner occupier)								
Social renter	0.68***	0.12	0.49***	0.14	0.45**	0.14	0.31*	0.15
Private renter	0.23+	0.13	0.34*	0.15	0.32*	0.15	0.09	0.13
LSOA level measures								
Disorder	0.23**	0.08	0.16+	0.09	0.15	0.09	0.14	0.09
Proportion of residents aged 15–29 (logged)	–0.02**	0.01	–0.02**	0.01	–0.02**	0.01	–0.02**	0.01
Proportion of residents born in the UK	–0.79*	0.31	–1.01**	0.36	–0.96**	0.36	–1.00**	0.36
Any drug use in previous year (ref: no)								
Yes					0.87***	0.12	0.83***	0.12
Stopped in car (ref: no)								
Yes							0.42**	0.13
Constant	2.70+	1.51	5.95***	1.76	5.48**	1.75	5.54**	1.75
ICC	0.08		0.13		0.08		0.09	
n	27,270		17,037		17,037		17,037	

Source: CSEW, 2008/2009 to 2010/2011.

Notes
+ $p<0.1$; * $p<0.05$; ** $p<0.01$; *** $p<0.001$.

seems much of the difference between ethnic minority and white groups was accounted for by factors such as different age and class structures (and, indeed, once control variables are introduced non-Muslim Asians were *less* likely than their white counterparts to have been stopped by police).

Elsewhere in the models shown in Table 5.4 it seems that it was variables that might be characterized as being associated with different routine activity patterns that were the most consistent predictors of the probability of experiencing a foot stop. All else equal, people with access to a car were less likely than others to experience such a stop; single people, the unemployed, those not in poor health, and recent victims of crime were all more likely to experience such an encounter. Most of these associations were robust to the inclusion of drug use in Model 3. Yet, beyond the simple moniker of 'routine activities' these variables may represent a number of factors. Availability to the police, of course; but they are also associated with membership of marginalized social categories, such as 'unemployed', and arguably 'victim of crime', that many accounts of policing suggest are 'police property', particularly prone to being objects of police attention. Notable in this regard is that all else equal those who lived in socially rented accommodation were more likely to have been stopped, while those with degrees were significantly less likely to have been stopped by the police. Since in both cases these are characteristics of individuals invisible to police officers, the variables must be acting as proxy measures for some other factor, with some aspect of social class being one possible candidate. Use of drugs in the past year was strongly and significantly associated with a higher probability of also having been stopped by police. Finally, the car stop measure, when added in Model 4, was strongly significant – people who had been stopped in a car were more likely to have been stopped while on foot. Yet, addition of this measure did little to alter the other coefficients in the model. One interpretation of this is that while there did indeed seem to be an emphasis on the usual suspects, this process was largely independent of the social groups or categories to which such individuals belonged.

Only three area-level variables remained significant in the models once individual-level factors were taken into account – disorder, proportion of young people and proportion of UK-born residents. Taking each in turn, it seems first that, independent of individual characteristics, people living in more 'disorderly' areas were more likely to have experienced a foot stop; but this association attenuated and lost significance once drug use at the individual level was taken into account. One interpretation here is that police stop activity is concentrated in areas with higher levels of disorder because there are in those areas more people who use drugs, and it is this which attracts the attention of police.

Second, people living in an area with a higher concentration of immigrants were significantly more likely to have been stopped by police. Yet, at the individual level, people who were born outside the UK were, at least in Model 1, somewhat less likely to have been stopped than their UK-born counterparts. It could be that at the individual level immigrants are less likely to be stopped by police because, for example, they on average use public space in a different way or are less likely to be involved in crime (Ewing *et al.* 2015; Sampson 2008). Yet, there are a number of reasons why police stop activity might be higher in areas with larger immigrant populations, for example because police activity may be differently calibrated in local areas that exhibit greater diversity and variation from the norm. There is also the possibility that police conduct more stop activity in such areas because they are specifically targeting immigrants for the purposes of internal border control (Franko Aas 2011; Weber 2011), although if this a major factor the association between immigrant status at the individual level and being stopped might have been expected to be the reverse of that actually identified.

Third, there was a relatively small *negative* correlation between the proportion of young people in an area and the probability of those living there having experienced a foot stop. This reverses the correlation between age profile and the probability of stops shown in Table 5.3. While at the individual level younger people are very much more likely to be stopped it does not appear that the proportion of younger people in an area – and therefore, in a general sense, of likely offenders – triggers greater police attention. Indeed the reverse may be true.

It is worth noting which variables were *not* significant in these models. Controlling for socio-demographic and other personal characteristics people who went to pubs and clubs were not more likely to have been stopped, and this was true even before drug use was taken into account. Similarly, people living in 'inner city' areas and London were not more likely to have been stopped by police than others. This last finding is particularly intriguing given the concentration of stop and search in the capital (see Chapter 6), and it suggests that once the characteristics of the *policed* are taken into account police in London were not behaving so differently from police elsewhere in England and Wales.

To test to 'race out of place' thesis interactions between ethnicity and area-level population composition was tested in Model 3. Variables and interaction terms that allowed consideration of whether (a) people from non-white ethnic minority groups were in a general sense more likely to have been be stopped if they lived in 'whiter' areas and (b) whether people from specific non-white groups were more likely to have been stopped in they live in 'whiter' areas. None of these interaction terms were significant, and there seems to be little support for the 'race out of place' thesis in this British dataset. People from ethnic minority groups were no more likely to have been stopped if they lived in an area with a greater proportion of white residents; similarly, people with white ethnicities were no more likely to have been stopped if they lived in an area with a larger visible ethnic minority population.

Models including interactions between age, gender and ethnicity were also tested. Did these three key socio-demographic characteristics interact (or intersect) to multiply the chances of particular groups or types of individuals being stopped? Most importantly, perhaps, did the statistical effect of age and gender on the probability of being stopped vary by ethnicity, such that youth and gender were more important predictors of stops for people from ethnic minorities? The idea that police stop activity is especially focused on young black men carries a particularly strong charge – and the evidence presented above confirms that being young, male and from certain ethnic minority groups was indeed associated with a higher chance of being stopped. Was this effective additive or multiplicative, though – if the latter were to be true this would suggest a substantially higher level of disproportionality than even that identified thus far.

To keep things simple – and bearing in mind the small numbers of people from most ethnic minority groups included in the sample – ethnicity was entered as a simple white/other dummy in a series of models that test this idea. Results suggested, first, that conditioning on the other variables in the model the probability of having experienced a foot stop fell more sharply with age for women than for men: older women were particularly unlikely to have been stopped. Second, there was no significant interaction between age and minority status: increasing age had the same negative association with the odds of a stop for young people from both white and minority groups. Third, there was a significant interaction between gender and minority status: white women were *more* likely to have been stopped than their minority group counterparts. Fourth, results from a model including a three-way interaction between age, gender and (white/other) ethnicity did not suggest that being from a visible ethnic minority group multiplied a young man's chances of being stopped; rather, the negative effect of age on the odds of being stopped was greater for women from ethnic minority groups. Older non-white women, that is, were *particularly* unlikely to have been stopped.

While the crudity of the ethnicity measure means these results are indicative at best they suggest that the intersection of age, gender and ethnicity may not have a multiplicative effect on the young, ethnic minority men's probability of experiencing a foot stop. Although they were still more likely to have experienced this form of police contact this statistical effect was additive in nature. Instead, age, gender and ethnicity seemed to interact in such a way that the negative association between age and police stops was greater for ethnic minority women than for others.

Car stops

Moving on to car stops, recall that variance component models suggested only 2 per cent the variance in experiences was explained at the LSOA level. As might be expected, the area in which people live has much less influence on their probability of being stopped by police while in a car. Given the lack of any meaningful area-level effect, standard binary logistic regression models were used to analyse experiences of car stops among the CSEW sample.

Tables 5.2 and 5.3 above suggest that at the bivariate level the predictors of experiencing car stops were broadly similar to those of foot stops, although there were some subtle differences. Younger people, men, people from most visible ethnic minority groups and single people were all more likely to have been stopped in a car. Similarly, those who went to pubs and clubs, who spent more time out home, and who used drugs were all more likely to have been stopped, as were those who had been stopped while on foot (strikingly, 22 per cent of those stopped on foot had also been stopped while in a car). Yet the unemployed, students and those without educational qualifications were *not* more likely to have experienced this form of police contact, in a direct reversal of the patterns seen in relation to foot stops. These slightly divergent findings presumably relate to the confounding effect of car access and use. People in work and/or in higher social classes are both more likely to own cars and, possibly, use them more than others. To reiterate, an individual's availability to police must have some effect on their chances of being stopped.

Table 5.5 displays results from a series of binary logistic regression models generated as before. Given the variables included in Model 1, that is, none of the other individual-level variables shown in Tables 5.2 and 5.3 were significant when added to the model (nor were the dummy indicators representing living in London and an 'inner city' area). The key finding from these models is that black Caribbeans, Asian Muslims and those with 'other' mixed ethnic identities were more likely to have been stopped in a car than their white counterparts. In distinction to the foot stop case, controlling for all the other variables shown police attention was disproportionality directed at people from these specific ethnic minority groups. Notable also, however, is the difference between ethnic minority groups. All else equal non-Muslim Asians and those with black African ethnicities were no more likely to have been stopped in a car than their white counterparts.

Other aspects of the models shown in Table 5.5 are familiar. Women were less likely to have been stopped than men, and older people less likely than younger people. People who seem likely to be more available to police – who spend more time out of the home, who go to pubs and clubs – were more likely to have been stopped, as were recent victims of crime, those not in good health, and in some models the unemployed. Once again, people with degrees were less likely to have been stopped while in a car (although this statistical effect was marginal), while social renters were more likely. Again, we are left with the idea that these variables are acting as proxies for some other factor, some unobserved aspect of social class, being the most likely candidate (coupled, perhaps, with the value of people's cars – police may choose to stop older, more 'beat up' models over newer, more expensive vehicles). People who used drugs and who had been stopped by police while on foot were also more likely to have been stopped while in a car. What these findings suggest is that once relevant confounds are taken into account the pattern of greater police attention toward people from (some) marginal social categories more clearly asserts itself – although, in the case of car stops, availability to police seems to be a more important predictor.

The interaction between age, gender and ethnicity was also tested, as before. Of the four interaction terms included – age/gender, age/ethnicity, ethnicity/gender and a three-way interaction – only the ethnicity/gender interaction proved significant, suggesting, as in the case of foot stops, that all else equal women from ethnic minority groups were less likely to have been stopped in a car than their white counterparts.

Table 5.5 What predicts experiences of car stops?

Results from binary logistic regression models predicting experience of a police car stop

	Model 1		*Model 2*		*Model 3*		*Model 4*	
	β	*se*(β)	β	*se*(β)	β	*se*(β)	β	*se*(β)
Survey year (ref: 2008/2009)								
2009/2010	0.09+	0.05	0.05	0.06	0.06	0.06	0.06	0.06
2020/2011	0.04	0.06	0	0.07	0.01	0.07	0.01	0.07
Individual level measures								
Gender (ref: male)								
Female	–0.47***	0.05	–0.50***	0.06	–0.47***	0.06	–0.45***	0.06
Age	–0.02***	0	–0.03***	0	–0.03***	0	–0.03***	0
Ethnicity (ref: White)								
Asian Muslim	0.56***	0.15	0.60***	0.17	0.64***	0.17	0.64***	0.17
Asian other	0.09	0.15	0.15	0.17	0.17	0.17	0.18	0.17
Black African	0.41*	0.2	0.42*	0.21	0.46*	0.21	0.46*	0.21
Black Caribbean	0.64***	0.19	0.54*	0.22	0.53*	0.22	0.52*	0.22
Mixed White and Black	0.43	0.3	0.32	0.34	0.31	0.34	0.28	0.34
Mixed other	0.41	0.28	0.54+	0.29	0.56+	0.29	0.58*	0.29
Other ethnic group	–0.17	0.22	–0.28	0.26	–0.25	0.26	–0.24	0.26
Educational attainment (ref: other)								
No qualifications	–0.03	0.07	–0.01	0.08	–0.02	0.08	–0.02	0.08
First degree or higher	–0.13*	0.06	–0.1	0.07	–0.09	0.07	–0.09	0.07
NS-SeC (ref: high professional)								
Lower professional	0.07	0.09	0.07	0.1	0.07	0.1	0.07	0.1
Employees	0.31***	0.09	0.36***	0.1	0.35***	0.11	0.35***	0.11
Routine occupations	0.13	0.1	0.14	0.11	0.13	0.11	0.13	0.11
Never worked	–0.09	0.19	–0.24	0.23	–0.24	0.23	–0.26	0.23
Not classified	–0.09	0.14	–0.15	0.15	–0.16	0.15	–0.2	0.15

Car access (ref: no)								
Yes	1.23***	0.09	1.10***	0.1	1.12***	0.1	1.14***	0.1
Time spent out of home on weekdays (hours)	0.08**	0.02	0.07*	0.03	0.07*	0.03	0.07*	0.03
Evenings spent in pub	0.11***	0.02	0.09***	0.03	0.08**	0.03	0.08**	0.03
Goes to clubs (ref: no)								
Yes	0.40***	0.07	0.39***	0.07	0.35***	0.07	0.35***	0.07
Employment status								
Part-time	–0.01	0.08	–0.01	0.08	–0.02	0.08	–0.03	0.08
Unemployed	0.22+	0.12	0.19	0.13	0.14	0.13	0.09	0.13
Economically inactive	–0.15+	0.08	–0.13	0.1	–0.14	0.1	–0.15	0.1
Health status (ref: good)								
Fair	0.14*	0.07	0.23**	0.08	0.21**	0.08	0.21**	0.08
Poor	0.18	0.12	0.17	0.16	0.16	0.16	0.15	0.16
Victim of crime (ref: no)								
Yes	0.36***	0.05	0.31***	0.05	0.29***	0.05	0.28***	0.05
Housing tenure (ref: owner occupier)								
Social renter	0.35***	0.07	0.33***	0.08	0.32***	0.08	0.31***	0.08
Private renter	0.15*	0.06	0.17*	0.07	0.16*	0.07	0.16*	0.07
Any drug use in previous year (ref: no)								
Yes					0.47***	0.08	0.44***	0.08
Stopped on foot in previous year (ref: no)								
Yes							0.49***	0.12
Constant	–3.18***	0.23	–2.79***	0.26	–2.92***	0.26	–2.98***	0.26
n	28,183		17,677		17,677		17,677	

Source: CSEW, 2008/2009 to 2010/2011.

Notes
+ $p<0.1$; * $p<0.05$; ** $p<0.01$; *** $p<0.001$.

Multiple stops

So far we have considered only whether people have experienced a stop or not. Yet, many experience multiple stops, often in a relatively short length of time but also, in many cases, over many years. Experiencing multiple police stops may be a particular issue for those involved. One police stop may be discounted (an even accepted as necessary), but being stopped multiple times may well begin to feel like, and indeed may be, persecution, as the experiences of people like Ken Hinds, stopped five or six times a year from the age of 14, attests (EHRC 2010).

CSEW respondents who indicated they had been stopped in the past year were asked how many times this occurred. Most (around 70 per cent) were indeed stopped only once, but a significant minority had therefore been stopped more than once. For the purposes of analysis, answers to this question were grouped into two: one stop only and two or more stops. The distribution of this variable by ethnicity is in Figure 5.3. This suggests significant ethnic disparities in the proportion of people stopped more than once. Some 12 per cent of *all* people with mixed black and white ethnicities reported being stopped more than once; nearly half of those from this group who had been stopped reported that this had happened more than once in the past year. Asian Muslims (9 per cent) and black Caribbeans (8 per cent) were also more likely

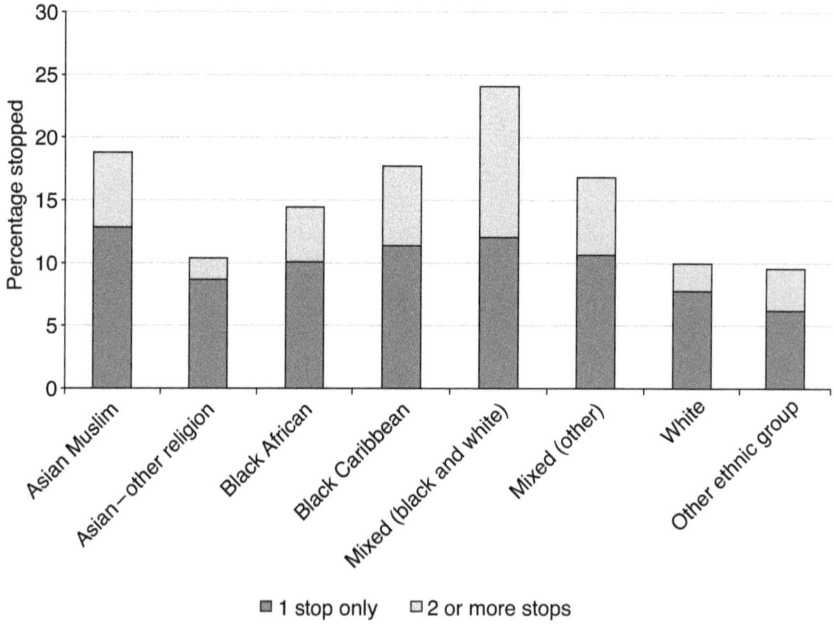

Figure 5.3 People from some ethnic groups are more likely to experience multiple stops in the same year.

Source: CSEW, 2008/2009 to 2010/2011.

than those from other groups to report multiple stops. By contrast, people from other ethnic minority groups reported multiple stops at roughly the same rate as those from the white group.

Regression modelling was used to further investigate the issue of multiple stops. Multinomial logistic regression models predicted the probability of being in each category of a three-category response variable: no stop; one stop; and two or more stops. The results of these models were intriguing (they are not shown here for reasons of space). Controlling for demographic factors only people from the black Caribbean group were more likely than those from the white group to report just one stop; but people with black Caribbean, Asian Muslim and mixed black and white ethnicities were *all* more likely to report multiple stops. To put it another way, people from these particular ethnic minority groups who experienced one stop in a given year were more likely than their white counterparts to go on to experience further stops that same year. These results suggest a significant concentration of multiple stop experiences among people from specific minority groups, who are stopped multiple times.

Outcomes of stops in the CSEW

What happened, then, once people had been stopped by the police? After being asked how many times they were stopped in the past year, CSEW respondents were directed to think about the last stop they experienced – specifically, whether it resulted in a search of themselves, the vehicle or someone else in it (for car stops) or of themselves or someone else they were with (for foot stops). Figure 5.4 shows that people from most ethnic minority groups were more likely than those from the white group to report that a search took place, with the Asian Muslim and black groups particularly likely to have experienced this. There is again a stark difference in the experiences of between Muslim and non-Muslim Asians. Over 30 per cent of the former reported a search after being stopped, compared with just 6 per cent of the latter. Note that a combined mixed group is shown used due to small sample sizes and, in general, the small numbers of people from ethnic minority groups in the sample mean that the estimates shown in Figure 5.4 should be treated with caution.

The relationship between the respondent's ethnicity and the probability of the last stop they experienced resulting in a search also held in multivariate analysis – see Table 5.6. The models shown were generated as before – a backward selection process was implemented to generate Model 1, with the final result that given the model shown none of the variables discussed above were significant, at the 10 per cent level, once added to it.[5] This model was then re-estimated using only the sub-sample who answered the self-report drug use module (Model 2), and finally the drug use variable was added (Model 3).

The most striking finding from Table 5.6 is that even controlling for other variables in the models people from the Asian Muslim, black African, mixed and 'other' ethnic groups were all more likely to have experienced a search once they had been stopped (with the proviso that some of the searches were of other

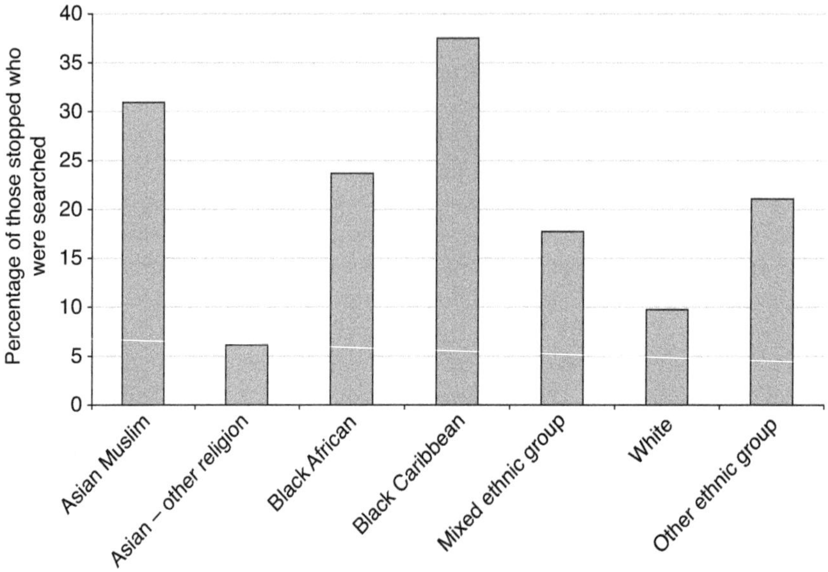

Figure 5.4 People from some ethnic groups are more likely to be searched once stopped.

Source: CSEW, 2008/2009 to 2010/2011.

people). But equally noticeable is that other characteristics were also associated with the experience of a search. Being male, young, unemployed, single, living in London, not having access to a car and the use of drugs were all characteristics associated with a higher probability experiencing a search once stopped by police. Yet there is some countervailing evidence: people with degree level qualifications were, having been stopped, more likely to have experienced a search; conversely, an individual who went to nightclubs was, all else equal, less likely to have experienced a search. These findings are hard to interpret, but it may be in the latter case that the 'routine activities' of people who go to nightclubs make them more available to be police to be stopped, thus boosting their number in the sample, but these stops do not necessarily result in a search, leading to an apparent negative association between being a 'clubber' and the probability of experiencing a stop once searched. Overall, though, it seems that not only is the experience of police stops concentrated among particular social groups and categories who might for a variety of reasons be considered to be socially marginal, but once stopped people from those same groups and categories were more likely than others to be searched. Finally, note also that searches were more likely after foot stops.

The CSEW also records the final outcome of the stop (and perhaps search). In terms of car stops some 31 per cent of those recorded in the sample resulted in some sort of 'criminal justice' outcome – such as an on the spot warning about an offence committed, an arrest, issue of a summons, issue of a fixed penalty notice or the issue of a vehicle defect rectification notice. Only 1 per cent of car stops resulted in an arrest. On the spot warnings (12 per cent) and Fixed Penalty Notices (12 per cent) were far more common. Turning to foot stops, only around 5 per cent resulted in a criminal justice outcome of some kind – 1 per cent in an arrest and 4 per cent in an on the spot warning for an offence committed.

Recall from Chapter 2 that compared with the large volume of research on stop and search relatively little is known about the far more numerous category of car stops. The CSEW data therefore provides some important insights into this mode of policing. While the fact that foot stops rarely resulted in an arrest or other outcome seems to underline the fact that their primary function is social control rather than simply the exercise of the law, car stops quite often resulted in what might loosely be termed a criminal justice response. While the reasons for this might be quite mundane – it may be easier for police to spot a problem or offence with a car or someone's driving than it is to spot a problem or offence when someone is simply walking down the street – it nonetheless an important finding, in as much as makes clear that police stops are multi-functional. In the case of car stops they serve, among other things, the important purpose of making the roads and driving safer. Yet, even here, it is people from marginal groups who are more likely to be stopped. Parking tickets and class repression, indeed.

Summary

To bring together the findings reported above we can return to the hypotheses laid out at the beginning of the chapter. First, even after a range of control variables were introduced people from some ethnic minority groups were still more likely than those from a white ethnic group to have been stopped by police. However there was important variation here. People from black and Asian Muslim ethnic groups appeared to be particularly badly affected by police stop and stop/search activity, as also were those with mixed ethnicities. By contrast non-Muslim Asians were generally *less* affected by police stops then their white counterparts. There was also little evidence, once relevant controls were introduced, of ethnic variation in experience of, specifically, police foot stops. In sum the results in relation to ethnicity present a mixed picture, and tend to support the idea that while police bias – whether active or implicit – does exist in relation to people from some ethnic minority groups this is not a blanket effect, and important differences in experience exist within the ethnic minority population.

Second, the modelling presented above tended to support the idea that police stop activity is directed disproportionality against less advantaged or marginal social groups and categories. The unemployed, those with health problems, living in social housing, in more disordered areas and in areas with more migrants were generally more likely to have been stopped by police. There was also evidence of the usual suspects effect, in that net of all controls those who had been stopped in one mode were more likely to have been stopped in the other.

Table 5.6 What predicts the probability of being searched once stopped?

Results from binary logistic regression models predicting the probability of being searched following a stop

	Model 1		*Model 2*		*Model 3*	
	β	*se(β)*	β	*se(β)*	β	*se(β)*
Survey year (ref: 2008/2009)						
2009/2010	0.1	0.16	0.04	0.18	0.06	0.18
2020/2011	0.12	0.19	0.06	0.21	0.04	0.22
Type of stop (ref: car stop)						
Foot stop	0.37*	0.18	0.37+	0.19	0.32+	0.19
Gender (ref: male)						
Female	–0.90***	0.17	–0.79***	0.18	–0.75***	0.19
Age	–0.03***	0.01	–0.04***	0.01	–0.03***	0.01
Ethnicity (ref: White)						
Asian Muslim	0.57+	0.3	0.64+	0.33	0.74*	0.34
Asian other	–0.37	0.58	–0.21	0.58	–0.22	0.6
Black African	0.97*	0.47	1.01*	0.49	1.06*	0.52
Black Caribbean	1.06**	0.39	0.64	0.46	0.62	0.47
Mixed ethnic group	0.54	0.42	0.69	0.43	0.79+	0.43
Other ethnic group	0.48	0.46	0.91+	0.52	0.98+	0.53
Social class (ref: managerial/professional)						
Employees	0.38+	0.21	0.41+	0.23	0.36	0.23
Routine	0.09	0.21	0.1	0.23	0.08	0.24
Never worked	0.68+	0.38	0.57	0.45	0.59	0.45
Not classified	0.29	0.26	0.15	0.28	0.13	0.28

Educational attainment (ref: other)						
First degree or higher	0.37+	0.19	0.53*	0.21	0.51*	0.2
No qualifications	0.3	0.19	0.37+	0.22	0.3	0.23
Car access (ref: no)						
Yes	–0.87***	0.19	–0.90***	0.21	–0.87***	0.21
Marital status (ref: married/partnership)						
Single	0.41*	0.18	0.45*	0.19	0.41*	0.2
Employment status (ref: all others)						
Unemployed	0.51*	0.25	0.58*	0.26	0.53*	0.26
Health status (ref: good)						
Fair	0.28	0.21	0.31	0.23	0.25	0.23
Poor	0.71*	0.34	0.5	0.43	0.43	0.43
Clubber? (ref: no)						
Yes	–0.36+	0.19	–0.41*	0.2	–0.49*	0.2
Lives in London (ref: no)						
Yes	0.83***	0.2	0.78***	0.21	0.76***	0.22
Any drug use in previous year (ref: no)						
Yes					0.63***	0.19
Constant	–1.03**	0.37	–0.85+	0.44	–1.09*	0.44
n	2,685		2,130		2,130	

Source: CSEW, 2008/2009 to 2010/2011.

Notes
+ $p<0.1$; * $p<0.05$; ** $p<0.01$; *** $p<0.001$.

Third, people's 'routine activities' had a significant effect on their chances of experiencing police stops. Car access was an important predictor not only of a greater chance of having experienced a traffic stop but of a lesser chance of experiencing a foot stop. Behaviours that seem likely to make people more 'available' to the police, such as going to pubs and clubs, were in some models associated with a greater probability of being stopped, as was being single (a variable that must imply a certain set of behaviours that, among other things, make an individual more available to the police). A further notable finding is that recent victimization was consistently associated with a higher probability of being stopped by police. It may be that behaviours associated with an increased probability of victimization are also associated with an increased probability of attracting police attention. It is also tempting to note that victimization and offending are often highly correlated, which might suggest that, all else equal, victimization may act as a partial proxy for offending above and beyond the drug use that was included in the models. Correspondingly police stop activity was consistently more likely to be experienced by – and thus surely more likely to be targeted at – people who had used illegal drugs in the past year. This is not surprising, and is also, in terms of the validity of the models shown above, reassuring. Given the preponderance of stop and search activity related to illegal drugs it would have be disturbing had such an association not been identified.

Fourth, police stop activity was higher in high crime areas (as measured by the self-reported victimization of CSEW respondents). This however appeared to be largely due to the individual characteristics of people living in those areas, and once these, and other area-level characteristics, were taken into account the link between crime and stops was broken. Equally, and fifth, police stop activity tended to be higher in more disadvantaged or 'disorderly' areas, those with a higher proportion of drug users, and those with a greater proportion of young people. These associations were again generally broken by the introduction of individual-level controls – with two important exceptions. Independent of their personal characteristics, people who lived in areas with a higher proportion of immigrants and, less consistently, more disorderly areas, were more likely to have been stopped by police while on foot. An important implication of these findings is that while police stop and search activity is indeed concentrated in higher crime, poorer areas it is largely – although not only – the characteristics of the people living there that 'attracts' police attention. It is people, not places, that seem to be the primary object of this type of police activity: as Bittner noted: 'the police are more likely to be found in places *where certain people live or congregate* than in other parts of the city' (1990: 98, emphasis added).

Sixth, there seems to be little evidence of 'race out of place' effect in this data. People from visible ethnic minority groups were not more likely to have been stopped by police if they lived in areas with larger majority group populations (and vice versa). This finding should be treated with caution, since it may be that had a different, in all likelihood smaller, area-level unit been used then such an effect could have emerged. In a general sense, though, it may serve to suggest an important distinction between the US and UK situations, and that it cannot simply be assumed that patterns identified in the US will be identified in the UK.

Finally, many of the same characteristics that predicted higher odds of being stopped also predicted higher odds of being searched once stopped. While there were some anomalous findings, the general pattern was clear: people from specific ethnic minority groups, the young, men, the unemployed, those not in relationships and drug users were all more likely to have been searched once stopped. Compared with others, greater or more invasive police power was more frequently deployed in relation to these groups.

Although not covered by the original hypotheses, it is worth underlining that both age and gender were consistently associated with the odds of being stopped (and searched). These are above all powers primarily used against men and against the young, a point that arguably deserves more attention than it often receives (Murray 2015). While it may seem self-evident, and indeed inevitable, that young men in particular are more likely to be stopped by the police, given that they are disproportionality likely to offend, we should recall that this is unlikely to be true for all forms of crime. The extent to which white-collar crime, for example, is concentrated among young men is much less clear. Which is to say of course that police stops are a tactic that takes aim not at all types of crime but at specific categories, which tend to both resonate with public perceptions of what 'real' crime is (violent crime, drug use, certain categories of volume crime, or what Bittner (1990: 5) referred to as 'residual crime') and which, in a process that surely has an element of circularity, comprise the bulk of the recorded crime data. Note, though, that young people were more likely to be stopped even after recent drug use was taken into account (the most common reason for a stop and search, at least, to be instigated). In this limited sense police stops were used more against young people *even after* their differential levels of offending were taken into account.

Taken together, these findings offer support to a number of theories concerning the distribution of police stop activity. Routine activities do seem to make some people more available to the police (and these may vary significantly across different ethnic groups and other social categories). Yet, there appears to be a proportion of ethnic and perhaps class-based disproportionality that cannot be explained away by routine activity variables, suggesting that notions of implicit (or explicit) bias, stereotyping and perhaps the association by police of particular ethnic groups with criminal and social threat retain important explanatory power. In short, since ethnic disproportionality persists even after the introduction of a wide range of statistical controls, the CSEW data provide evidence that racial profiling, of some kind, is occurring. Moreover, as proposed by conflict and perhaps also group threat theories, stop activity is directed at marginalized individuals and, perhaps, areas. The England and Wales data presented here correspond with US research on the extent to which police activity is concentrated in disadvantaged areas (e.g. Fagan *et al.* 2010), albeit that in the final analysis that is the characteristics of the people living there, not the area itself, which seems to be most important in terms of attracting police attention.

Consensus theory finds less support – stops and/or searches do not appear to be consistently, or specifically, targeted at high crime areas, although they are indeed targeted at people who break the law (by using drugs).

Yet, support for all these theories is often contradictory. Most notably, not all minority groups were consistently singled out; individuals from the cluster of ethnic minority groups which arguably pose the greatest economic (competitive) 'threat' to the white population, non-Muslim Asians, were not more likely to be stopped: group 'threat', if it is present, seems not to be of an economic nature. Two basic demographic factors that transcend most others – age and gender – are the most consistent predictors of being stopped, and this association is independent of factors including routine activities and drug use. Being young had an effect on the probability of being stopped even when controlling for some of the things young people are more likely to do. Race out of place had little explanatory power in the CSEW data – but owning and/or using a car was arguably *the* strongest predictor of being stopped by police.

Overall, one is left with the sense that police stop – and search – activity, while certainly directed at particular places and, more importantly, types of people, does not 'fit' neatly into any of the theoretical paradigms outlined in Chapter 4. It is in a sense both too loose, used in a diverse range of situations and locations, and too restricted, concentrating on very particular social categories: young not old, men not women, some minority groups not others; people disadvantaged across some categories but not others; areas disadvantaged by poverty and disorder, but not necessarily by crime.[6]

How to explain this? It may be that part of the problem with existing theoretical approaches is that they position stop/searches as a police response to *external* stimuli. Police certainly do respond to specific events – for example major crimes – by stepping up stop and search. They also respond to governmental priorities, such as the 'war on drugs' and knife-crime, by instigating major stop and search programmes, such as cordons at major transport hubs. But the extent of the use of the power to stop people – millions of times each year – belies the idea that these responsive activities comprise the reasons for the bulk of police stops.

Instead of positioning it as a response to crime per se, stop and search, and the wider police practice of stopping people going about their business and asking them to account for themselves, is perhaps better conceptualized as a *disciplinary power*, the application of which stems from some of the basic structures underlying the institution of police in a context such as England and Wales. The distribution of stop experiences across social and geographic space stems not so much from external pressures placed on police, nor necessarily from active bias on the behalf of individual officers or some form of institutional racism (although all may be important factors at some times and in some places), but from the basic structures of policing as it has developed in the UK and indeed many other contexts. Positioned thus street stops can be seen as a fundamental aspect of police practice which is *prior to* the pressure on officer behaviour exerted by processes of social conflict, group threat, stereotyping and so forth, albeit that these processes will moderate and mediate the effect stop activity has on individuals and areas. The distribution of stop/searches can be best explained, therefore, if it is viewed as an expression of *the police power*, and of the basic imperative *to police* – the effort of the state, and its agents, to maintain a diffuse notion of social order defined by a need to reproduce existing power relations and extant normative conceptions propriety and right. This being the case, those that do not fit into or challenge this order in some way (possibly by merely existing) are inevitably the special targets of police and, therefore, of police stops. But so, equally, are those who break the law and those using the public highway. All such individuals and groups are targets of police.

Notes

1 Around half of these searches result from a foot stop, and around half from a car stop.
2 Obtained from www.nomisweb.co.uk/census/2011.
3 This was created via factor analysis of seven CSEW items that covered respondents' assessments of the extent to which issues such as noisy neighbours, teenagers 'hanging around', vandalism, rubbish and drunk and disorderly people were a problem in their local area (defined as the area within 15 minutes' walk of their residence). All seven items loaded very strongly onto one underlying factor, labelled disorder. To generate the LSOA level measure the mean score of this variable among the residents of each LSOA was taken.
4 Four Census measures were used to construct this index: proportion of households in socially rented accommodation; proportion of households with no car; percentage unemployed; and proportion of lone parent households. The proportion of ethnic minority and young residents are commonly included in such scales – however these were excluded here as they were included as separate measures in the analysis.
5 Robust standard errors, with clustering at the LSOA level, was preferred due to the sparseness of the data. None of the LSOA level measures proved significant in these models.
6 The extent to which the disproportionalities identified in this chapter constitute the misdirection of police resources (in as much as the 'wrong' people are being stopped) is moot, given the data at hand, but it is tempting to conclude that the extent of the disproportionalities identified above imply yet again that this form of policing does not contribute much in terms of the 'fight against crime' (Delsol 2015).

References

Allen, J., El Komy, M., Lovabakke, J. and Roy, H. (2005). *Policing and the Criminal Justice System – Public Confidence and Perceptions: Findings from the 2003/04 British Crime Survey*. Home Office Online Report 31/05.

Ariza, J.J.M. (2014). Police-initiated contacts: young people, ethnicity, and the 'usual suspects'. *Policing and Society* 24(2): 208–223.

Ashby, M.P.J. and Tompson, L. (2015). Routine activities and proactive police activity: A macro-scale analysis of police searches in London and New Work City. *Justice Quarterly*. Online.

Bittner, E. (1990). *Elements of Police Work*. Boston: Northeastern University Press.

Bradford, B. and Loader, I. (2016). Police, crime and order: The case of stop and search, in Bradford, B., Jauregui, B., Loader, I. and Steinberg, J. (eds) *The SAGE Handbook of Global Policing*. London: SAGE.

Delsol, R. (2015). Effectiveness, in Delsol, R. and Shiner, M. (eds) *Stop and Search*. Basingstoke: Palgrave Macmillan.

EHRC (2010). *Stop and Think – A Critical Review of the Use of Stop and Search Powers in England and Wales*. London: Equalities and Human Rights Commission.

Ewing, W.A., Martínex, D.E. and Rumbour, R.G. (2015). *The Criminalization of Immigration in the United States*. American Immigration Council Special Report, July 2015.

Fagan, J., Geller, A., Davies, G. and West, V. (2010). Street stops and broken windows revisited: Race and order maintenance policing in a safe and changing city, in Rice, S. and White, M (eds) *Exploring Race, Ethnicity and Policing: Essential Readings*. New York: New York University Press, 309.

Franko Aas, K. (2011). 'Crimmigrant' bodies and bona fide travellers: Surveillance, citizenship and global governance. *Theoretical Criminology* 15(3): 331–346.

Gulliford, M.C., Ukoumunne, O.C. and Chinn, S. (1999). Components of variance and intraclass correlations for the design of community-based surveys and intervention studies: Data from the Health Survey for England 1994. *American Journal of Epidemiology* 149(9):876–883.

Hedges, L.V. and Hedberg, E.C. (2007). Intraclass correlation values for planning group-randomized trials in education. *Educational Evaluation and Policy Analysis* 9(1): 60–87.

Lea, J. (2003). Institutional racism in policing: The Macpherson report and its consequences, in Matthews, R. and Young, J. (eds) *The New Politics of Crime and Punishment*. Cullompton: Willan.

Murray, K. (2015). *The Proactive Turn: Stop and Search in Scotland*. PhD Thesis, University of Edinburgh.

ONS (2010). *Standard Occupational Classification 2010*. Volume 1: *Structure and Descriptions of Unit Groups*. Basingstoke: Palgrave Macmillan/Office for National Statistics.

ONS (2012). 2011 *Census: Population and Household Estimates for England and Wales, March 2011*. London: Office for National Statistics.

Sampson, R. (2008). Rethinking Crime and Immigration. *Contexts* 7(1): 28–33.

Sampson, R. (2012). *Great American City*. Chicago: Chicago University Press.

TNS-BMRB (2010). *British Crime Survey 2009–10 Technical Report*. London: TNS-BMRB.

TNS-BMRB (2011). *British Crime Survey 2010–11 Technical Report*. London: TNS-BMRB.

Waddington, P., Stenson, K. and Don, D. (2004). In proportion: race, and police stop and search. *British Journal of Criminology* (44): 889–914.

Weber, L. (2011). 'It sounds like they shouldn't be here': Immigration checks on the streets of Sydney. *Policing and Society* 21(4): 456–467.

6 The distribution of stop and search

Evidence from Police Force Areas

The analysis presented in Chapter 5 demonstrated that even controlling for potential confounders such as age, place of residence, social class, drug use and routine activities, people from some ethnic minority groups were still more likely than their white counterparts to have experienced police stops. Evidence for ethnic disproportionality in the experience – and use – of this police power therefore remains strong. There was evidence, too, of other forms of disproportionality. People from socially disadvantaged or marginalized groups were consistently more likely to have been stopped by police: most notably, victims of crime, the unemployed, those living in socially rented accommodation and those in poor health. It seems that the uneven social distribution of police stop activity is not limited to an emphasis on young men and people from minority ethnic groups, but rather extends to other types of individuals and groups as well. A complicating factor was that car ownership, hardly a marker of social disadvantage, strongly predicts experience of police stops, because so many of these are traffic stops. The basic underlying issue seems to be that stop and search is used as a controlling, disciplinary tool as much as, if not more than, a crime-fighting tool, and is correspondingly focused on groups thought to be in need of such interventions. Overall, the suggestion might be that it is not the fact that this power exists that is necessarily the problem, but rather the *extent* and *unevenness* of its application.

Thus far the emphasis has been on the experience of the broad category of police stops at the individual level, albeit that area-level factors were also examined. In this chapter the discussion moves on to consider data at a very different level of aggregation – the Police Force Area (PFA) – and the specific power to stop and search as laid out in PACE and other legislation. PFAs are the major unit of police organization in England and Wales. They generally correspond with local political boundaries such as counties (as in Devon and Cornwall, or Norfolk) and/or with metropolitan areas (as in Greater Manchester, the London Metropolitan Police Service (MPS) and West Midlands Police). Police forces in England and Wales have significant operational autonomy and different cultures; they report quite widely varying 'policing outcomes', for example in terms of arrest and conviction rates (Home Office 2015), and serve areas with varying populations and levels of socio-economic deprivation.

At the threshold it would seem variation in the way these different, yet also of course similar, organizations use a key police power is likely to be of interest. Moreover, beyond organizational and cultural differences across PFAs the switch from micro-level analysis of the CSEW to macro-level analysis at the PFA level is justified, in part, simply by the very significant level of variation in the use of stop and search across different forces. During the decade starting in 2002/2003 the MPS, the heaviest user of stop and search, used the power *10 times* more frequently, per head of population, than the PFAs that used it the least (see below, and also Borooah 2010; Miller 2010). This is a mode of policing that is very much more common in some parts of the country than in others. Yet, despite this being a well-known phenomenon (EHRC 2010) there has been very little attempt to explain this variation beyond noting that London is something of a special case, not only in terms of the intensity with which stop and search is used in the capital, but also in terms of the challenges faced by the MPS in policing it.

Why, then, do some police forces use stop and search much more than others? What factors might contribute to this variation? Drawing on the discussion and results from the previous chapter, three plausible factors that might explain this variation suggest themselves. First, stop and search might be a police response to variation in levels of crime. This is in essence is a consensus theory explanation – police activity rates would be expected to be higher, and more intrusive, in regions with higher levels of crime, not least because police will be responding to the wishes of residents to deal with this issue.

Second, given the strength of the association between individuals' marginality and their probability of experiencing a police stop, it does not seem unreasonable to suggest that PFAs serving populations with higher levels of social deprivation (which, for current purposes, can be treated as a proxy measure of or even simply conflated with marginality) will have higher levels of stop and search. This is an idea that resonates with conflict theories of police activity and, in essence, the idea that the police activity serves in an important sense to patrol the boundaries between the haves and the have-nots, and that policing functions to control or discipline the latter.

Third, given, again, the strong predictive link between ethnic minority status and the probability of being stop/searched demonstrated in Chapter 5, we might expect that stop and search will be higher in areas with larger ethnic minority populations and particularly, perhaps, larger black or Asian populations. This is once more a conflict theory prediction, although it also relates closely to questions of statistical discrimination and institutional racism. Conflict theory would suggest that police activity will be more intense, perhaps even harsher, in areas with large minority populations, since these populations are considered to be more in need of controlling or disciplining; theories of discrimination or institutional racism would suggest police activity is more intense in areas with large minority populations due to assumptions about likely levels of offending in those areas (because police believe black people offend more, they will use stop and search more in areas with larger black populations).

Another way to frame these hypotheses is in terms of Dubber's notion of police power and, in particular, his idea that 'police' is less concerned with criminality than with the control of marginal or 'difficult' populations. Here, we would still expect the level of deprivation and size of minority population to predict the level of stop and search. But we might also expect that the link between crime and stop and search to be much more tenuous. Because police activity may not, from a sociological perspective and in the final analysis, be primarily about 'fighting crime' (Brodeur 2010) perhaps levels of crime will not have any straightforward link with stop and search activity. To put it another way, based on Dubber's account, stop and search and the wider category of police stops can be positioned as practices that stem from, and reflect, application of police power as part of the fundamental effort of the state to control and exert discipline on its population. Since the targets of this power are not necessarily 'criminals' or offenders, but rather social categories considered challenging or troubling, perhaps the application stop and search varies less according to the level of crime than might otherwise be expected. Moreover, a further implication of applying Dubber's insights in the context of stop and search, which in many senses seems so obvious it hardly needs stating, is that all else equal stop and search will be used where there are more police (where there are more police there is more policing). We would therefore expect to find a strong correlation between the number of police officers per head of population and the rate at which stop and search is used.

Data

To address the issues raised above a dataset was constructed by drawing on various official sources of PFA level data, primarily those published for a number of years by the Home Office (HO), Ministry of Justice (MoJ), and Officer for National Statistics (ONS). Despite the PFA level variation noted above, something that seems worthy of further exploration, the choice of PFA as the unit of analysis was essentially enforced, as this is the lowest unit of aggregation at which statistics on stop and search are published on any consistent basis. Ideally, smaller units of geographical aggregation would also have been used in this chapter.

The final dataset comprised PFA level data on:

- Stop and search (incidence, prevalence, disproportionality, and arrest rate)
- Recorded crime (crime identified to and recorded by the police)
- CSEW crime (estimates of the level of vicitimization for each PFA derived from the CSEW)
- Police numbers (number of serving officers in a given PFA)
- Complaints against the police (as recorded by the Independent Police Complaints Commission)
- Population and other socio-demographic data (derived from the 2001 and 2011 Census data)

Data were collected for a number of years, starting from 2002/2003 and running through to 2010/2011. An important feature of the dataset is therefore that it contains multiple (yearly) entries for each PFA, and thus comprises a longitudinal or panel dataset, a fact taken into account in the analyses presented below.

Key measures

While broadly self-explanatory, some of the measures used in this chapter nevertheless require some elucidation. Most importantly, the response variable is the number of stops within a PFA in a given year per 1,000 population of that PFA. This variable turned out to be highly skewed (since a few police forces use the power very much more than the majority of others); the natural log was taken to correct for this skew.

The explanatory variables are, first, CSEW crime rates. Obtained from the regular 'Crime in England and Wales' reports, these were used in preference to the police recorded crime figures as the latter are endogenous to the response variable (stop and search can, and does, 'produce' significant numbers of detected crimes). Both CSEW personal and household crime were used; the measure of personal crime, in particular, contains many offences thought to be 'susceptible' to stop and search (Miller *et al.* 2000), such as street crimes, the incidence of which in a given area might stimulate stop and search activity. However, by definition, since they are based on self-reported victimization, neither measure covers drug offences, and this is an important omission in the analysis. It is perhaps best to treat both as proxy measures of the 'overall' level of crime in a given area, rather than necessarily relating to the particular types of crime police might use stop and search 'against' in any direct manner.

The measures of crime were entered into the models in two different ways. First, the average personal and household crime rates for each PFA over the entire period in question (2002/2003 to 2010/2011) were calculated from the individual yearly data – this measure can be thought of as representing the 'structural' level of crime in a given PFA. Second, the yearly level measures were also used and, given the inclusion of the mean levels of crime in the models, can be interpreted as showing the statistical effect of deviations from the mean level of crime in an area on the use of stop and search (see below). All these measures of crime were strongly inter-correlated; however, robustness checks suggested this did not cause a problem in the models.

Second, the size of the ethnic minority population was represented by two variables, percentage black and percentage Asian.[1] These were themselves generated by taking the means of the figures from the 2001 and 2011 Censuses for the PFA concerned; since the dataset covers the period 2002/2003 to 2010/2011, the mean of the two Census values is a suitable overall measure. These measures were strongly correlated ($r=0.76$). The focus on the black and Asian population, rather than the ethnic minority population as a whole, was desirable because other measures of interest, particularly in relation to ethnic disproportionality, applies primarily to these groups.

Third, a measure of deprivation was created in the following fashion. Adapting the approach taken by Sutherland *et al.* (2013) and others, data on the following measures at the PFA level were collated from both the 2001 and 2011 Censuses: proportion of households in socially rented accommodation; proportion of households with children and no adults in employment; proportion of lone parent households; proportion of households with no access to a car; proportion of individuals who were long-term unemployed; proportion of individuals who have never worked. Exploratory Factor Analysis (EFA), using PFA level data and both Census years suggested all these measures loaded very strongly onto a single factor – one implication is therefore that relative deprivation, at the PFA level, was largely stable over the period in question. Factor scores were extracted and used as a measure of social deprivation in subsequent analysis; these can again be thought of, broadly, as representing the overall level of deprivation for a given PFA over the period 2001 to 2011. It is worth noting at the outset that despite their size and internal heterogeneity there was significant variation in levels of deprivation across different PFAs. Looking at the individual measures used to construct the overall deprivation measure, the proportion of households living in socially rented accommodation in 2011, for example, ranged from a low of 11 per cent to a high of 24 per cent. Similarly, the proportion of long-term unemployed ranged from 1 per cent to 3 per cent. PFAs serve populations with quite widely varying levels of social deprivation (which, to reiterate, I am treating here as broadly synonymous with marginality).

The final explanatory variables were (a) the number of police officers per 1,000 population, obtained from the regular Home Office publications on police force strength; (b) the proportion of young people (aged 16–29) living in an area (i.e. the proportion of the population within which offending is likely to be concentrated, and toward which police attention is likely to be directed), again calculated from Census data; and (c) population density. With regard this last variable, it does not seem unreasonable to suggest that stop and search will be 'easier' for forces serving areas of high population density; and population density is, of course, likely to be highly correlated with social deprivation (cities are densely populated and likely to suffer significant levels of deprivation). This measure was again calculated as the mean of the 2001 and 2011 population densities for each PFA.

Provisos

A number of initial provisos are in order. First, data for the MPS and City of London police were combined, where possible, to enable comparison across different data sources, leaving 42 areas in the final dataset (where combination was not possible, MPS data were used to represent London as a whole). Second, 'stop and search' refers here to what are identified in HO and MoJ outputs as 'Searches conducted under Section 1 of PACE and other legislation', the exact composition of which has changed somewhat over time. Note also that data pertaining to stops that did not result in a search were not included in the analysis.

Third, the period covered by the data is essentially bookended by the two Census years, meaning that the data derived from the Census can be tied closely to the police data. This does mean however that the decline in levels of stop and search that occurred from 2010/2011 onwards is not captured by this analysis. Finally, the analysis presented here is firmly of a descriptive nature – the purpose is to sketch out variation in the use of stop and search across different PFAs and suggest some potential reasons for this variation.

PFA level variation in the use of stop and search

Figure 6.1 demonstrates the extent of variation in the use of stop and search across different PFAs. It shows the mean stop and search rate (per 1,000 resident population) for each of the 42 PFAs (the figure for London excludes the City of London police) for the years 2002/2003 to 2010/2011. As many years of previous research would suggest (e.g. EHRC 2010; Miller *et al.* 2000) the MPS used stop and search substantially more often than any other force. In fact across the period covered in only two years was the stop and search rate higher in a force outside London than it was in the capital (Cleveland in 2002/2003 and West Midlands in 2004/2005).

Beyond this, what is perhaps most striking in Figure 6.1 is the extent to which otherwise similar forces use stop and search to very differing degrees. HMIC publishes lists of 'most similar groups' (MSGs) of police forces in a regular basis: these are groupings of PFAs based on similarities in demographic, economic and social characteristics related to crime. While these change somewhat over time, most forces have a fairly consistent set of 'similar' counterparts. To pull out just three points of comparison, according to the HMIC criteria Hampshire and Essex are similar forces, yet each year the former conducted on average over twice as many stops and searches on a per capita basis as the latter. Similarly, Nottinghamshire is grouped with South Yorkshire, but the latter used stop and search around three times as much as the former. Finally, the MPS is grouped with West Midlands, yet used stop and search around five times as much. Similar comparisons could be made right across the data, between, for example, Suffolk and Norfolk, or Cleveland and Durham.

What explains the extent of this variation? As mentioned above, most obviously having more police officers in an area may mean more are available for this type of activity. Figures 6.2a and 6.2b show this is, indeed, the case, whether we examine ratios – number of stops per capita by number of officers per capita – as in Figure 6.2a; or absolute numbers – total number of stops by total number of officers – as in Figure 6.2b. At the simplest level, the strength of the correlation between the number of officers available and the use of stop and search appears to support the idea that stop and search is in an important sense a function, or an exemplar, of the basic activity of policing; to reiterate, where there are more police there is more policing.

To investigate the association between rates of stop and search and the other variables of interest, as a first step a series of random effects (multi-level)

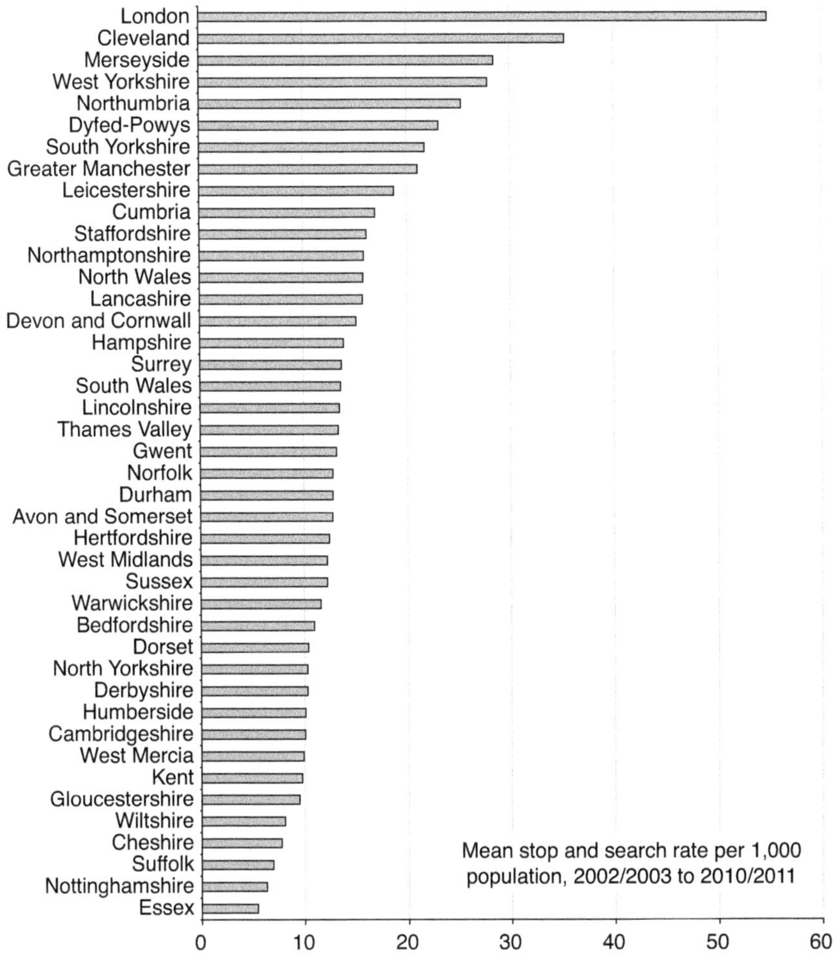

Figure 6.1 The use of stop and search varies significantly over different Police Force Areas.

Source: Home Office.

regression models were estimated, each predicting the logged number of searches per 1,000 population in a police force area in a given year. In these models individual yearly data-points (level 1) were 'nested' within PFAs (level 2). Results are shown in Table 6.1.

Model 1 in Table 6.1 is an empty 'variance components' model, showing that over 70 per cent of the variation in stop and search rates is explained at level 2. In other words, *most* of the variance in the use of stop and search can be explained at the PFA level, or *across* PFAs, rather than at the level of year-on-year variation *within* PFAs. This finding reiterates, therefore, the extent of variation in the use of stop and search across different PFAs shown in Figure 6.1.

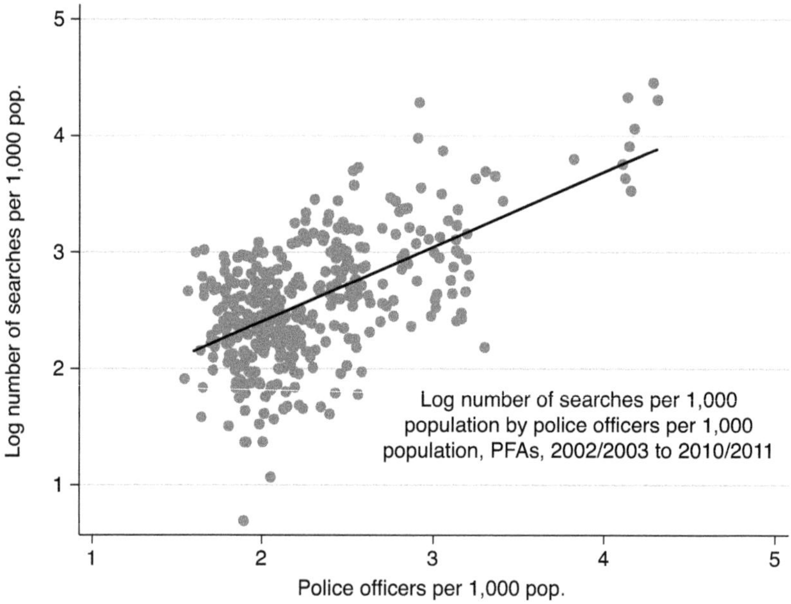

Figure 6.2a Where there are more police per capita, there is more stop and search.
Source: Home Office and others.

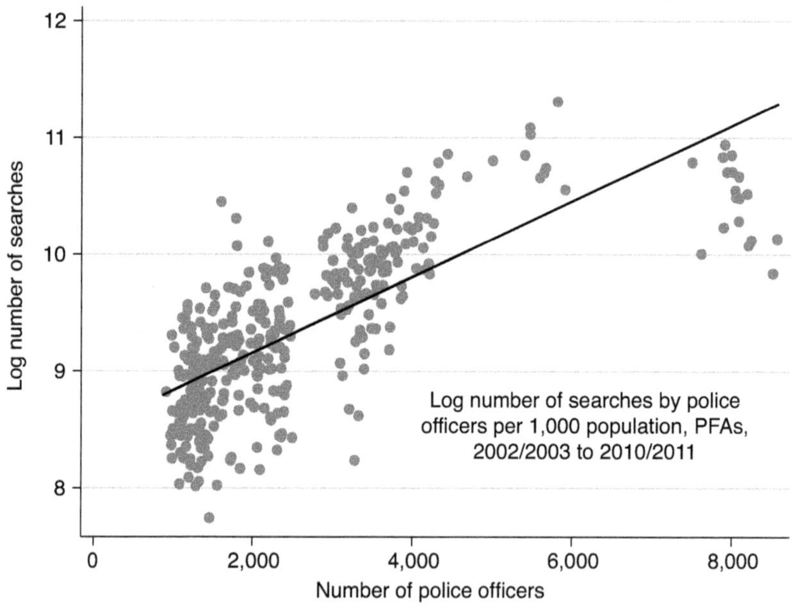

Figure 6.2b Where there are more police, there is more stop and search.
Source: Home Office and others.

Models 2 and 3 in Table 6.1 add level 1 (within year) predictor variables: personal and household victimization rates, and police numbers per capita. We find, first, that there is no association between levels of crime, measured on this basis, and the use of stop and search. It seems that areas with similar levels of crime in a given year could, and did, use stop and search at very different rates or, to put it another way, within PFAs, higher levels of crime in a particular year were not associated with greater use of stop and search that same year. Second, however, and as suggested above, there was a very strong association between the number of police officers per capita and the rate of stop and search. In the context of a multi-level model this suggests that, within PFAs, if more police were available in a given year the use of stop and search tended to be higher in the same year. Note also that the ICC falls substantially on the addition of the measure of police numbers (by 28 per cent to 0.56). A significant proportion of between PFA variation in the use of stop and search is explained simply by the number of police officers available to use the power.

Models 4 to 9 in Table 6.1 add PFA-level (level 2) explanatory variables. The emphasis thus shifts to the influence of what might be thought of as the structural characteristics of the different PFAs, and to explaining *across* PFA variation. We find that, as predicted, across PFAs those with higher levels of deprivation, larger ethnic minority populations, and greater population densities all tended to have significantly, and substantially, higher rates of stop and search. Intriguingly, we also find that the mean level of personal crime in a given PFA across the period in question was, on average, associated with higher levels of stop and search (model 4), although there was no association between mean level of household crime and stop and search rates. One interpretation here is that while year on year variation in crime has little effect on the use of stop and search, the power is used more in areas where there are structurally (or persistently) higher levels of personal crime.

Table 6.2 displays results from models that take the analysis further by entering multiple explanatory variables. Three models are shown. The first includes most of the predictors used above (the proportion of black and Asian residents is represented by a combined measure due to the high correlation between the two measures and the similarity of their statistical effects on levels of stop and search rates, as shown in Table 6.1) except police per head population and within year crime rates. It also includes year and a quadratic effect of year to take into account the secular trend in the use of stop and search, which grew substantially over the period in question (see Chapter 2). The results shown echo the fact that the use of stop and search first grew over time, then at the end of the period in questions fell back somewhat.

The key finding here, however, is that the 'structural' level of personal crime and the level of social deprivation were both positive, and independent, predictors of the level of stop and search. In other words, holding constant the level of crime, stop and search was used more in PFAs with higher levels of social deprivation. Equally, though, holding deprivation constant, stop and search was used more in areas with higher personal crime. However, perhaps rather perplexingly

Table 6.1 Do the characteristics of PFAs predict the use of stop and search?

Mixed effects models predicting stop and search rate per 1,000 population (logged)

Standardized betas	*Model 1*	*Model 2*	*Model 3*	*Model 4*	*Model 5*	*Model 6*	*Model 7*	*Model 8*	*Model 9*
CSEW personal crime		–0.03							
CSEW household crime		0.03							
Police per head of population			0.52**						
CSEW personal crime (mean)				0.38+					
CSEW household crime (mean)				–0.13					
Social deprivation					0.51**				
Proportion aged 15–29						0.47**			
Proportion Black							0.34**		
Proportion Asian								0.35**	
Population density									0.42**
ICC	0.71	0.7	0.56	0.7	0.62	0.64	0.68	0.68	0.66
n	378	378	378	378	378	378	378	378	378

Source: Home Office and others.

Notes

\+ $p<0.1$;

* $p<0.05$;

** $p<0.01$.

stop and search was all else equal used *less* in areas with higher structural levels of household crime. This was however a 'residual' effect that emerged only conditional on personal crime, and in a model which excluded structural personal crime there was no association between household crime and stop and search rate. One interpretation of this finding might be that if two forces had the same level of personal crime the one with more household crime used stop and search less, perhaps because resources were diverted to other interventions.

Once the number of police per 1,000 population is entered (Model 2) the picture changes. Most notably the coefficient for social deprivation lost significance once police numbers were added to the model. This suggests that there was more stop and search in PFAs in areas with more socially more deprivation *because there are more police in those areas*, and this effect was, at least to some extent, independent of the level of crime. Figure 6.3 supports this argument – there was a strong linear association between the level of deprivation in a PFA and the number of police officers per head. PFAs with the most deprived populations had over twice as many police as those with the least deprived populations (although the figure needs to be read with some caution as the deprivation measure is simply the mean for each PFA between 2001 and 2011, while police numbers are recorded each individual year). Moreover, further analysis (results not shown here) demonstrated that even controlling for all the other variables shown in Table 6.2 a significant link between levels of deprivation and numbers of police persisted.

By contrast the associations between the structural level of crime and stop and search are not altered by addition of the police numbers variable, suggesting that there was a link between the use of the power and crime, on these measures, which was independent of the number of police. Note also that the ICC for the model remains very high (0.57), suggesting that while a considerable amount of the variation in the use of stop and search at the PFA level was explained by the variables in the model (primarily, by year and police numbers) most was not, and there seems to be unobserved factors 'driving' the across PFA variation in the use of the power.

Finally, Model 3 in Table 6.2 tests for the importance of year-on-year variation in the level of crime as a predictor of stop and search rates. Given inclusion of the structural crime variables in the models, the interpretation of the yearly coefficients would be in terms of deviation from the mean – a positive coefficient would imply that stop and search increased when there was more crime than normal in a PFA in a given year. In the event neither coefficient was significant, suggesting that police use of stop and search, at the PFA level at least, is not sensitive to yearly variation in crime rates.

In sum, these findings, exploratory as they are, correspond quite closely with those discussed in Chapter 5. While there is a correlation between the 'structural' level of personal crime and the use of stop and search, the power does not appear to be used more when police in a particular PFA are faced with an increase in the level of crime, conforming to the idea that consensus theories of police activity have relatively little to offer when thinking about stop and search

Table 6.2 What are the PFA-level correlates of stop and search?

Mixed effects models predicting stop and search rate per 1,000 population (logged)						
	Model 1		*Model 2*		*Model 3*	
	β	*se(β)*	β	*se(β)*	β	*se(β)*
Year	0.13*	0.03	0.09*	0.04	0.09*	0.04
Year squared	–0.01*	0	–0.00+	0	0	0
PFA level variables						
CSEW household crime (mean)	–0.10*	0.04	–0.08*	0.04	–0.09*	0.04
CSEW personal crime (mean)	0.34*	0.14	0.31*	0.13	0.32*	0.13
Social deprivation	0.32*	0.09	0.14	0.11	0.14	0.11
Proportion age 15–29	0.05	0.09	0.05	0.08	0.05	0.08
Proportion Black/Asian	–0.02	0.07	–0.02	0.06	–0.02	0.06
Population density	–0.01	0.01	–0.01	0.01	–0.01	0.01
Within year variables						
Police per head of population			0.47*	0.17	0.47*	0.17
CSEW household crime					0.01	0.01
CSEW personal crime					–0.01	0.01
Constant	1.11	1.53	0.06	1.48	0.07	1.48
n	378		378		378	
ICC	0.60		0.57		0.57	

Source: Home Office and others.

Notes
+ $p<0.1$;
* $p<0.05$.

in England and Wales. By contrast conflict theories seem to have more purchase, at least in as much as it seems there is a link between higher levels of deprivation and greater use of stop and search, seemingly because such areas have more police per head of population. The idea that the police exist at least in part to control and/or discipline the disadvantaged or marginalized appears to find some support in the data. Yet there is little evidence that stop and search was used more in areas with higher ethnic minority populations; or, at least, that it was deprivation and crime which seemed to lead to greater use of stop and search in areas with large minority populations. This finding, apparently in contradiction to those in Chapter 5, which suggested that evidence for ethnic effect on police stops could not be 'explained away' by socio-demographic factors, demonstrates the difficulty of moving between different levels of analysis and between data from different sources – more research is needed on these issues.

How, then, might the high ICCs shown in Table 6.2 be explained? There seem to be important characteristics of PFAs, not covered by the variables included in the models, which influence the distribution of stop and search. One obvious candidate is variations in the crime mix across different areas; that is, different areas may have higher levels of the type of crime 'susceptible' to

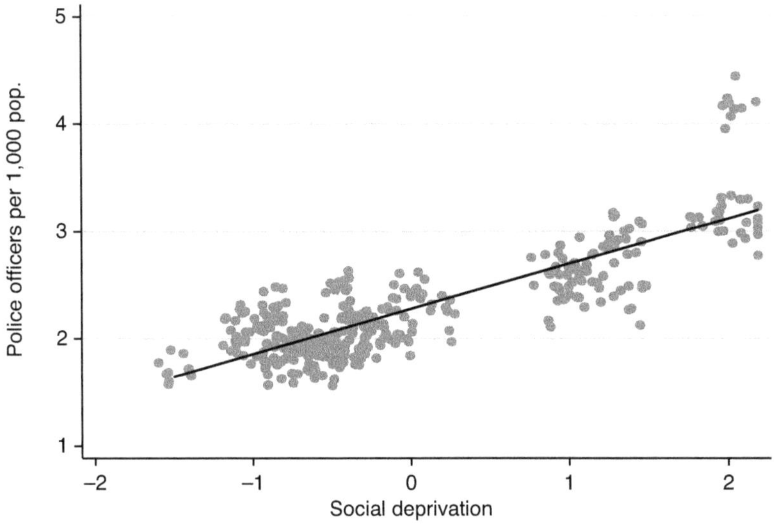

Figure 6.3 PFAs with more deprived populations have more police.

Source: Home Office and others.

targeting by stop and search. Future research could profitably explore this idea, too. Another possible explanation for some of the PFA-level variation in the use of stop and search is the cultures of different forces. While the extent to which 'police culture' is a defining aspect of policing in England and Wales is unclear – the police often seem much like any other organization (Bradford *et al.* 2014; Myhill and Bradford 2013) – there is little doubt that police culture can be an important guide to officer's behaviour (Loftus 2009; Reiner 2010; Waddington 1999). For example, and most pertinently, not only might the 'canteen culture' identify particular types of individual or groups as particularly worthy of police attention (Loftus 2009; Way and Patten 2013), but the nature and embeddedness of this culture may vary from force to force and have a differential effect on officers deciding when, and how much, to use stop and search powers. Other organizational factors, less cultural than managerial, may also have an effect. Senior officers might be a significant influence, setting the agenda and encouraging or discouraging, implicitly or explicitly, particular types of behaviour or modes of policing.

External factors will also be in play. This is most obviously the case when it comes to London. At least some of the difference between the MPS and other forces must surely be explained by the stresses placed on this particular force as a result of policing a city unlike any other in the country, home to the greatest concentration of political, cultural and financial power and also (and relatedly) target of most terrorist threats and location of the most important instances of organized dissent. Given these issues it is perhaps not surprising that the MPS uses stop and search more than any other force, although many might argue that the extent of this difference is hard to justify.

Finally, the trend for an increase, then decrease, in the use of stop and search over the period in question may be down to a combination of internal and external factors. On the one hand the period covered in this chapter starts not long after the publishing of the Stephen Lawrence report and a low point in the use of stop and search (see Chapter 2). Part of the initial upward trend may indicate increasing confidence to use the power among the police as memories of, and the controversy around, the report faded. On the other hand, 9/11 and subsequent events may have acted as something of an exogenous shock, spurring increased police activity in relation to certain areas and communities. Yet, equally, the decline in the use of stop and search toward the end of the decade may be explained at least in part by the growing pressure on police to address the issue of disproportionality (Delsol and Shiner 2015), as well as debate around excessive use of s.44 and s.60 powers.

The overall impression, then, is of a power that is both linked the basic practice of – even urge to – police, but which is also shaped in important ways by processes operating at organizational *and* wider societal levels. The distribution of stop and search appears to be to a seemingly important extent reflective of the distribution of police. Where there are more officers, the power to police is used (or applied) with greater frequency, although this is not to discount that the power was used more in areas 'structurally' higher levels of crime and in those with higher levels of social deprivation – in the latter case simply because there were more police in those areas. The application of this power was not however invariant across time or space, illustrating how a range of different forces might come together to shape police practice and behaviour.

The distribution of disproportionality

Thus far this chapter has considered only the overall distribution of stop and search – the mere fact of its presence or absence. However the *quality* of the use of the power is also important and, in particular, the distributive fairness of its application is of key interest. As described in Chapter 5 there seems to be a significant element of this disproportionality that cannot be explained away by other factors. Even controlling for demographic, behavioural and area-level characteristics, including personal drug use, people from several key minority groups were more likely to be have been stopped than their white counterparts. To what extent, then, does disproportionality in stop and search, specifically, vary across different PFAs?

The immediate answer to this question is: by a considerable amount. This is well known (Borooah 2010; Miller *et al.* 2000; EHRC 2010), and Figure 6.4 reiterates the point. It shows the mean level of disproportionality over the 2002/2003 to 2010/2011 period for each PFA, where mean disproportionality is calculated as the mean of the Asian and black disproportionality rates published by the HO and later MoJ. The chart therefore plots the mean of a mean and should be treated with caution. The basic illustrative point is sound, though:

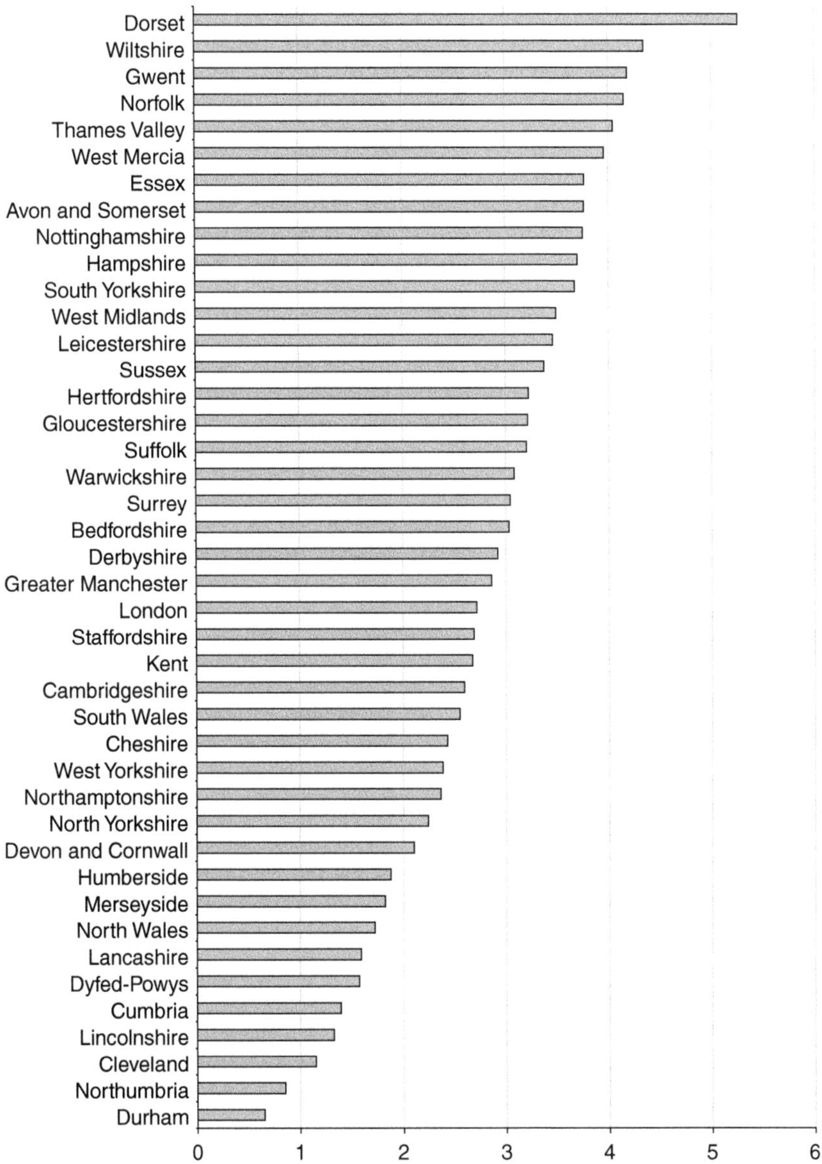

Figure 6.4 Disproportionality in stop and search varies significantly by PFA.

Source: Home Office.

there was very significant variation in disproportionality rates across PFAs. Dorset, Wiltshire, Gwent, Norfolk and Thames Valley all have mean disproportionality rates higher than four (meaning that in an overall sense people from black and Asian groups were four times more likely to be stopped and search than their white counterparts); conversely Northumbria and Durham had disproportionality rates of less than one, implying that in these PFAs white people were more likely to be stopped than their Asian or black counterparts (it should be noted that the ethnic minority population of both areas is very low). While the absolute differences between PFAs should be treated with some caution, the data so demonstrate that stop and search is indeed very much more disproportionate in some areas compared with others.

To complete the picture, Table 6.3 shows results from a series of random effects models predicting the mean disproportionality within PFA years. Variables as before are included as predictors (although proportion of children and population density are excluded on conceptual grounds – it is hard to envisage why either should have an association with disproportionality). Model 1 is the empty variance components model – the simple message here is that over half the variation in disproportionality is explained at the PFA level (rather than at the level of yearly variation within PFAs). Model 2 adds the PFA level variables, whole Model 3 adds within year predictors.

There are four key messages from Table 6.3. First, there was a very strong secular trend in disproportionality, with levels increasing during the first part of the period in question and subsequently declining. Second, controlling for the other variables in the model, it seems that when stop and search was used more this tended to produce somewhat *less* disproportionate outcomes; to put it another way, disproportionality was higher on average when stop and search was used less (although this association was significant only at $p<0.1$). Third, disproportionality tended to be lower in PFAs with higher levels of social deprivation, although this correlation disappeared when the within year measures were added. Fourth, and perhaps most importantly, disproportionality was *higher* in areas where the black and Asian population was greater. Note that the ICC is barely reduced by the addition of explanatory variables – most of the variation at the PFA level remains unexplained.

These results are in many ways rather difficult to interpret. Why, for example, should disproportionality have increased, then fallen over the period in question, independent of such factors as crime rates and the intensity of the use of the tactic? Why, all else equal, is disproportionality lower when stop and search is used more? One explanation here might be the fallout from the 7/7 London terrorist attacks in 2005 (which fell toward the beginning of the period) and then, later, a different kind of fallout from the continued debate over the Stephen Lawrence affair and allegations of racism in the MPS, the aftermath of the Jean Charles De Menezes trial in 2007, and then the events of the G20 demonstration in 2009. As noted above, police may be susceptible or responsive to outside pressures and developments, and this may affect the *way* stop and search is conducted as well as the *level* at which it is conducted.

Table 6.3 What are the PFA-level correlates of disproportionality?

Random effects models predicting ethnic disproportionality in stop and search

	Model 1		*Model 2*		*Model 3*	
	β	*se(β)*	β	*se(β)*	β	*se(β)*
Year			0.59*	–0.1	0.67*	–0.11
Year squared			–0.05*	–0.01	–0.05*	–0.01
PFA level variables						
CSEW household crime (mean)			0.15	–0.1	0.14	–0.1
CSEW personal crime (mean)			–0.51	–0.36	–0.39	–0.36
Social deprivation			–0.68*	–0.2	–0.36	–0.28
Proportion Black/Asian			0.27*	–0.12	0.28*	–0.12
Within year variables						
CSEW household crime					–0.04+	–0.02
CSEW personal crime					0.03	–0.04
Stop and search rate (logged)					–0.28+	–0.15
Police per head of population					–0.5	–0.47
Constant	2.82*	–0.16	1.16	–1.15	3.00+	–1.63
n	378		378		378	
ICC	0.57		0.57		0.56	

Source: Home Office and others.

Notes
+ $p<0.1$;
* $p<0.05$.

A second question is the negative association between social deprivation and disproportionality. It may be that stop and search is ethnically more evenly distributed in PFAs with higher levels of deprivation because in those areas the range of potential targets is in some sense greater (the proportion of the population in need of social control and disciplining is larger in such areas), meaning that people from ethnic minorities do not suffer so disproportionately from the drive 'to police'.

Finally, disproportionality is higher in areas with larger minority populations, a finding that would appear to fit quite neatly into the conflict theory and group threat hypotheses outlined in the previous chapter. On this account, when minority populations are larger they provide a greater threat to dominant groups and interests, probably of a subjective or ideological nature, thus stimulating greater police attention – and therefore greater disproportionality. Moreover, the finding that disproportionality is higher in areas of lower social deprivation might be interpreted in a similar way – perhaps the 'threat' from ethnic minority groups is more keenly felt in areas with less deprivation. But why, conditioning on the other variables in model, is disproportionality lower when stop and search is used more? Perhaps there is an element of 'practice makes perfect' here. It may be that in two areas with otherwise similar populations police in the area that used stop and search more simply got a bit better at dealing with some of the issues that led to disproportionality (such as, for example, implicit bias).

While some of these interpretations seem appealing, given the history of stop and search in England and Wales, the absence of corroborating evidence from elsewhere, either in the present volume or further afield, should caution against leaping to conclusions. Perhaps all that can be said at this stage is, yet again, that more research is needed on all these important issues.

Summary

What implications arise from the apparent distribution of stop and search across PFAs that is sketched out above? First, to reiterate, there is evidence that stop and search is used more in areas with higher numbers of disadvantaged residents. As both conflict theory and Dubber's conceptualization of the nature of the police power would suggest, stop and search is an important extent concentrated in areas containing more marginalized populations.

Second, it seems at least plausible that police organizational culture explains, to a significant degree, the variation observed across different PFAs. This is true in the case of both the incidence of stop and search and its disproportionality. This, it seems to me, only strengthens the notion that this is an aspect of police activity strongly linked to, and highly representative of, some of the basic underlying structures – or perhaps purposes – of the institution of police. If 'to police' is to act on an imperative to regulate and control (as well as to 'fight crime' and assist the public) we might well expect variation in the expression of this imperative across different police organizations not (only) as a result of external stimuli but (also) as a result of their internal structures, organization and culture. To borrow from Bourdieu (1990; see also Chan 1997), it might be that the *field* of policing is defined by and oriented toward regulation and control, particularly of marginal populations. This is something that all police organizations by definition work toward. However the *habitus* of different officers, differentially inculcated by the particular forces they work for, encourages or predisposes them to attempt this end in different ways, leading to significant variation in the use of stop and search across time and space.

Finally, there is ample space in the data above for circumstance and contingency. The extent of the London effect may be at least partly due to the culture of the MPS – but it is also a result of the particular context, and challenge, of policing in the capital. It seems these elements of local context may mediate or moderate the use of stop and search, shaping the extent of its application but not fundamentally affecting the underlying thrust behind the use of the power. Yet if this claim is correct it amounts to an insistence that the use of stop and search, like any other mode of policing, results in the final analysis from the choices made by police officers and/or organizations. These may be influenced or shaped by external factors and processes – indeed this must be the case – but it always remains a choice, and, given that, another route could always have been taken.

Note

1 The PFA-level measures utilizing census data were generated by matching data aggregated at the Unitary Authority (UA) level to the relevant PFA. Data at the UA level were collected online; the figure for each PFA was then calculated as the mean of its constituent UAs. This means that the figure for the proportion of black residents in a PFA (for example) used in this analysis will differ somewhat from the actual figure for that PFA (since it is the mean of the relevant UA figures). This approach was necessary because suitable 2011 Census measures at the PFA level were not available at the time the dataset was created. The mean figures calculated are however suitable proxy measures, and arguably may even provide a better estimate of the 'spread' of populations within a PFA.

References

Borooah, V.K. (2010). Racial disparity in police stop and searches in England and Wales. *Journal of Quantitative Criminology* 27(4): 453–473.

Bourdieu, P. (1990). *The logic of practise*. Cambridge: Polity Press.

Bradford, B., Quinton, P., Myhill, A. and Porter, G. (2014). Why do 'the law' comply? Procedural justice, group identification and officer motivation in police organizations. *European Journal of Criminology* 11(1): 110–131.

Brodeur, J.-P. (2010). *The Policing Web*. Oxford: OUP.

Chan, J. (1997). *Changing Police Culture: Policing in a Multicultural Society*. Melbourne: Cambridge University Press.

Delsol, R. and Shiner, M. (eds) (2015). *Stop and Search*. Basingstoke: Palgrave Macmillan.

EHRC (2010). *Stop and Think – A Critical Review of the Use of Stop and Search Powers in England and Wales*. London: Equalities and Human Rights Commission.

Home Office (2015). *Police Powers and Procedures England and Wales, Year Ending 31 March 2015*. London: Home Office.

Loftus, B. (2009). Police occupational culture: Classic themes, altered times. *Policing and Society* 20(1): 1–20.

Miller, J. (2010). Stop and search in England: A reformed tactic or business as usual? *British Journal of Criminology* 50(5), 954–974.

Miller, J., Bland, N. and Quinton, P. (2000). *The Impact of Stops and Searches on Crime and the Community*. Police Research Series Paper 127. London: Home Office.

Myhill, A. and Bradford, B. (2013). Overcoming cop culture? Organizational justice and police officers' attitudes toward the public. *Policing: An International Journal of Police Strategies & Management* 36(2): 338–356.

Reiner, R. (2010). *The Politics of the Police* (4th edn). Oxford: Oxford University Press.

Sutherland, A., Brunton-Smith, I. and Jackson, J. (2013). Collective efficacy, deprivation and violence in London. *British Journal of Criminology* 53(6): 1050–1074.

Waddington, P.A.J. (1999). *Policing Citizens: Authority and Rights*. London: University College Press.

Way, L.B. and Patten, R. (2013). *Hunting for Dirtbags*. Boston: Northeastern University Press.

7 Stops, trust and legitimacy

The previous chapters have shown that police stops are unevenly distributed across social and geographic space. People who live in some types of area, and, in particular, those who belong to certain social groups or categories, are significantly more likely to be stopped than others. Once stopped, they are often also more likely to be searched. In the present chapter the discussion turns to the effect these experiences might have on the trust they invest in, and the legitimacy they grant to, the police. What implications for police–public relations arise from this form of police activity?

All encounters between police officers and citizens are 'teachable moments' (Tyler *et al.* 2014), generating and communicating information concerning the status of the parties involved, the relationship between them, and their mutual positions within wider social structures and processes. The behaviour of police officers indicates to people the extent to which the police behave in a fair manner, are effective, abide by the rules, direct their attention toward the right ends and seek to achieve these via normatively justifiable means (Bradford *et al.* 2009; Jackson *et al.* 2012, 2013; Sunshine and Tyler 2003; Tyler and Fagan 2008; Tyler *et al.* 2015; Van Damme 2015). Furthermore, officer activity contains information concerning not only the police (their trustworthiness and legitimacy) but also about the citizen: about the moral worth the officer assigns to them and their positions with social groups the police both represent and partially define (Bradford *et al.* 2014; Loader and Mulcahy 2003; Parmar 2011; Waddington 1999). Contacts between police and public can also have significant downstream implications. This is particularly likely to be the case for police-initiated, enforcement-oriented encounters, such as police stops, not least because these are moments where the citizen, and perhaps also the police, have much at stake – for the citizen, of course, one possible outcome is arrest and entry into the criminal justice system. Experimental and longitudinal research has shown that public experiences of police-initiated encounters are associated not only with legitimacy judgements (Mazerolle *et al.* 2011, 2012) but, in a much wider sense, with subsequent behaviour, including offending behaviour (Wiley and Esebenson 2016; Slocum *et al.* 2016).

In this chapter and the next Tyler's procedural justice model is used as a framework for exploring, first, the implications for trust, legitimacy and compliance that arise from the experience of being stopped and/or searched, and second, linking to literatures concerned with the role of the criminal justice system as an engine of identity formation and transformation, the associations between the experience of procedural justice or injustice during police stops and the social identities of those stopped is considered. Street and traffic stops, like all police behaviours, can affect not only what people think of the police but also what they think of themselves. Police unfairness, in particular, can serve to shunt feelings of belonging and affect away from groups associated with the police and perhaps towards other, more marginal or indeed problematic identities.

In both chapters data from a number of survey sources are used. The two most important are the CSEW, as introduced in Chapter 5, and the London Metropolitan Police Public Attitudes Survey (PAS – Stanko and Bradford 2009; Stanko *et al.* 2012). The PAS is a large-scale, representative survey of Londoners that shares some characteristics with the CSEW but unsurprisingly has a far greater emphasis on public attitudes toward the police. Other sources are also used, however, and in keeping with the practice elsewhere in the book they are introduced as they become relevant to the discussion.

Procedural justice, trust, legitimacy and belonging

Procedural justice theory is, in essence, a model of authority in group settings, and of the relationship between individuals and organizations/institutions that have power over them. It posits that at the heart of public experiences of policing are assessments of the way in which officers exercise their power and authority. Procedural justice refers to impartiality and the fair, respectful and even-handed use of power. Numerous studies show how the exercise of authority via the application of fair process strengthens the social bonds between individuals and authorities and enhances trust between them (Tyler and Huo 2002; Sunshine and Tyler 2003; Tyler 2006).

Three organizing concepts in procedural justice theory are that, first, people tend to be sensitive to signs and symbols that communicate information about their status and position within a group (De Cremer and Tyler, 2005); second, the way police treat people communicates their status within the group the police represent (Blader and Tyler 2009), often characterized as the nation, state or community (Bradford *et al.* 2014; Jackson and Bradford 2009; Loader and Mulcahy 2003; Reiner 2010; Waddington 1999); and third that significant numbers of people in a given context valorize this identity and make it an important aspect of their sense of self (Bradford forthcoming). The experience of procedural justice during encounters with police promotes among those involved the idea that they and the police are in some sense 'on the same side'. During such interactions police communicate messages about their own trustworthiness, about the status and 'inclusion' they assign to the individual concerned, and about whether they conceive of their relationship with them as one based on shared group membership. Fair treatment promotes trust and encourages a sense of shared group membership. Of particular relevance in the current context is the idea that, in a symmetrical sense, procedural *injustice* can communicate stigmatization by legal authorities resulting from their application of negative stereotypes (Tyler and Wakslak 2004). If people perceive that the way police officers treat them is based not on what they are doing, but on their race, gender, or age, police behaviour undermines trust and carries negative identity implications, raising critical questions about whether those on the receiving end are accorded rights pertaining to membership of the group police represent (or the rights accorded to group members in good standing), or whether they have been assigned by police to a different group identity that may be less valorized by police, by others in society and, indeed, by themselves.

Despite the centrality of social identity in Tyler's theory it is important to keep in mind that procedural justice has a significant evaluative component (Bradford 2014). Procedurally fair police behaviour can demonstrate to citizens that the police are behaving in a normatively justifiable manner – after all, the police are, or at least should be, in the business of 'doing justice'. On this account, police actions are held up against a set of commonly shared norms and values, for example, that everyone involved in a dispute should be able to have their say, and officers and organization are found wanting if they do not allow this to happen.

Procedural justice and the sense of trust it engenders are linked to satisfaction with particular encounters and, in a more general sense, to legitimacy. As described in Chapter 3, the legitimacy of the police *from the perspective of the policed* can be characterized as (a) the extent to which people believe that the police have a valid right to power and influence; and (b) the types of opinions and actions such a belief engenders. Following ongoing work investigating the nature of police legitimacy in diverse social contexts (Jackson *et al.* 2012, 2014; Jackson and Gau 2015), the analysis presented below assumes that the police can be considered to be legitimate when individuals perceive that police officers act in morally valid ways, when they believe that the police abide by the rules and procedures intended to govern their behaviour, and when they voluntarily offer their consent to police activity. Seen in these terms, legitimacy can be seen as partly dependent on people's assessments of the behaviour *of* the police (e.g. citizens make assessments of whether or not the police follow the rules and act in normatively justifiable ways) and partly dependent on their motivations or behaviour in relation *to* the police (e.g. citizens act in ways that indicate their consent to the role of the police – or they do not). Most research finds that assessments of (or trust in) the instrumental effectiveness of police are far less important than procedural justice as predictors of legitimacy (although few would claim that effectiveness is ever entirely unimportant).

Procedural justice, trust and legitimacy – and indeed social identity – have all, furthermore, been linked to people's readiness to cooperate with the police and abide by the law. On the one hand, people are motivated to follow the rules – the laws – of groups to which they feel they belong; they are also more likely to cooperate with group representative and act on behalf of the group (Bradford *et al.* 2015). On the other hand, granting the police legitimacy involves ceding it the right to determine proper behaviour, whether this relates to the law itself or the imperative for people to assist the police in their duties when called on to do so. Furthermore, identification with the police, which is strengthened by fair use of authority, also helps promote a sense that police power is morally justified (Jackson *et al.* 2012, 2013), further strengthening the links between procedural justice, legitimacy and cooperation (we are motivated to support authorities we believe 'do the right thing'). One obvious implication here is that police activity that undermines trust and legitimacy will, in the long run, make policing more difficult, as people withdraw from cooperating with officers and are encouraged to see offending behaviour as a possible – or more desirable – 'action-alternative' (Wikström *et al.* 2012).

While there is an increasing amount of evidence, from multiple national contexts, underpinning the procedural justice model, the existence of a 'procedural justice effect' in any one social context cannot be assumed but must be tested for. Particularly relevant for current purposes is the idea that procedural justice may be less important – less salient, less predictive of trust and legitimacy, and less identity relevant – to people from minority and otherwise socially marginal groups (Huo *et al.* 1996; Murphy and Cherney 2012). There are a number of reasons for suggesting that this might be the case.

First, the centrality of shared group membership in procedural justice theory may make it inapplicable in contexts where individuals or groups feel distanced or alienated from the group identity police represent. Under such conditions, people may be less attuned to the identity-relevant aspects of officer behaviour, they may care less about procedural justice, and procedural injustice may have less of an impact on their legitimacy judgements and propensities to cooperate. Caring less about procedural justice, marginalized individuals may be more instrumentally minded and place relatively greater emphasis on questions of effectiveness when forming legitimacy judgments and making decisions about acts of cooperation. Alternatively, they place little weight on *any* aspect of police performance when making such judgements. Second, the experience of being stopped, particularly among those for whom it is a regular occurrence, may not have the knock-on effects on trust, legitimacy and other outcomes if they become inured to the experience, or if they expect so little from the police that any one encounter has little effect on them. Third, irrespective of their relationship with police and the wider social categories involved, instrumental concerns may simply be more important to some people in some times and places. Most pertinently, people who live in high crime areas, or who are recent victims of crime, may quite reasonably care more about the instrumental effectiveness of the police than about fairness issues. Finally, some people may expect less from the police during encounters – due to cynicism, a simply lack of expectation or a regular experience of poor service – and therefore react less strongly to poor (unfair) treatment than others who may expect more from the police (Reisig and Chandek 2001). All this suggests that among those who are most likely to be stopped this type of encounter might have less of an effect on their trust and legitimacy judgements than would otherwise be the case.

Conversely, it might be that contact experiences count for *more* among marginalized groups. As their status is less certain in relation to the social groups the police represent, people from such groups are more attuned to the inclusion and status relevant 'messages' contained in police behaviour (Bradford 2014; Bradford *et al.* 2014). This would suggest a stronger association between contact experiences and trust among such groups – which would make, of course, the potentially damaging effect of stop encounters on trust and legitimacy even more acute.

In the discussion that follows consideration of some of these ideas is used as a way to explore the potential effect of stop and search on public trust and police legitimacy. I start however with a rather more straightforward question – what types of stop and search experiences do people have, and how do they judge them?

Judgements about and satisfaction with police behaviour during stop/searches

Recall that procedural fairness is characterized by neutrality, voice, respectfulness, openness and dignity. Unfortunately the CSEW contains only a limited range of variables relating to assessments of stop experiences. One item does however address a key element of procedural justice – whether the respondent felt they were *given a reason* for being stopped (using a simple binary yes/no question). Being informed of the reason for police behaviour may indicate to those involved that the police have a reason for what they are doing, that this reason is a good one, and that they respect the individual's right to know this reason (Mazerolle *et al.* 2012).

Table 7.1 shows that there was some variation in experiences across foot and car stops. Looking first at the former, less than one in five of those stopped while on foot were *not* given a reason for the stop. Yet, there was also variation across the socio-demographic categories shown. Notably, people from non-white ethnic groups were significantly less likely to have been given a reason for the stop. Similarly, younger people were less likely than older people to have been given a reason, as were unemployed people and students, people in routine and semi-routine occupations, single people and those living in socially rented accommodation. In multivariate analysis (binary logistic regression modelling – results not shown here for reasons of space) just two factors were found to be the most important predictors of the odds of not being given a reason for the stop: people from non-white ethnic groups were much less likely to have been given a reason for the stop, as were those who were unemployed.

When it came to car stops, overall only 8 per cent of those stopped were not given a reason by the officers involved: it seems that police making traffic stops are generally very good at explaining why they stopped drivers (cf. MacQueen and Bradford 2015). There was however still significant variation in people's experience of police behaviour in this regard. Again, people from non-white ethnic groups were less likely to be provided with a reason for the stop, as were younger people and the unemployed. Multivariate analysis (again not shown) confirmed that young people, those from non-white ethnic groups and, in this instance, men, were significantly less likely to have been given a reason for the stop.

In sum, people from some of the groups identified in Chapter 5 as being the *most* likely to be stopped by police were also the *least* likely to given a reason as to why the officers concerned initiated the encounter. Not only is police stop activity unevenly distributed across social as well as geographic space, but the way police behave during these encounters is, at least from the perspective of the individuals experiencing them, also inconsistent. While it is important to note that in most cases a reason for the stop was provided by police – a finding that chimes with research that has shown police are generally good at handling these encounters and displaying key elements of procedural justice (MacQueen and Bradford 2015) – it nevertheless seems that people from particular marginal or excluded groups were less likely feel they had been fairly treated by the officers who stopped them.

Overall satisfaction with stops

In addition to being asked whether they had been given a reason for the stop CSEW respondents who reported experiencing a police stop are also asked how satisfied they were 'overall' with the way the police treated them. Responses were on a four-point scale ranging from 'very satisfied' to 'very dissatisfied' – this was dichotomized into 'satisfied' and ''dissatisfied' for analysis. This measure is particularly useful as procedural justice has consistently been shown to the most important predictor of satisfaction with police contact. As Table 7.2 shows, overall satisfaction rates were high, but there was again some important variation across key socio-demographic variables.

In relation to foot stops, just over one-quarter (27 per cent) to those stopped indicated they were dissatisfied to some degree with the way the police treated them. It is once more notable that people from some of the groups most likely to be stopped by police were also the most likely to be dissatisfied with the way police handled the encounters. Those from non-white ethnic groups were more likely to be dissatisfied than their counterparts from white groups, for example, as were younger people, men, the unemployed, single people, those in poor health and those living in socially rented accommodation. The strongest correlate of dissatisfaction by far, though, was whether a search took place. Nearly half of those searched were dissatisfied overall with the way the police handled the encounter.

Regression modelling was again used to investigate in a little more detail (results not shown). This process revealed that the strongest predictors of satisfaction were being given a reason for the stop and whether a search took place – once these factors were taken into account few other variables were statistically significant in the model. Being given a reason for the stop was associated with greater odds of satisfaction (firmly in line with procedural justice theory); being

Table 7.1 People's treatment during police stops is uneven

Proportion of those stopped who were not given a reason: by socio-demographic characteristics

	Foot stops		*Car stops*	
	%	n	%	n
Age				
16–18	*27*	168	*11*	128
19–21	*30*	71	*12*	137
22–24	*27*	51	*5*	155
25–34	*11*	113	*8*	456
35–44	*12*	68	*5*	478
45–54	*3*	59	*6*	389
55–64	*14*	61	*10*	269
65–74	*19*	23	*7*	151
75 plus	*0*	8	*12*	76
Gender				
Female	*22*	413	*9*	1,326
Male	*18*	209	*5*	903
Ethnicity (8 categories)				
Asian Muslim	*27*	19	*13*	57
Asian – other religion	*27*	7	*9*	51
Black African	*58*	9	*11*	33
Black Caribbean	*36*	15	*17*	36

	Foot stops		*Car stops*	
	%	n	%	n
Economic activity status				
Employed	*16*	327	*7*	1,614
Unemployed	*36*	92	*15*	109
Student	*25*	90	*7*	71
Looking after family	*6*	13	*4*	92
Long term sick	*19*	43	*5*	84
Retired	*9*	36	*10*	240
Educational attainment				
First degree or higher	*18*	80	*8*	488
Below degree level	*21*	411	*8*	1,371
No qualifications	*21*	131	*8*	380
Social class (NS-SeC)				
Professional	*11*	115	*7*	740
Intermediate/self-employed	*14*	141	*7*	734
Routine and semi-routine	*23*	187	*9*	561
Never worked/long term unemployed	*32*	43	*14*	45
Not classified	*26*	136	*8*	159

Mixed (Black and White)	*32*	11	*26*	14
Mixed (other)	*0*	3	*14*	16
White	*19*	548	*7*	2,004
Other ethnic group	*27*	10	*12*	23
Ethnicity (2 categories)				
White	*19*	548	*7*	2,004
Other	*32*	74	*14*	235
Country of birth				
UK	*21*	561	*8*	1,959
Other	*18*	61	*7*	276
Victim of crime				
Yes	*20*	265	*7*	799
No	*22*	366	*8*	1,440
Relationship status				
Single	*27*	342	*7*	1,788
Married/cohabiting	*12*	280	*9*	451
Health status				
Good/very good	*23*	486	*8*	1,819
Fair	*11*	102	*8*	326
Poor/very poor	*20*	33	*4*	90
Housing tenure				
Owner/occupier	*19*	274	*7*	1,416
Socially rented	*15*	158	*7*	342
Privately rented	*27*	190	*10*	481
All stopped	*21*	622	*8*	2,239

Source: CSEW 2008/09, 2009/10 and 2010/11.

Note
unweighted *n*'s.

Table 7.2 Dissatisfaction with police behaviour during stops is unevenly distributed

Percentage dissatisfied: by socio-demographic characteristics

	Foot stops		*Car stops*	
	%	n	%	n
Age				
16–18	*34*	167	*27*	129
19–21	*38*	71	*19*	138
22–24	*36*	51	*21*	154
25–34	*17*	113	*24*	456
35–44	*11*	67	*23*	478
45–54	*21*	59	*16*	389
55–64	*14*	61	*18*	268
65–74	*9*	23	*15*	151
75 plus	*0*	8	*16*	74
Gender				
Female	*15*	208	*17*	902
Male	*32*	412	*23*	1,325
Ethnicity (8 categories)				
Asian Muslim	*39*	18	*23*	57
Asian – other religion	*18*	7	*24*	51
Black African	*64*	9	*36*	33
Black Caribbean	*56*	15	*46*	36

	Foot stops		*Car stops*	
	%	n	%	n
Economic activity status				
Employed	*24*	325	*20*	1,614
Unemployed	*32*	92	*32*	109
Student	*34*	89	*29*	71
Looking after family	*25*	13	*11*	92
Long term sick	*26*	44	*24*	84
Retired	*6*	36	*16*	238
				24
Educational attainment				
First degree or higher	*16*	80	*22*	488
Below degree level	*29*	409	*21*	1,370
No qualifications	*27*	131	*19*	379
Social class (NS-SeC)				
Professional	*22*	114	*20*	738
Intermediate/self-employed	*14*	140	*20*	734
Routine and semi-routine	*28*	189	*20*	561
Never worked/long term unemployed	*38*	43	*33*	46
Not classified	*36*	134	*25*	158

Mixed (Black and White)	*37*	10	*49*	14	**Relationship status**				
Mixed (other)	*0*	3	*19*	16	Single	*34*	279	*22*	450
White	*25*	548	*19*	2,003	Married/cohabiting	*17*	341	*20*	1,787
Other ethnic group	*11*	10	*38*	23					
					Health status				
Ethnicity (2 categories)					Good/very good	*27*	484	*21*	1,819
White	*25*	548	*19*	2,003	Fair	*24*	102	*21*	325
Other	*38*	72	*31*	234	Poor/very poor	*47*	33	*27*	90
Country of birth					**Victim of crime**				
UK	*29*	559	*21*	1,957	Yes	*27*	253	*24*	800
Other	*16*	61	*18*	277	No	*27*	367	*19*	1,437
Housing tenure					**Searched?**				
Owner/occupier	*19*	273	*20*	1,416	Yes	*49*	124	43	157
Socially rented	*36*	157	*29*	340	No	*20*	495	19	2,079
Privately rented	*31*	190	*18*	481					
					All stopped	*27*	620	*21*	2,237

Source: CSEW 2008/09, 2009/10 and 2010/11.

Note
Unweighted *n*'s.

searched was associated with lower odds of satisfaction. Conditioning on these variables black Caribbeans were less likely to be satisfied with a foot stop than those from the white group. However levels of satisfaction did not significantly vary between the other visible minority groups and the white group (although this may just be a function of the small sample sizes involved). Intriguingly, being born in the UK was associated, on average, with lower levels of satisfaction: perhaps those born in the UK are more prepared to be critical of the police, or expect more of officers and are therefore more likely to be disappointed by what transpires during personal contact with them.

Turning to the more prevalent car stops, just over one-fifth (21 per cent) of those stopped were dissatisfied in some way – once more, the impression is that police handle car stops rather better than foot stops. Equally, it seems yet again that those from some of the groups most likely to be stopped are also the most likely to be dissatisfied with the ensuing encounters – for example those from many visible ethnic minority groups, younger people, men, the unemployed, those in ill health and those who live in socially rented accommodation. Regression modelling of satisfaction with car stops again found that, first, those who were given a reason for the stop where more likely to be satisfied than those not given a reason. Second, being searched was consistently associated with lower levels of satisfaction. Third, conditioning on the other variables in the model, people from the mixed, 'non-Muslim' Asian and black Caribbean groups were all less likely to be satisfied than their white counterparts. People living in socially rented accommodation were significantly less likely to be satisfied than others, as were people born in the UK.

Experience of unsatisfactory stops

It seems then that ethnicity is an important variable predicting differential subjective experiences of police stops, as were other key socio-demographic variables and, of course, as what actually transpired during the encounters (although it is important to bear in mind that we do not know from the CSEW data how police actually behaved, but rather how respondents *thought* they behaved). Another way to look at the distribution of police stops is to examine who has experience of *unsatisfactory* stops (see Jackson *et al.* 2013). As discussed below, unsatisfactory contact experiences are strongly linked to lower levels of trust, legitimacy and cooperation. If negative experiences of policing are clustered among certain social groups, types of individual, or areas, this would be concerning not only on the basis of equity but also in terms of the ability of the police to work with such individuals or communities to deal with issues of crime and disorder.

Bivariate statistics suggest there is indeed a significant social clustering of negative experiences. Overall, less than 3 per cent of people reported having an unsatisfactory stop (car or foot) experience in the past year. Notably this rose to 5 per cent of Asian Muslims and black Africans, 9 per cent of black Caribbeans and 12 per cent of those with mixed black and white ethnicities, suggesting much higher levels of unsatisfactory experiences within those groups. While this last figure should be treated with some caution, due to the small sample size (n= 133) it is also quite remarkable; more than *one in nine* of people with Mixed black and white ethnicities reported a negative police stop experience in the 12 months before interview. Similarly, 4 per cent of people living in social housing reported an unsatisfactory stop, as did 4 per cent of recent victims of crime and 8 per cent of the unemployed.

This issue is examined in more depth in analysis shown in Table 7.3, which returns to the multi-level modelling framework used in Chapter 5. The modelling approach replicates that taken there. Each of the three models shows the results of a multi-level binary logistic regression model predicting the probability of having experienced an unsatisfactory car *or* foot stop in the previous 12 months. Tested as predictors in Model 1 were all the explanatory variables covered in Chapter 5. To ensure the model was as parsimonious as possible a stepwise approach was again taken to model selection – given the final set of explanatory variables shown in Model 1 none of the other individual or area-level variables specified in Chapter 5 were significant when added to this model. As before, Model 1 was estimated using the full sample; Model 2 replicates this model, but includes only those who answered the self-report drug use module; while Model 3 adds the drug use variable.

As found previously there was significant clustering in experiences at the LSOA level, this time of course in experiences of *unsatisfactory* police stops (an empty variance components model suggested around 18 per cent of the variance in this variable was explained at the LSOA level). The experience of unsatisfactory police stops is not evenly spread across different areas but is rather concentrated more in some than in others. The key findings are however shown in Model 3 in Table 7.3, which includes on the drug use variable. Holding constant the other variables in the model, the probability of having experienced an unsatisfactory stop in the last year was higher among men compared with women, younger people, people from most ethnic minority groups, the UK-born, unemployed people, those living in socially rented accommodation, victims of crime, and those who had used drugs in the past 12 months. Notably, once individual-level variables were taken into account the only area-level variable to retain significance was the dummy variable representing whether the respondent lived in an 'inner city' area. None of the LSOA level measures proved significant, suggesting that once again it is types of people rather than types of places that predict differential experiences of policing, albeit that the ICC values for all three models suggest unexplained variance at the LSOA level.

As was the case in the overall distribution of police stops in Chapter 5 it seems that experiences of unsatisfactory police stops are clustered among certain types of people, often those who might be considered marginalized, excluded or 'police property'. There are some countervailing points, though, most notably in relation to car access (lack of access to a car can be marker of disadvantage). On the whole, it would seem that people with cars are more available to police and more likely to be stopped (most stops are car stops), and therefore more likely to experience an unsatisfactory stop.

Table 7.3 What are the correlates of experiences of unsatisfactory police stops?

Multi-level binary logistic regression models predicting probability of experiencing an unsatisfactory police stop

	Model 1		*Model 2*		*Model 2*	
	β	*se*(β)	β	*se*(β)	β	*se*(β)
Survey year (ref: 2008/2009)						
2009/2010	0.26**	0.10	0.23*	–0.11	0.26*	–0.11
2020/2011	0.23+	0.12	0.18	–0.13	0.19	–0.13
Individual level measures						
Gender (ref: male)						
Female	–0.98**	0.10	–0.99**	–0.10	–0.93**	–0.11
Age	–0.08**	0.01	–0.13**	–0.02	–0.11**	–0.02
Age squared	0.00**	0.00	0.00**	0.00	0.00**	0.00
Ethnicity (ref: White)						
Asian Muslim	0.77**	0.28	0.88**	–0.29	0.96**	–0.29
Asian other	0.56+	0.30	0.58+	–0.30	0.61*	–0.30
Black African	0.94**	0.35	0.78*	–0.37	0.85*	–0.37
Black Caribbean	1.59**	0.27	1.40**	–0.29	1.37**	–0.29
Mixed White and Black	1.18**	0.40	0.97*	–0.43	0.98*	–0.43
Mixed other	–0.14	0.63	–0.07	–0.62	–0.02	–0.62
Other ethnic group	0.41	0.40	0.35	–0.42	0.43	–0.42
Country of birth (ref: outside UK)						
United Kingdom	0.65**	0.19	0.54**	–0.20	0.52**	–0.20

Employment status (ref: all others)						
Unemployed	0.65**	0.16	0.56**	–0.17	0.49**	–0.17
Car access (ref: no)						
Yes	0.52**	0.14	0.33*	–0.14	0.38**	–0.14
Housing tenure (ref: owner occupier/private renter)						
Social renter	0.49**	–0.12	0.49**	–0.13	0.47**	–0.13
Health status (ref: good)						
Fair	0.08	–0.13	0.06	–0.15	0.01	–0.15
Poor	0.50*	–0.20	0.25	–0.26	0.21	–0.26
Evenings spent in pub	0.12**	–0.04	0.06	–0.05	0.02	–0.05
Victim of crime (ref: no)						
Yes	0.47**	–0.09	0.41**	–0.10	0.35**	–0.10
Area level measure						
Inner city area (ref: no)						
Yes	0.30*	–0.14	0.35*	–0.15	0.33*	–0.15
Any drug use in previous year (ref: no)						
Yes					0.81**	–0.12
Constant	–2.93**	–0.39	–1.68**	–0.46	–2.02**	–0.47
ICC	0.14		0.05		0.05	
n	28,616		18,004		18,004	

Source: CSEW 2008/09, 2009/10 and 2010/11.

Notes

+ $p<0.1$; * $p<0.05$; ** $p<0.01$; *** $p<0.001$.

This last point goes the heart of the matter. The correspondence between the findings shown in Table 7.3 and those discussed in Chapter 5 is of course not surprising, since the single biggest predictor of experiencing an *unsatisfactory* police stop is presumably experiencing a stop in the first place (as well, it seems, as being searched). What this correspondence suggests however is that the structural position of certain social groups or types of individual in relation to the police predisposes them toward having poor quality contacts with officers *if for no other reason than that they have higher rates of contact.* Even if police behave with entirely consistent levels of procedural fairness across the different groups and types of people they stop and perhaps search, some of those groups will still experience different levels of problematic or 'bad' police contact because they experience more stops and searches in the first place. This is not to discount the idea that police do behave differently in relation to different types of groups of people – far from it. As shown in Table 7.1, there was significant variation in the way people felt they were treated during 'their' stop. Nor can we exclude the possibility that even if police behaviour during stops was consistent across groups the decision on whom to stop in the first place is biased or problematic in some way (see, again, Chapter 5). The underlying point, though, is that the motivation to control and discipline particular population groups that is embodied in and enacted by police will likely generate differential experiences of policing that stem not only, or even primarily, from the vagaries of individual officer's behaviour but also from the distribution of activity this motivation produces.

All that being said the experience of people from most visible ethnic minority groups was once again markedly different to that of the white group. Controlling for a wide range of factors including unemployment, access to a car and drug use, people from Asian and black ethnic groups were significantly more likely to have experienced an unsatisfactory police stop in the 12 months before interview. Not only are people from many ethnic minority groups more likely to be stopped by police, they are more likely to be searched, more likely to be unhappy with such encounters and thus, overall, have significantly higher rates of unsatisfactory police contact. This may, as we will see below, have significant implications for the trust and legitimacy judgements of people from those groups.

Linking contact experiences to trust, legitimacy, cooperation and compliance

As described above, the procedural fairness of people's treatment by police officers can be thought of as carrying two interlinked and mutually reinforcing sets of meanings and messages. Fairness (or unfairness) has an evaluative component. When police treat someone *unfairly* this may communicate to them that officers are not wielding their power in an appropriate or justifiable way, that they are untrustworthy, and that they are not playing by the rules. Fairness also has an affective component, and based on social-psychological understandings of the role of group membership in people's lives, procedural justice theory stresses that treatment at the hands of important group representatives such as the police carries status-relevant messages concerning individuals' inclusion in and relationship with the groups the police represent: nation, community or 'society'. Police behaviour may therefore carry a double load, communicating to citizens both that the police are legitimate holders of the power vested in them (or not) and that the person involved is included and respected in the group the police represent (or not). Experiences related to both these 'pathways' may influence the extent to which people trust, and grant legitimacy to, the police.

Contact experiences and trust in the police

A number of questions in the CSEW address trust in the police. While they cover conceptually different issues (such as trust in police fairness and community engagement) answers tend to be very highly correlated with each other, all drawing on one underlying factor or latent construct that can be labelled simply as 'trust in the police'. This is likely to be partly an artefact of the survey design – the questions are asked immediately after one another it the questionnaire – and it is in general preferable to distinguish between, for example, trust in police fairness and effectiveness (Hough *et al.* 2013; Jackson and Bradford 2010 – the PAS allows this distinction to be drawn more clearly, and is considered below). A combined measure of trust was therefore created via factor analysis: question wordings and factor loadings are shown in Table 7.4.

Table 7.5 shows results from a series of linear regression models predicting the trust variable.[1] The four models are estimated as before: first using the full sample (Models 1 and 2), then using only the respondents who answered the self-report drug use survey (Model 3), then finally adding self-reported drug use (Model 4).

Table 7.4 Trust in the police: items and factor loadings

How much (do) you agree or disagree with each of the following statements about the police in your local area?	*Std Factor loading*	R^2
...can be relied upon to be there when you need them	0.74	0.54
...would treat you with respect if you had contact with them	0.67	0.45
...treat everyone fairly regardless of who they are	0.66	0.44
...can be relied on to deal with minor crimes	0.73	0.53
...understand the issues that affect this community	0.77	0.59
...are dealing with the things that matter to people in this community	0.84	0.70
Taking everything into account I have confidence in the police in this area	0.92	0.85
Chi^2	1249.3	
Degrees of freedom	9.00	
p-value	<0.00005	
RMSEA	0.06	
CFI	0.99	
TLI	0.99	

Source: CSEW 2008/2009, 2009/2010 and 2010/2011.

Table 7.5 What are the correlates of trust in the police?

Multi-level linear regression models predicting trust in the police

	Model 1		*Model 2*		*Model 3*		*Model 4*	
	β	*se*(β)	β	*se*(β)	β	*se*(β)	β	*se*(β)
Survey year (ref: 2008/2009)								
2009/2010	0.03*	0.01	0.02	0.01	0.01	0.02	0.01	0.02
2020/2011	0.10***	0.02	0.09***	0.02	0.08***	0.02	0.07***	0.02
Individual level measures								
Gender (ref: male)								
Female	0.15***	0.01	0.13***	0.01	0.09***	0.02	0.08***	0.02
Age	–0.01***	0	–0.02***	0	0	0	0	0
Age squared	0.00***	0	0.00***	0	0	0	0	0
Ethnicity (ref: White)								
Asian Muslim	0.1	0.06	0.12*	0.05	0.12	0.07	0.11	0.07
Asian other	0.07	0.05	0.09	0.04	0.05	0.05	0.04	0.05
Black African	0.05	0.06	0.08	0.06	0.1	0.07	0.09	0.07
Black Caribbean	–0.24***	0.06	–0.20***	0.06	–0.18*	0.07	–0.18**	0.07
Mixed White and Black	–0.36***	0.1	–0.33***	0.09	–0.31**	0.11	–0.31**	0.11
Mixed other	0.1	0.09	0.12	0.09	0.07	0.1	0.06	0.1
Other ethnic group	0.05	0.06	0.06	0.06	0.01	0.07	0	0.07
Country of birth (outside UK)								
United Kingdom	–0.24***	0.02	–0.23***	0.02	–0.26***	0.03	–0.26***	0.03
Employment status (ref: employed)								
Part-time	–0.01	0.02	–0.02	0.02	0.01	0.02	0.01	0.02
Unemployed	–0.13***	0.04	–0.11**	0.04	–0.07	0.04	–0.06	0.04
Economically inactive	–0.03	0.02	–0.03	0.02	0.02	0.03	0.02	0.03

Health status (ref: good)								
Fair	–0.12***	0.02	–0.11***	0.02	–0.13***	0.02	–0.13***	0.02
Poor	–0.20***	0.03	–0.19***	0.03	–0.28***	0.04	–0.28***	0.04
Housing tenure (ref: owner occupier)								
Social renter	0.01	0.02	0.02	0.02	0.01	0.02	0.01	0.02
Private renter	0.04*	0.02	0.03	0.02	0.03	0.02	0.03	0.02
Victim of crime (ref: no)								
Yes	–0.21***	0.02	–0.20***	0.02	–0.23***	0.02	–0.22***	0.02
Area level measures								
Percentage of population aged 15–29 (LSOA)	0	0	0.00*	0	0.00*	0	0.00*	0
Percentage Black (logged) (LSOA)	0	0.01	0	0.01	–0.01	0.02	–0.01	0.02
Percentage born in UK (logged) (LSOA)	–0.15*	0.07	–0.14*	0.07	–0.12	0.09	–0.12	0.09
Deprivation (LSOA)	–0.02*	0.01	–0.02*	0.01	–0.03*	0.01	–0.03*	0.01
Victimization rate (LSOA)	0.09**	0.04	0.09**	0.04	0.11*	0.04	0.11*	0.04
Disorder (LSOA)	–0.18***	0.01	–0.17***	0.01	–0.17***	0.02	–0.17***	0.02
Contact with police (ref: none)								
Stopped and satisfied			0.04	0.02	0.05	0.02	0.05*	0.02
Stopped and dissatisfied			–0.70***	0.04	–0.71***	0.05	–0.69***	0.05
Self-initiated and satisfied			0.25***	0.02	0.24***	0.02	0.24***	0.02
Self-initiated and dissatisfied			–0.63***	0.03	–0.63***	0.03	–0.63***	0.03
Any drug use in previous year (ref: no)								
Yes							–0.17***	0.03
Constant	1.14***	0.33	1.13***	0.32	0.78	0.41	0.82*	0.41
ICC	0.03		0.03		0.02		0.02	
n	25,600		25,600		16,302		16,302	

Source: CSEW 2008/2009, 2009/2010 and 2010/2011.

Notes
+ $p<0.1$; * $p<0.05$; ** $p<0.01$; *** $p<0.001$
Models also control for: educational attainment, NS-SeC, marital status, car access, time spent out of home, attending pubs/clubs, and whether respondent lived in London or an ‘inner city’ area. Coefficients are omitted for visual ease.

Findings across all four models are quite consistent, although there was some variation across the different specifications. There was, first, surprisingly little variation in trust by ethnicity – but, consistently, those from black Caribbean and mixed black and white groups expressed lower levels of trust than their white counterparts. Another perhaps surprising finding was that, all else equal, people born in the UK evinced less trust in the police than those born elsewhere (see Bradford *et al.* 2016). Elsewhere, the models suggest that the unemployed were less trusting in the police than others; being in poor health was associated with lower levels of trust; recent victims of crime tended to trust less than non-victims, and drug users also trusted less than those who did not use drugs. Unlike in previous models area-level predictors retained significance once individual-level correlates were taken into account. All else equal trust tended to be lower in more disadvantaged and disorderly areas, but higher in areas with a greater non-UK-born population (see, again, Bradford *et al.* 2016) and in areas with more victimization.

Most importantly for current purposes, though, was that unsatisfactory stop experiences had what was the largest negative statistical effect on trust in the police of any variable included in the models ($\beta \approx 0.7$). For comparison, this is a statistical effect roughly three times the size of that associated with being a victim of crime. 'Self-initiated' contacts with police were broadly symmetrical (Bradford *et al.* 2009; Myhill and Bradford 2012; Skogan 2006; Van Damme 2015) in their association with trust – satisfactory contacts seemed to enhance trust, while unsatisfactory contacts damaged trust. Yet the statistical effect of police stops appears to be almost entirely *asymmetrical*. The statistical effect of satisfactory stops on trust was negligible, while the statistical effect of unsatisfactory stops was large and strongly significant, suggesting that the net effect of this type of police activity is to undermine trust among those who experience it.

It is notable also that adding the contact variables in Model 2 did not change to any great degree the coefficients of the other variables in the model (compare Model 1 with Model 2 in Table 7.5). This is interesting in terms of the argument that some social groups or types of people have lower trust because they have problematic contact with police. If this was the case, adding the contact variables should have at least attenuated the associations elsewhere in the models – for example between ethnicity or unemployment and trust. This did not, in general, occur. One possible explanation is that there are two different and somewhat independent processes shaping people's trust in the police. On the one hand, people experience policing as individuals, and draw lessons from their contact with officers concerning, for example, the trustworthiness of police. Yet they also experience policing as members of social groups or categories, and 'membership' of these groups or categories may predict trust independent of personal experience. The two most obvious examples of this latter process might be the lower levels of trust among black Caribbeans and victims of crime. The former is an ethnic group with a long history of problematic relationships with police and experiences of police racism – indeed, black Caribbean ethnicities in Great Britain can be argued to have formed partly in response to police prejudice and discrimination (Gilroy 1987) – while the latter is of course a categorical distinction relating to people's experiences of crime. In both cases is might make sense to claim that membership of these groups will predict trust independent of actual experiences of police contact (because there is a particular cultural orientation toward police, or because there are concerns about crime and victimization). Interactions with police officers contain a potential for altering levels of trust that is in large part distinct from these background factors.

Do people from different social categories react to police stops in the same way?

Personal contact with police officers, particularly during stop encounters, has a significant and, in the case of stop encounters, almost entirely negative statistical effect on trust in the police. Do people from different social groups or categories react to contact with the police in different ways, though? This question is particularly pertinent in the current context, given the concentration of stop experiences among certain groups and individuals who might be considered socially marginal and/or alienated from the police and wider identities associated with police. As discussed above, perhaps being stopped has less effect on trust than might imagined because of the types of people who tend to be stopped and the different ways they read police activity?

Figure 7.1 summarizes the results from a series of linear regression models predicting trust in the fairness of the police, specifically. The response variable was created by taking the mean of two survey items (Cronbach's $\alpha=0.72$), 'The police would treat you with respect if you had contact with them for any reason' and 'The police treat everyone fairly regardless of who they are' (see Hough *et al.* 2013). These are the two CSEW questions that relate most clearly to procedural justice, and, if people are differentially sensitive to the messages in officer behaviour we might expect stop experiences to have a different statistical association with this aspect of trust across different social categories. In essence, this is a hypothesis that suggests personal experience counts less towards general trust judgements for some people compared with others. Included as predictors in each model were survey year, age, gender, the key explanatory variable (ethnicity, age, employment status etc. – the model for age therefore only contained year, gender and age), and finally two dummy variables representing experience of positive, and negative, stop encounters. The models also allowed interactions between contact experience and the key explanatory variable. Predicted scores on the trust measure where then calculated for those who have had no stop contact and those who have had unsatisfactory stop contact, which allows the statistical effect of negative stop encounters on this aspect of trust to be charted.

Strikingly, the statistical effect of unsatisfactory stop experiences on trust in police fairness was similar across all the social categories shown. Regardless of categorization, people who had recent experience of an unsatisfactory police reported lower levels of trust police fairness. Even more strikingly, while there was no significant interaction at all between ethnicity and stop experience, across

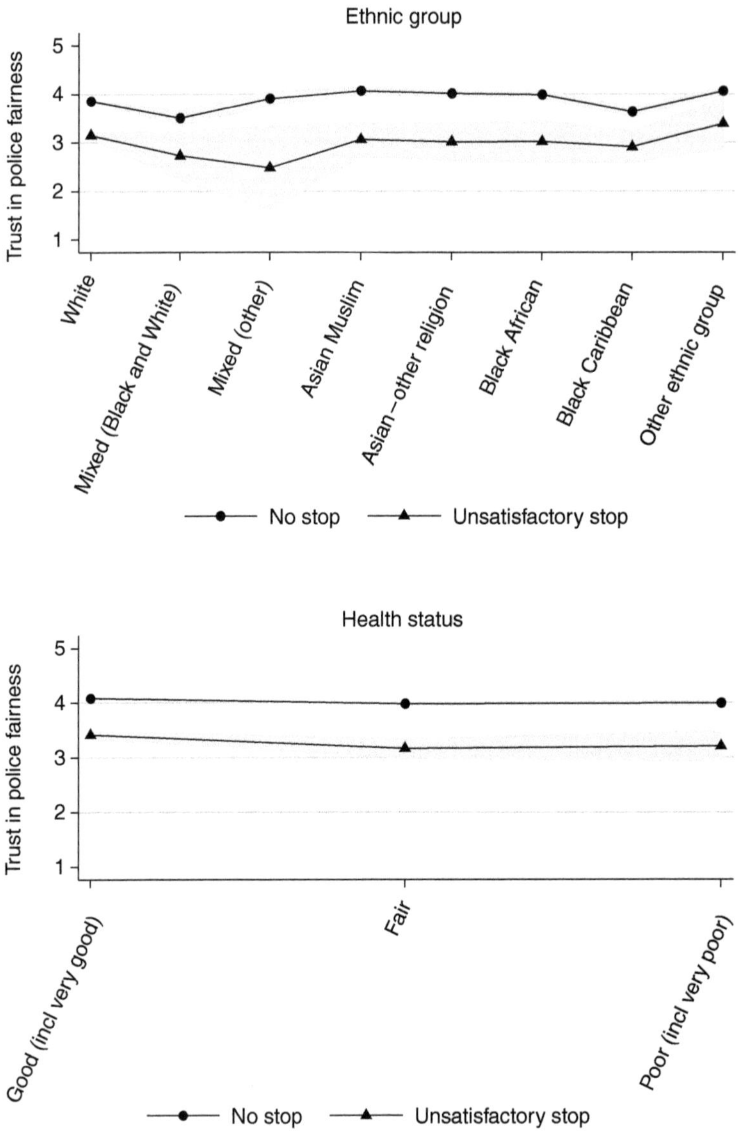

Figure 7.1 Different people tend to react to police stops in similar ways.

Source: CSEW 2008/2009, 2009/2010 and 2010/2011.

Note

Trust in police fairness: Mean=3.85; Std. Dev.=0.77; Min=1; Max=5.

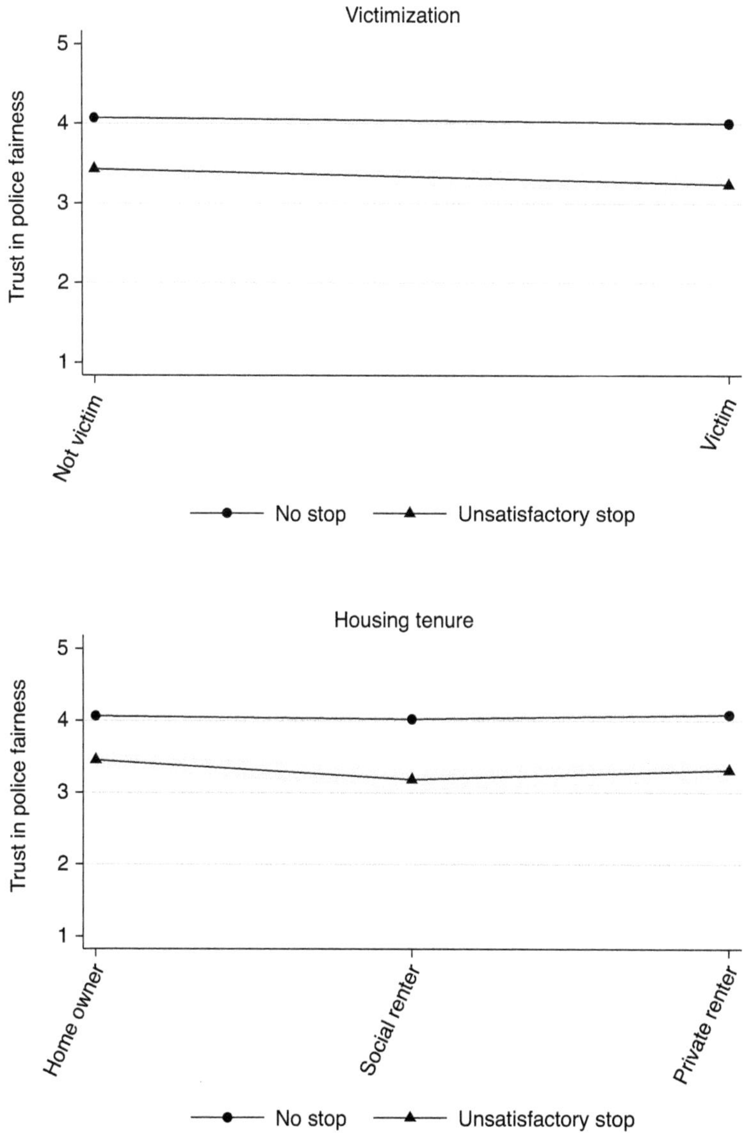

Figure 7.1 Continued

continued

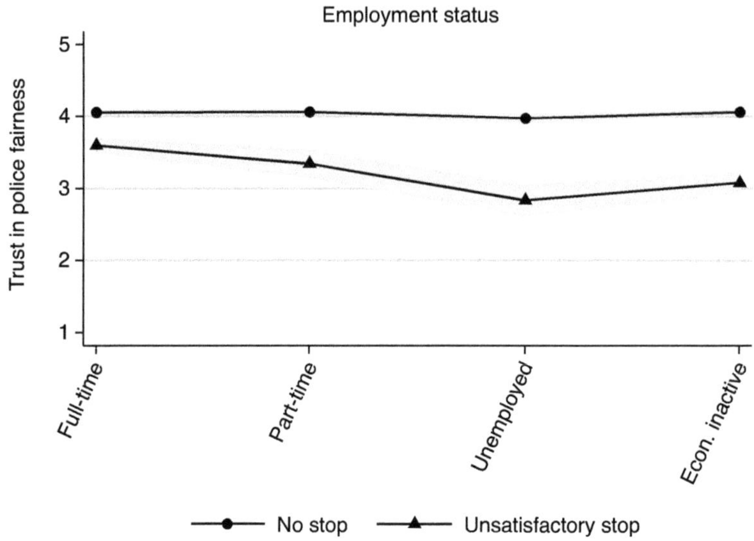

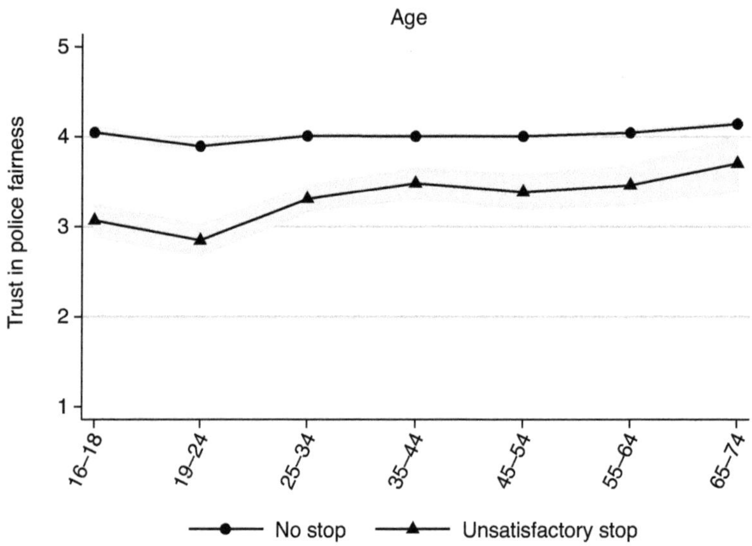

Figure 7.1 Continued

all the other variables shown people from more marginal social groups appeared to react somewhat *more* strongly to negative stop experiences. The association between unsatisfactory stops and (lower) trust in police fairness was stronger among recent victims of crime, those not in good health, people living in socially rented accommodation, the unemployed and economically inactive, and younger people. Not only are people from these groups more likely to experience negative police stops, they appear to be more likely to come away from them with lower trust in the fairness of the police.

Moreover, for all groups, and compared with not having experienced a stop, positive contacts were *not* associated with significantly higher levels of trust in police fairness (results not shown here for reasons of space). As noted above and described in many other studies, the statistical effect of police-initiated contact on trust in the police is largely or entirely asymmetrical, although there is some experimental evidence that under certain conditions, the use of procedural justice during police stops can enhance public trust (Mazerolle *et al.* 2011, 2012).

Contact, public trust and police legitimacy

Thus far the discussion has focused solely on the associations between police stops and public trust. Yet procedural justice theory draws on a much wider range of concepts – legitimacy, cooperation and compliance, as well as ideas such as group value and group engagement. To fully understand the potential effect being stopped and/or searched might have not only on people's relationship with the police but on their law-related behaviour, sense of self, and relationships with wider social formations, we need to move beyond the limited set of variables available in the CSEW. In the remainder of this chapter I draw upon the London Metropolitan Police's Public Attitude Survey (PAS), a population representative sample survey of Londoners that has been conducted in the capital for a number of years (Jackson *et al.* 2012; Stanko and Bradford 2009; Stanko *et al.* 2012). Several iterations of the PAS have fielded a range of questions concerning, for example, police legitimacy.

Within the PAS series Q1 of the 2009/2010 survey is of particular interest. This quarter contained a range of questions that measured trust in the fairness of the police, trust in effectiveness, legitimacy, and propensities to cooperate with the police. Research has consistently demonstrated strong links between trust (particularly trust in fairness), legitimacy and propensity to cooperate. Using the available items, factor analysis was used to derive composite measures of each concept (in a manner similar to that described above for the measure of trust) that allow consideration of the role procedural fairness plays in shaping legitimacy and cooperation among groups with differential exposure to police stop activity. The measures of fairness, effectiveness and cooperation are all fairly straightforward (although note that the 'fairness' scales also contains measures of community engagement, making it very similar in content to the BCS scale used above). However, the measurement of legitimacy requires a little further explanation.

Two measures of police legitimacy were derived from the PAS data. In line with the discussion in Chapter 3, the measures used draw on recent developments in the conceptualization of legitimacy in the literature (Jackson and Gau 2015). Accordingly, the first measure of legitimacy – *normative alignment* – is a measure of the extent to which people believe the police share and operate according to a shared, general, normative framework. One question used in this scale, for example, asked respondents to assess the extent to which 'the police usually act in ways that are consistent with my own sense of what is right and wrong'. The second measure – *duty to obey* – was a measure of respondent's sense that they had a duty to obey the directives of police officers and, in doing so, express their consent to the authority of the police. Observed indicators for this scale included 'You should do what the police tell you, even if you disagree'.

Tracing the paths from contact, through trust, to legitimacy and cooperation

Procedural justice theory proposes that the empirical legitimacy of the police will be based most importantly on individuals' fairness judgements. Trust and legitimacy will in turn be associated with propensities to cooperate with the police and other similar behaviours: people are more likely to aid and assist authorities or organizations they trust and perceive to be legitimate (Murphy *et al.* 2008; Sunshine and Tyler 2003; Tyler and Fagan 2008; Van Damme *et al.* 2013). A crucial factor influencing the extent to which people trust and legitimize the police will therefore be their assessment of manner in which it (or more correctly its representatives, i.e. officers) treats them and/or the manner in which they imagine they would be treated should they have such contact. Contact experiences should therefore be associated with trust in the police; trust in the police should be associated with legitimacy judgements; and most of the effect of contact on legitimacy should be mediated by trust judgments.

A conceptual model of the processes envisioned by the procedural justice is displayed in Figure 7.2. Naturally in reality all these processes are likely to be circular and reciprocal with, for example, the extent to which people trust the police influencing how they experience encounters with officers. There is however significant evidence from panel and experimental studies that trust – and indeed police legitimacy – is affected by personal contact with officers (Bradford *et al.* 2014; Mazerolle *et al.* 2011, 2012; Myhill and Bradford 2012; Slocum *et al.* 2016; Tyler and Fagan 2008); people do change their opinions of the police as a result of personal contact with police officers.

The PAS data are in full accord with the CSEW, and indeed many other studies, in that here, too, 'police-initiated' contacts, of which police stops are the most important and numerous example in the PAS sample,[2] have a net negative statistical effect on trust in both the fairness and the effectiveness of the police. Figure 7.3 plots the simple bivariate association between police initiated contact and the measures of trust, legitimacy and cooperation. Contacts judged

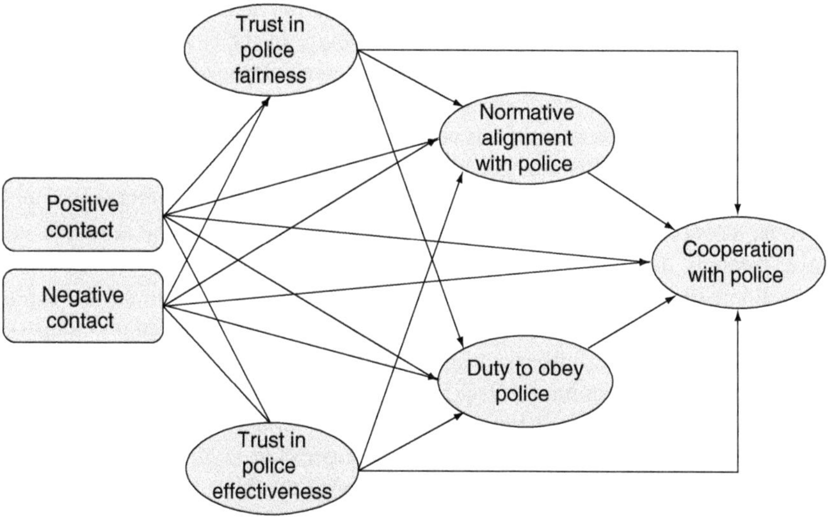

Figure 7.2 Police contact, trust, legitimacy and cooperation: a conceptual map.

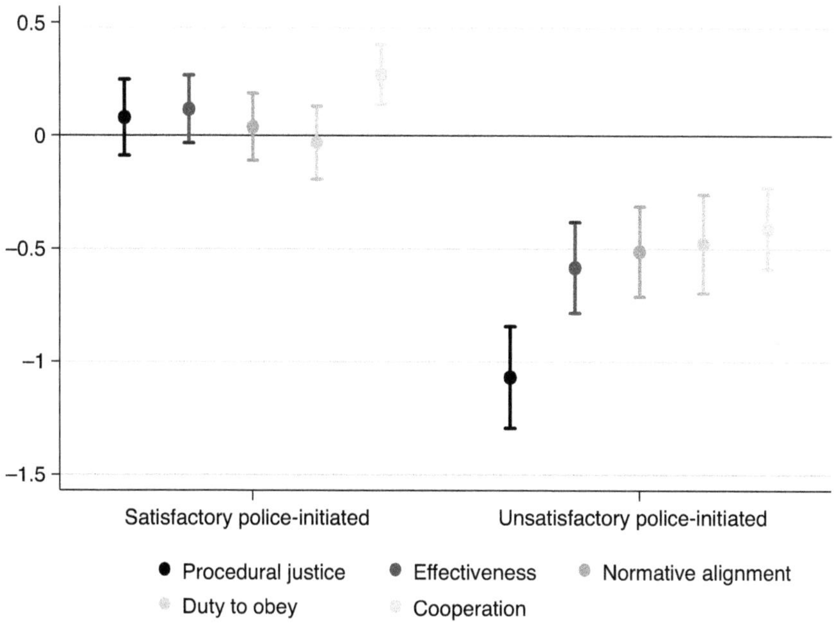

Figure 7.3 Police-initiated contact tends to undermine trust and legitimacy.

unsatisfactory had a negative association with trust, while those judged satisfactory had a negligible positive association; similar associations play out in terms of both components of legitimacy. However, in the case of self-assessed propensity to cooperate with the police the association with police-initiated contact was rather more symmetrical, resulting in a net zero overall association between police-initiated contact and cooperation.

Rather than repeat this analysis in more depth – the links between personal contact, trust and legitimacy being well-covered in the existing literature – I will move on to examine the possible downstream implications stop and search as we move through the procedural justice 'process' shown in Figure 7.2. Prior research has shown that, in the British context at least, the most important pathways through the model summarized in the figure moves from contact experience, via trust in police fairness, to normative alignment with the police and on to cooperation and compliance (Jackson *et al.* 2012, 2013). That is, procedural justice is the most important predictor of normative alignment, and normative alignment is the most important predictor of cooperation. A key question is thus, again, whether this pathway is of equal importance for those who are both more likely to experience stop and search activity and more likely, for a variety of interrelated reasons, to be socially marginal or excluded.

It might be suggested once more that procedural justice could be a less important predictor of legitimacy among people from marginal or excluded groups because the behaviour of the police, as a representative of dominant social categories, is less 'identity-relevant' to them. Under such conditions the affective path linking procedural justice to legitimacy might be weaker. Yet, conversely, it may be that procedural justice is *more* important when an individual is marginalized or excluded because they are more attuned to those social processes – for example the way they are treated by police officers – that can serve to either reproduce and instantiate that exclusion, or ameliorate it by fostering a firmer sense of value and belonging. A similar argument might be made in relation to the normative alignment component of legitimacy and, for example, cooperation with police. A sense of normative alignment with police might lack salience, or be simply irrelevant, to those pressured or stigmatized by their position toward the bottom of various social hierarchies, weakening the association between legitimacy and cooperation among such groups and individuals.

To test whether, first, trust in police procedural justice was differentially associated with normative alignment with police across different social groups and categories, a series of linear regression models predicting this measure of legitimacy. Each contained gender, trust in police procedural fairness and trust in police effectiveness. Key explanatory variables were added to different models: age (which was retained as a covariate in the subsequent models), ethnicity, employment status, housing tenure, victimization, and disability status;[3] each model also tested an interaction between the explanatory variable concerned and the procedural justice measure. Results from the six resulting models are summarized in Figure 7.4.

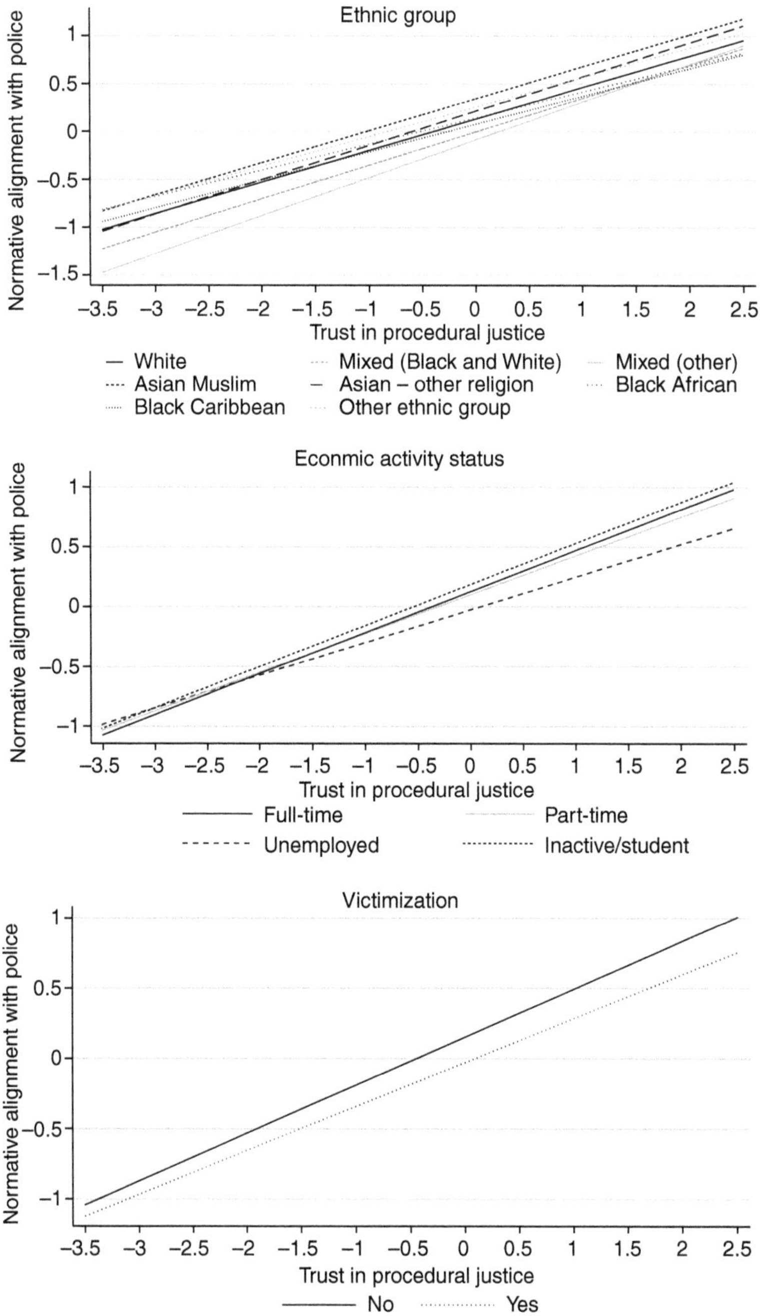

Figure 7.4 The association between procedural justice and legitimacy is relatively constant across social categories. *continued*

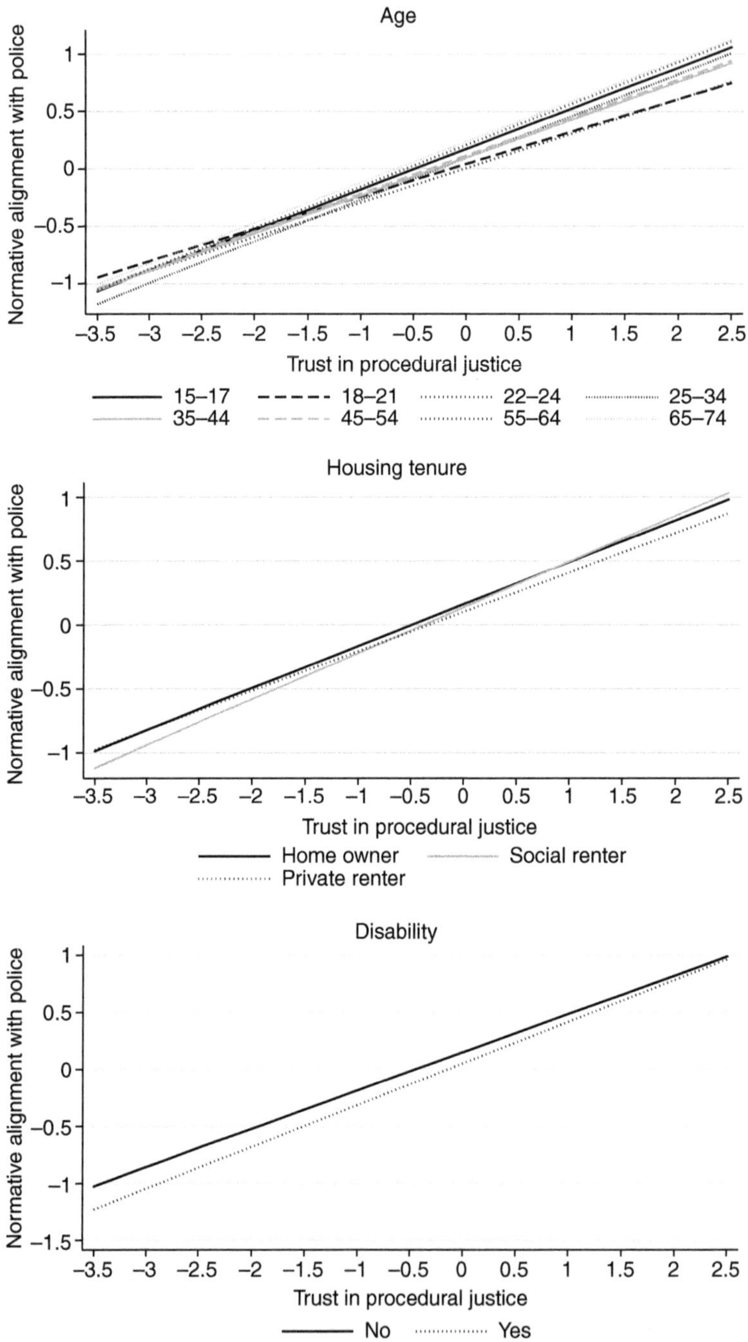

Figure 7.4 Continued

The results appear conclusive. There was essentially no variation in the strength of the association between people's trust in the procedural fairness of the police and their sense of normative alignment with officers and institution across any of the categories tested. The nature of the statistical association between procedural justice and this component of legitimacy did not vary by ethnicity, age, employment status, housing tenure, disability status or victimization. Results (not shown) from a series of models predicting duty to obey, the other component of legitimacy assessed here, produced almost identical results. People who come from social groups more likely than others to experience police-initiated contacts such as stop and search seem, in London at least, to place no more or no less emphasis on procedural justice than others less likely to experience such contact

Turning to the association between normative alignment and propensity to cooperate with the police, the above process was repeated, this time with legitimacy (normative alignment and duty to obey) as explanatory variables and cooperation as the response variable. Interactions between the same six variables and normative alignment, as predictors of cooperation, were tested, and results are shown in Figure 7.5. The picture is, again, one of overwhelming similarity in the strength of the association between normative alignment and cooperation. The only significant interactions were in the employment status model (the legitimacy/cooperation link was very slightly weaker among the economically inactive) and the housing tenure model (people living in privately rented accommodation tended to place slightly more emphasis on this component of legitimacy than others) – these interaction effects were not large, however, as the charts show. This process was again repeated, testing for interactions with duty to obey; here, it seemed duty to obey may be a less important predictor of cooperation for the unemployed, and more important for home owners. Again, however, the picture was one of a general homogeneity in the association between this aspect of legitimacy and cooperation.

Viewed from one perspective the implications of these findings are clear. The key relationships proposed by the general procedural justice model shown in Figure 7.1 seem to be largely invariant across the social categories investigated; one key implication may be that, while people in socially marginal categories may be more likely to experience police stops than others, they generally draw similar lessons in terms of trust, legitimacy and the possibility for cooperation with the police than those with arguably easier relationships with the police. Those socially marginal or excluded across a variety of categories (age, ethnicity, employment, housing, victimization, disability) do not appear by dint of their background or experience to place any less or indeed any more emphasis on the fairness and legitimacy of the police than others.

Viewed from another perspective, however, this is something of a puzzle. Under various iterations of the procedural justice model, procedural fairness should be less important to those who feel they do not share group membership with the police, or more important to those who feel they do share a group with police, but feel marginal within it. Yet there is no consistent evidence for link

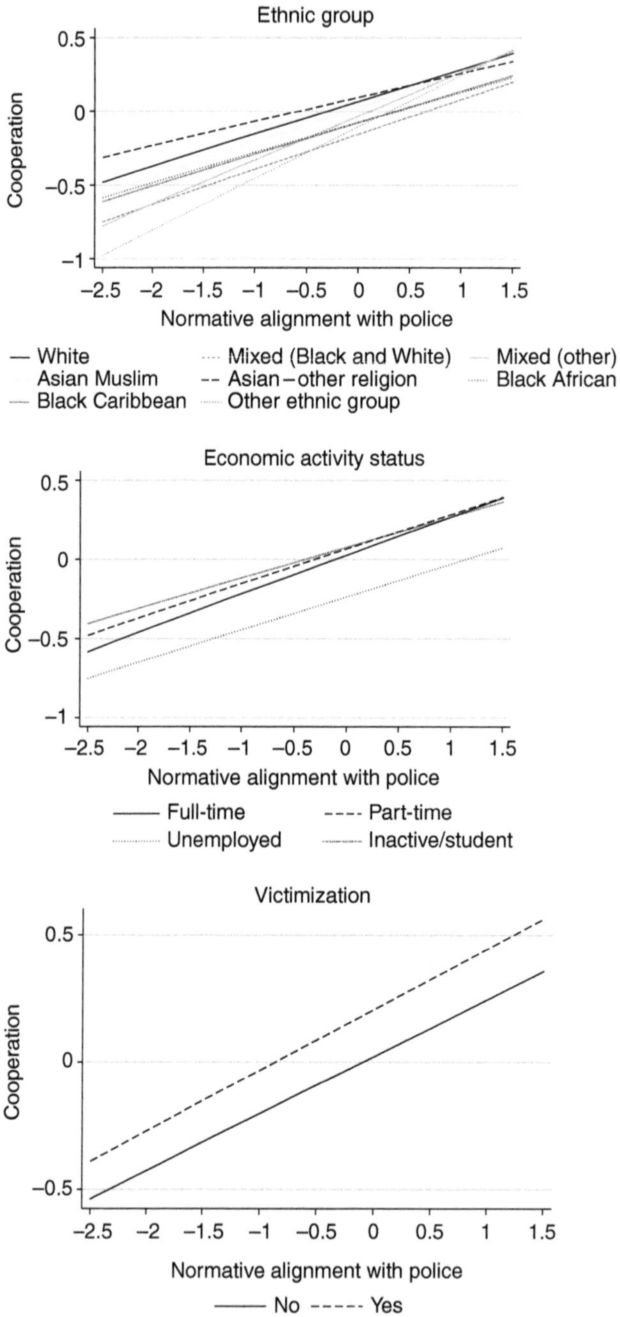

Figure 7.5 The association between legitimacy and cooperation is relatively constant across social categories.

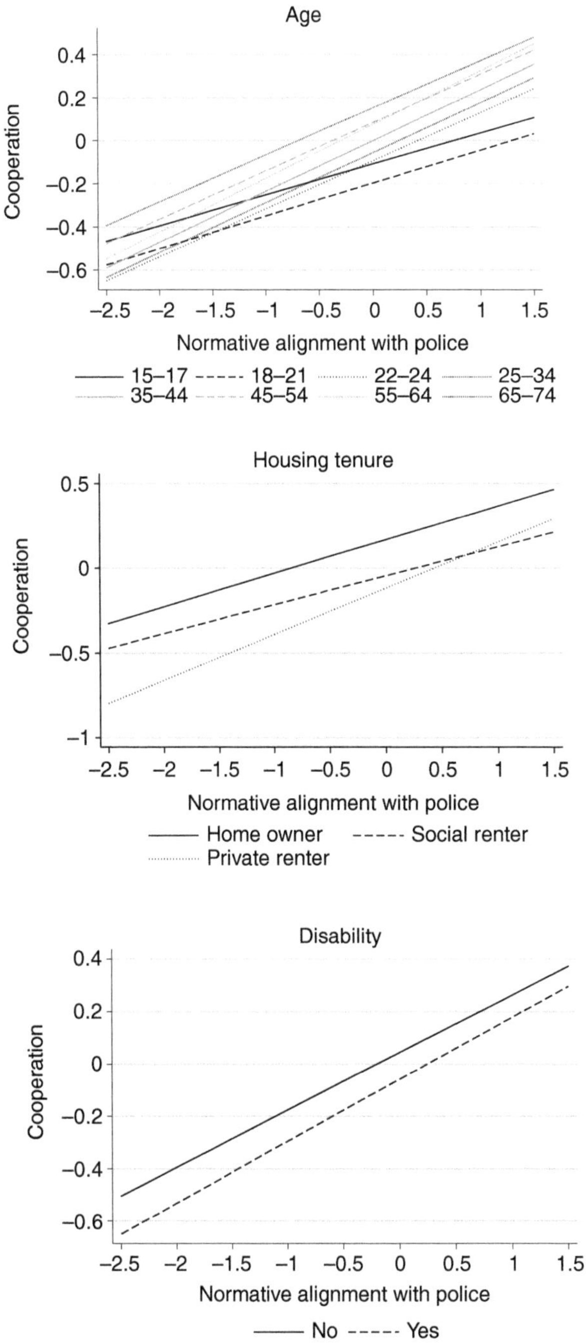

Figure 7.5 Continued

between social exclusion and a weaker procedural justice effect. The most likely reason is that a basic sense of affiliation with social groups the police represent does not vary systematically across the social categories tested. People may be objectively disadvantaged within the group the police represent, but they still feel themselves members of it (and, recall, they appeared more attuned to police behaviour when forming judgements about the procedural fairness of the police).

It is also likely that reasons for the close correlations between procedural justice, legitimacy and cooperation are not exhausted by factors relating to group dynamics and processes. There are reasons why procedural justice, for example, enhances legitimacy other than that it promotes a sense of shared group belonging that turn motivates the legitimation of group authorities. Most obvious here is the idea that by acting in procedurally fair manner the police demonstrate they are behaving in an appropriate, legal manner – that they are doing the right thing – and that this motivates people to behave in an appropriate, reciprocal manner (Jackson *et al.* 2012). There may even be an element of an evaluative social contract here. Police garner legitimacy – public compliance, deference and support – when they demonstrate that they have *earned* these things.

Compliance with the law

Described above are consistent links between negative contact experiences, lower trust and lower legitimacy, and that people's propensities to cooperate with officers are undermined when they do not trust or hold the police to be legitimate. Yet this does not exhaust the potential negative effects of stop and search and other police–public interactions judged negatively by the citizens involved. I will consider here just one of these – the links between procedural justice and compliance, while the next chapter moves on to some further implications of police behaviour judged to be unfair.

It is a central claim of procedural justice theory that fairness is linked, via legitimacy, to compliance with the law. Legitimate legal authorities influence the behaviour of those they govern (Kelman and Hamilton 1989), for example by activating personal commitment toward the law as a guide for behaviour, or by promoting a sense of duty toward the authority and the group it represents (Tyler 2006). People feel it is right to obey the rules of groups to which they feel they belong and to which they feel normatively and socially aligned. There is by now a considerable volume of empirical evidence for such a 'procedural justice effect', although it is not yet fully conclusive, and there are significant methodological doubts remain around this aspect of procedural justice theory. Most notably, most research examining the procedural justice/offending pathway has relied on self-reported offending, and few studies have used longitudinal or experimental designs to look at 'real-world', externally verified, offending (for an exception see Paternoster *et al.* 1997). The causal effect of procedural fairness on compliance behaviour has yet to be proven.

Notwithstanding continued scepticism about the extent to which police procedural justice and legitimacy really are causally linked to offending, and while much of Tyler's own research has concentrated on the United States, recent studies in the UK (Jackson *et al.* 2012; Bradford *et al.* 2015) and Australia (Murphy *et al.* 2016) have echoed US research in finding strong associative links between procedural justice, legitimacy and compliance. Jackson *et al.* (2012), for example, report on findings from a nationally representative sample survey of England and Wales. They found strong statistical associations between perceptions of police procedural fairness, the perceived legitimacy of the police, and levels of self-reported offending in relation to minor, 'everyday' crimes. As predicted, individuals who granted the police more legitimacy were less likely to report breaking the law. Also as predicted, the links between perceptions of police effectiveness and legitimacy were much weaker and, crucially, there was no association between perceived risk of sanction and compliance. Contra deterrence theory, people who believed that the risk of sanction was high were not more likely to comply with the law – but people who perceive the police to be fair *were* more likely to do so.

The PAS allows consideration of the possible implications of personal contact with police officers for compliance (or offending). Figure 7.6 shows the results of a structural equation model predicting self-reported offending in relation to two 'everyday' crimes (buying stolen goods and fly-tipping). The explanatory variables duplicate those used above; the ultimate response variable is a binary

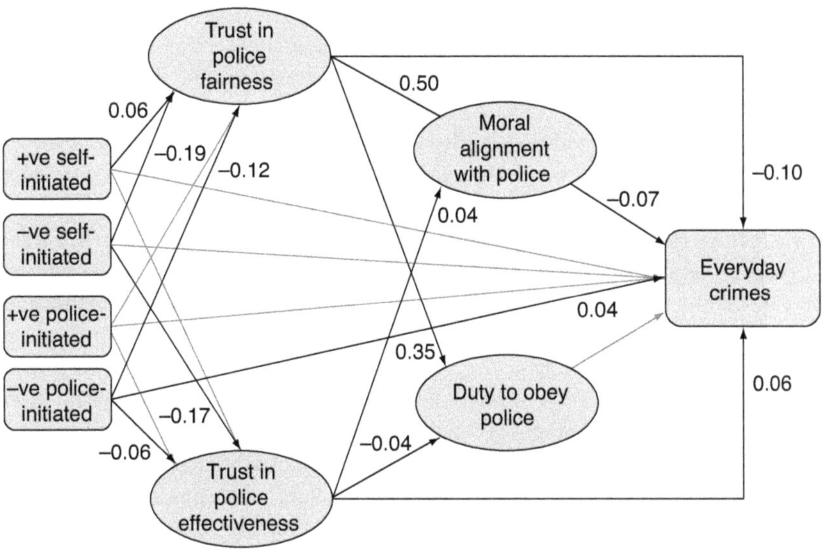

Figure 7.6 Greater trust in police fairness, and higher legitimacy, predict lower probability of self-reported offending.

Notes
Trust variables allowed to covary; legitimacy variables allowed to covary; all regression coefficients significant at 5 per cent level; non-significant paths shown as faded.
Chi-Square=3823.1; d.f.=229; $p<0.00005$.
RMSEA=0.06; CFI=0.98; TLI=0.97.

indicator coded 1 if a respondent admitted to 'ever' committing one of the two offences in the past year and 0 if they did not. One feature of the model requires additional explanation. Direct paths were allowed from the contact variables to the compliance variable. In theory, the model therefore controls for the fact that people who commit crimes may be more likely, for any number of reasons, to both have contact with the police and to judge that contact poorly. In other words, any direct statistical effect of (positive or negative) contact on compliance behaviour may have nothing to do with a 'procedural justice effect' but rather be explicable in terms of some other set of factors. Once this possibility is taken into account in the model, however, any indirect effect of contact on compliance, via procedural justice and legitimacy, may be more firmly attributed to the influence of procedural fairness, via legitimacy, on compliance. Of course, since the model reports statistical correlations only it cannot prove causal effects but only imply them, and the results in Figure 7.6 should be interpreted very much in this light.

The model appears to confirm the findings of Jackson *et al.* (2012). Procedural justice predicts both components of legitimacy, and legitimacy (as 'normative alignment') predicts compliance. People who think the police are fair, and who grant them legitimacy, are less likely to say they break the law, at least in relation to the two crimes covered. However, the real interest here is the indirect statistical effect of police-initiated contact experiences on compliance (via trust and legitimacy judgements). Effects decomposition suggests that unsatisfactory police-initiated contact had a significant indirect statistical effect on compliance ($\beta=0.02$; $p<0.05$) (added to the direct effect shown in the figure ($\beta=0.04$; $p<0.05$) this gives a total effect of $\beta=0.05$, with rounding error). Satisfactory police-initiated contact had no significant effect on compliance, direct, indirect or total. Since the model conditions on the direct links between police contact and offending, this finding opens up the possibility that people who experienced unsatisfactory police-initiated contact were, because such contact damaged trust and reduced legitimacy, more likely to have committed one of the two offences. The regression weights are of course small, although this is to be expected. Single instances of contact with the police are unlikely to have large effects on people's offending behaviour.

While these findings have to be treated with some caution they at least hint at the possibility that police stop and search activity, in as much as it is experienced as unfair, can damage trust and legitimacy and potentially encourage people to break the law. They thus correspond with research that has suggested that contact with criminal justice agents – often but not always the police – can be actively criminogenic (McAra and McVie 2007, 2012). That is, there is something about such contact, and entry into the criminal justice system, which promotes a level of offending among individuals who experience it above and beyond what they would have engaged in without such contact. Labelling theory is frequently drawn upon to explain this: people labelled as offenders are more likely to take on such identities and act on them, while at the same time being so labelled closes down non-criminal avenues of behaviour by, for example, making it more difficult to find a job. I will pick up this point and expand on it in the chapter that follows.

Summary

This chapter has described the likely effects of the experience of police stops and searches on public trust and the legitimacy of the police, at least among those subject to this forms of police activity. Consistent with other studies, the primary conclusion is that the net effect of stop activity on trust and legitimacy is negative. On average, those who have recently experienced this form of police contact evince lower trust in the police and grant less legitimacy. This effect seems to arise not because police consistently mishandle such encounters, because they do not (see Table 7.2 above). Rather, it is because the association between police stops, trust and legitimacy is asymmetrical. The more numerous 'satisfactory' stops have little or no positive statistical effect on opinions, but the less numerous 'unsatisfactory' stops have a large negative effect. The latter outweighs the former, resulting in the overall negative association. This means that police stops likely damage not only trust and legitimacy but also have knock on effects on cooperation and offending. People who have been stopped by police are less likely to say they would cooperate with the police in the future – and they may even be more likely to offend.

The analysis presented above also demonstrated that poor quality, unsatisfactory experiences of police stops are not evenly spread across the population, but are instead concentrated within particular social categories, most but not all of which can be described as marginal in some way (recall that the most important exception was car owners, who are considerably more likely than others to have experienced an unsatisfactory police stop). There appear to be three interrelated reasons for this. First, people from such groups are more likely to be stopped in the first place. Even if officers behaved in an entirely even-handed manner across the range of police–public encounter, since a proportion of such contacts will always 'go wrong', those individuals would therefore be likely to experience more unsatisfactory contacts purely as function of the more frequent encounters they have with police. Second, though, there is evidence that people from these same groups are treated in a less procedurally fair manner by police. Younger people, those from ethnic minority groups, the unemployed and those not in good health were less likely to have been given a reason for the stop, for example. Third, people from these groups were also more likely to be searched once stopped (see Chapter 5), and being searched was a very strong predictor of dissatisfaction. It seems that people from marginal social groups therefore suffer a double penalty – they are more likely to be stopped, and they are treated differently by police when they are.

Yet, people from these categories seemed to read their encounters with police in ways very similar to others from less disadvantaged social categories. The associations between contact and trust, procedural justice and legitimacy, and legitimacy and cooperation were broadly invariant across all the categorizations featured above. This is important for two reasons. First, it suggests that people from marginal social groups, who may have high levels of contact with the police, do not tend to become inured to such contact but rather continue to experience it as a moment containing much information concerning the police and their relationship *with* the police (which is not to say that specific individuals do not indeed become inured or even permanently estranged as a result of high levels of police contact). Encounters between officers and citizens continue to be teachable moments even among those who have a lot of contact with police.

Second, and relatedly, these findings underline the fact that public trust *in* and the legitimacy *of* the police are embedded in a constant process of negotiation, debate and sometimes contest. Because each contact remains a teachable moment then each contains the potential for shifting or switching the relationship between police and public – most often, due to the asymmetry effect, in a negative direction. Police stops are, precisely, moments in which the legitimacy of the police is challenged and perhaps undermined.

Notes

1 Note that only stops and self-initiated contacts are included to cover contact experiences. While other forms of police-initiated contact are included in the CSEW, changes to question wordings in 2010/2011 mean these are not directly comparable across all the survey years covered in this analysis. The numbers involved also tend to be very small.

2 Due to the much smaller sample size of the PAS (n=5,120) treating police stops as a separate category was problematic. I therefore combined stops with other forms of police initiated contacts – some 4 per cent of the sample reported some sort of police-initiated contact in the previous year, ranging from stop/searches to being contacted as a witness.

3 A question about general health was not available in the PAS so disability is used as an alternative.

References

Blader, S. and Tyler, T.R. (2009). Testing and expanding the group engagement model. *Journal of Applied Psychology* 94: 445–464.

Bradford, B. (2014). Policing and social identity: Procedural justice, inclusion, and cooperation between police and public. *Policing and Society* 24(1): 22–43.

Bradford, B. (in press). The dog that never quite barked: Social identity and the persistence of police legitimacy, in Bosworth, M., Hoyle, C. and Zedner, L. (eds) *Changing Contours of Criminal Justice: Research, Politics and Policy*. Oxford: Oxford University Press.

Bradford B., Hohl, K., Jackson J., and MacQueen, S. (2015). Obeying the rules of the road. *Journal of Contemporary Criminal Justice* 31(2): 171–191.

Bradford, B., Huq, A., Jackson, J. and Roberts, B. (2014). What price fairness when security is at stake? Police legitimacy in South Africa. *Regulation and Governance* 8(2): 246–268.

Bradford, B., Jackson, J. and Stanko, E.A. (2009). Contact and confidence: Revisiting the impact of public encounters with the police. *Policing and Society* 19(1): 20–46.

Bradford, B., Murphy, K. and Jackson, J. (2014). Officers as mirrors: Policing, procedural justice and the (re)production of social identity. *British Journal of Criminology* 54(4): 527–550.

Bradford, B., Sargeant, E., Murphy, T. and Jackson, J. (2016). A leap of faith? Trust in the police among immigrants in England and Wales. *British Journal of Criminology* Online First.

De Cremer, D. and Tyler, T.R. (2005). Am I respected or not?: Inclusion and reputation as issues in group membership. *Social Justice Research* 18(2): 121–153.

Gilroy, P. (1987). *There Ain't No Black in the Union Jack*. London: Routledge.

Home Office (2015). *Police Powers and Procedures England and Wales, Year Ending 31 March 2015*. London: Home Office.

Hough, M., Bradford, B., Jackson, J. and Roberts, J. (2013). *Attitudes to sentencing and trust in criminal justice: Exploring Trends from the Crime Survey of England and Wales*. London: Ministry of Justice.

Huo, Y.J., Smith, H.J., Tyler, T.R. and Lind, E.A. (1996). Superordinate identification, subgroup identification, and justice concerns: Is separatism the problem; is assimilation the answer? *Psychological Science* 7: 40–45.

Jackson, J. and Bradford, B. (2009). Crime, policing and the moral order: On the expressive nature of public confidence in policing. *British Journal of Sociology* 60(3): 493–522.

Jackson, J. and Bradford, B. (2010). Measuring public confidence in the police: Is the PSA23 target fit for purpose? *Policing: A Journal of Policy and Practice* 4(3): 241–248.

Jackson, J. and Gau, J.M. (2015). Carving up concepts?: differentiating between trust and legitimacy in public attitudes towards legal authority, in Shockley, E., Neal, T.M.S., PytlikZillig, L. and Bornstein, B. (eds) *Interdisciplinary Perspectives on Trust: Towards Theoretical and Methodological Integration*. New York: Springer.

Jackson, J., Bradford, B., Hough, M., Myhill, A., Quinton, P. and Tyler, T.R. (2012). Why do people comply with the law? Legitimacy and the influence of legal institutions. *British Journal of Criminology* 52(6): 1051–1071.

Jackson, J., Bradford, B., Kuha, J. and Hough, M. (2014). Empirical legitimacy as two connected psychological states, in Mesko, G. and Tankebe, J. (eds), *Trust and Legitimacy in Criminal Justice: European Perspectives*. Cham: Springer.

Jackson, J. Bradford, B., Stanko, B. and Hohl, K. (2013). *Just Authority? Trust in the Police in England and Wales*. London: Routledge.

Kelman, H.C. and Hamilton, V.L. (1989). *Crimes of Obedience*. New Haven, CT: Yale University Press.

Loader, I., and Mulcahy, A. (2003). *Policing and the Condition of England*. Oxford: Oxford University Press.

McAra, L. and McVie, S. (2007). Youth Justice? The impact of system contact on patterns of resistance from offending. *European Journal of Criminology* 4(3): 315–345.

McAra, L. and McVie, S. (2012). Negotiated order: Towards a theory of pathways into and out of offending. *Criminology and Criminal Justice* 12(4): 347–376.

MacQueen, S. and Bradford, B. (2015). Enhancing public trust and police legitimacy during road traffic encounters: results from a randomized controlled trial in Scotland. *Journal of Experimental Criminology* 11(3): 419–433.

Mazerolle, L., Bennett, S., Antrobus, E. and Eggins, E. (2011). *Key Findings from the Queensland Community Engagement Trial*. CEPS Briefing Paper June 2011.

Mazerolle, L., Bennett, S., Antrobus, E. and Eggins, E. (2012). Procedural justice, routine encounters and citizen perceptions of the police: Main findings from the Queensland Community Engagement Trial (QCET). *Journal of Experimental Criminology* 8(4): 343–366.

Murphy, K., and Cherney, A. (2012). Understanding cooperation with police in a diverse society. *British Journal of Criminology* 52: 181–201.

Murphy, K., Bradford, B. and Jackson, J. (2016). Procedural justice or deterrence? What motivates compliance behavior in a longitudinal study of tax offenders. *Criminal Justice and Behavior* 43(1): 102–118.

Murphy, K., Hinds, L. and Fleming, J. (2008), Encouraging Cooperation and Public Support for Police. *Policing and Society* 18(2): 138–157.

Myhill, A. and Bradford, B. (2012). Can police enhance public confidence by improving quality of service? Results from two surveys in England and Wales. *Policing and Society* 22(4): 397–425.

Parmar, A. (2011). Stop and search in London: Counter terrorist or counter-productive? *Policing and Society* 21(4): 369–382.

Paternoster, R., Brame, R., Bachman, R. and Sherman, L.W. (1997). Do fair procedures matter? The effect of procedural justice on spouse assault. *Law and Society Review* 31: 163–204.

Reiner, R. (2010). *The Politics of the Police* (4th edn). Oxford: Oxford University Press.

Reisig, M.D. and Chandek, M.S. (2001). Effects of expectancy disconfirmation on outcome satisfaction in police–citizen encounters. *Policing: An International Journal of Police Strategies and Management* 24: 88.

Skogan, W.G. (2006). Asymmetry in the impact of encounters with police. *Policing and Society* 16: 99–126.

Slocum, L.A., Wiley, S.A. and Esbensen, F.-A. (2016). The importance of being satisfied: A longitudinal exploration of police contact, procedural injustice, and subsequent delinquency. *Criminal Justice and Behavior* 43(1): 7–26.

Stanko, E.A. and Bradford, B. (2009). Beyond measuring 'how good a job' police are doing: the MPS model of confidence in policing. *Policing: A Journal of Policy and Practice* 3(4): 332–330.

Stanko, E.A., Jackson, J., Bradford, B. and Hohl, K. (2012). A golden thread, a presence amongst uniforms, and a good deal of data: Studying public confidence in the London Metropolitan Police, *Policing and Society* 22(3): 317–331.

Sunshine, J. and Tyler, T.R. (2003). Moral Solidarity, identification with the community, and the importance of procedural justice: The police as prototypical representatives of a group's moral values. *Social Psychology Quarterly* 66(2): 153–165.

Tyler, T. (2006). *Why People Obey the Law* (2nd edn). New Haven: Yale University Press.

Tyler T.R. and Fagan J. (2008). Legitimacy and cooperation: Why do people help the police fight crime in their communities? *Ohio State Journal of Criminal Law* 6: 231–276.

Tyler, T.R. and Huo, Y. (2002). *Trust in the Law: Encouraging Public Cooperation with the Police and Courts*. New York: Russell Sage Foundation.

Tyler, T.R. and Wakslak, C.J. (2004). Profiling and police legitimacy: procedural justice, attributions of motive, and acceptance of police authority. *Criminology* 42: 253–281.

Tyler, T.R., Fagan, J.A. and Geller, A. (2014). Street stops and police legitimacy: teachable moments in young urban men's legal socialization. *Journal of Empirical Legal Studies* 11(4): 751–785.

Tyler, T.R., Jackson, J. and Mentovich, A. (2015). The consequences of being an object of suspicion: Potential pitfalls of proactive police contact. *Journal of Empirical Legal Studies* 12(4): 602–636.

Van Damme, A. (2015). The impact of police contact on trust and police legitimacy in Belgium. *Policing and Society* Online First.

Van Damme, A., Pauwels, L.J.R. and Svensson, R. (2013). Why do Swedes cooperate with the police? A SEM analysis of Tyler's Procedural Justice Model. *European Journal on Criminal Policy and Research* 21(1): 15–33.

Waddington, P.A.J. (1999). *Policing Citizens: Authority and Rights*. London: University College Press.

Wikström, P.-O, Oberwittler, D., Treiber, K. and Hardie, B. (2012). *Breaking Rules: The Social and Situational Dynamics of Young People's Urban Crime*. Oxford: Oxford University Press.

Wiley, S.A. and Esbensen, F.-A. (2016). The Effect of Police Contact: Does Official Intervention Result in Deviance Amplification? *Crime and Delinquency* 62(3): 283–307.

8 Policing as classificatory action

The preceding chapter described how police stops, because they are often experienced as procedurally unfair, have a net negative effect on public trust and the legitimacy of the police. Yet procedural (in)justice is also linked to social identity, and research has suggested that negative encounters with the police can affect people's identities in relation to groups the police represent (Bradford 2014; Bradford *et al.* 2014) and, perhaps, push them toward alternate 'providers' of group membership and belonging or into a state of anomie. Moreover, police stops, searches and cognate practices can be important sites of police intelligence gathering and data collection – processes that can ascribe quite different forms of identity onto those caught up in them. The extent to which (a) stop and search 'outcomes' feed into police intelligence systems (HMIC 2013) and (b) the initiation of stop/searches is based on intelligence (Chainey and Macdonald 2012) is often unclear. Yet there can be little doubt that in a general sense people who are stopped and particularly searched, either on foot or in a vehicle, register on the 'radar' of the police, and once registered remain on it, potentially for some time. Their details may be entered into local or national databases, but perhaps more importantly they 'become known' to local officers. Above all, police stops can be sites for the collation of data on 'the usual suspects' (McAra and McVie 2005), with significant implications for the people so coded, in relation, for example, to the extent they subsequently enter into the criminal justice system

Police stop activity can thus be argued to having subjective (or affective) *and* objective (or material) effects on people's lives. At stake during such encounters is not only the way individuals think and feel about police as a result of their experiences of the activity of officers – as discussed in Chapter 7 – but also the way they think about themselves, about others around them and, in the final analysis, about their willingness and ability to participate fully in society. Moreover, while the discussion has thus far focused the extent to which police attention is focused on marginal social categories as if these simply pre-existed such attention, it is clear marginality is also the product of institutional processes and that the police play a key role in its production. People's life chances can be altered and diminished as a result of the classificatory aspects of policing, as Manning (2010: 187) insists:

> *policing is an allocative and reallocative agency in the sense that it shifts the burdens of those encountered, altering their life chances, opportunities for work, and attachment to society and, by inaction or tolerance, adding to the success of others.*
>
> (Emphasis in original)

In this chapter the allocative and reallocative aspects of police stops are explored in relation to the subjective and objective identities of those subject to them. The discussion starts by outlining in a little more detail the role and place of social identity in procedural justice theory, a key underlying claim of which being that police practices perceived as fair or unfair can activate and strengthen, or attenuate and undermine, identification with the superordinate social category police represent. While it is important to underline that this is a complicated, recursive and non-linear process – for example, people's identity judgements are likely to shape the way they 'receive' and process the information encoded in police activity – a clear implication is that police stops experienced as unfair weaken people's sense of affiliation with the group(s) police represent.

To pick up the argument initiated in the preceding chapter the resonance here with labelling theory (Becker 1963; Ericson 1975) is apparent: people's social identities are symbolically as well as bureaucratically defined by their interactions with police officers, and both processes may have important consequences. There are of course differences between procedural justice theory, on the one hand, and labelling theory, on the other. The latter is often interested primarily in the implications for individuals of being assigned to specific, negatively valorized bureaucratic categories, such as delinquent, offender or prisoner (Akers 1999), which became their 'master status', shaping experience and future behaviour. Procedural justice theory, by contrast, is concerned with a largely subjective notion of identity that revolves around affiliation with social groups that are, at least in some general sense, positively valued by the individual concerned. Yet despite these differences the affinities between the two theories remain strong, and, together, these perspectives may provide insight into the extent that police stops are a generative practice that serves to create and reproduce particular social categories and the membership thereof. Being stopped by the police labels someone as a (potential) offender, makes them 'known' to police, can trigger their inclusion in various databases or the extension of their records within those databases, and can shift or alter their sense of self and belonging within society.

The chapter proceeds from here in four parts. Section one summarizes the role of social identity in procedural justice theory, before section two goes on to present some evidence, from two different surveys, as to the association between procedural (in)justice during police stops and the identity judgements of those stopped. Section three considers the objective or material implications that can arise for those experiencing such contact, while the final section concludes with consideration of the joint consequences of these processes, both for the individuals concerned and the wider practice, and indeed success, of policing.

Procedural justice and social identity

Procedural justice theory, particularly in its 'group engagement model' iteration (Blader and Tyler 2003), is premised on the idea that the behaviour of group authorities (here, the police) 'does things' to the identities of group members, and that this process has implications for issues of trust, legitimacy, cooperation and compliance. On this account, when people experience – and judge – the behaviour of authorities such as police officers, they draw on that behaviour to provide information about the assessment of the officer, a 'proto-typical group representative' (Sunshine and Tyler 2003), of their value, moral worth, and social standing within the group the police represent. Being treated with dignity and respect, experiencing neutral decision-making and open, transparent communication that flows both ways suggests to people that they are included and have status and worth within this group (Blader and Tyler 2003, 2009; De Cremer and Tyler 2005). This generates feelings of pride and self-value, strengthens group identification, and motivates legitimation of the group's structures of authority, compliance with its rules, and cooperation within and on its behalf. When people's treatment by police is lacking across some or all of the same criteria their sense of value and worth within the group may be undermined, damaging trust, legitimacy, cooperation and compliance, and ultimately triggering, perhaps, withdrawal from the group. On this account, one reason why people react so strongly to perceptions of its fairness is that this fundamentally challenges their sense of self, the extent to which they feel secure in their social environment, and perhaps even their sense of connection with their fellow citizens.

Two key questions are, therefore, what is the group the police represent within a particular context, and do significant numbers of people in that context feel some sort of identification with or affiliation with this group? The police, like any other social institution, are of course polysemic, representing multiple meanings to different individuals and groups. For some, police are an important source of authority in society, or are simply the body charged with keeping citizens safe. For others, they represent an oppressive state or economic system, and/or constitute a *threat* to the safety of individuals or groups who do not fit in to or whom demur from that system. To reiterate the argument made in Chapter 2, from an objective point of view police are all these things at once, albeit that in the final analysis they most importantly represent and enforce economic and other forms of inequality because these are the status quo, and the police stand for the status quo.

Yet, from the subjective point of view of the policed there is significant evidence that a quite particular set of meanings cohere around the police in Great Britain, at least, and probably also more widely. Sociological and other accounts regularly position the police as representative of the nation-state (Oliveira and Murphy 2015) or the community of citizens and as associated with a particular set of identities have been suggested to revolve around the idea of the 'law-abiding citizen' (Bradford *et al.* 2014, 2015; Jackson *et al.* 2012). The subjective content of this identity is important because identity it is closely related to action (Burke and Stets 2009). Identities exist in mutually reinforcing relationships with roles, and enacting roles associated with identities serves to reproduce and substantiate one's sense of self. When an identity revolving around 'citizenship' is made salient – for example by the experience of procedural fairness at the hands of a police officer – attendant roles may include law-abidingness and a willingness to cooperate with group authorities. Conversely, police behaviour that serves to denigrate and exclude does not motivate the same role-related behaviours – not least because an individual's sense that they need to live up to role expectations is diminished when they feel excluded from related group identities. Such behaviour may even encourage *other* role-related behaviours as people begin to take on the roles attendant to being marginalized, pushed out or excluded.

An important point here is that this is a group identity and set of attendant roles with which most people in England and Wales feel some relationship. They may affiliate themselves with this particular identity or they may not, but it is a valid point of reference for them and, equally importantly, the police represent it *to* them and they use police activity as a way of thinking about their relationship with this group. Naturally, it is perfectly possible to feel oneself to be a 'law-abiding citizen' and not care about police behaviour one way or the other, to feel the police to be profoundly unfair, or to feel one needs to *break* a law or two in order to maintain one's sense of value and self-worth (for example during a direct action protest). The claim here is merely that, from an empirical perspective (a) the police represent this type of identity to significant numbers of people, (b) it is associated with a set of roles or normative behaviours that revolve, among other things, around law-abidingness and (c) stronger identification will *on average* be associated with greater engagement in role-related behaviours.

An emerging body of research suggests that procedural justice may indeed be associated with social identity and, through this, people's law-related behaviour. For example, Tyler and Huo (2002) found that people's identification with the United States was related to perceptions that police were legitimate, while Huo (2003) found that identification with the US was also positively related to perceptions that police were procedurally fair (see also Bradford forthcoming; Oliveira and Murphy 2015). Using a representative panel survey of Australians, Bradford *et al.* (2014) found experiences of police procedural justice were, when positive, associated with stronger identification as a 'law-abiding Australian citizen'; experiences of police procedural injustice were associated with weaker identification. In addition, a sense of affiliation with this identity was very strongly associated with police legitimacy – people who identified more strongly as law-abiding citizens were very much more likely to feel a sense to duty to obey the instructions of police officers.

A study conducted in Scotland (ScotCET – Bradford, Hohl *et al.* 2015) presented very similar findings; moreover, this latter research suggested that strong identifiers were significantly less likely to report a propensity to break traffic laws, suggesting exactly the sort of link between social identity and offending found in the labelling and system contact literature. Finally, Bradford (2014) reported findings that suggested these effects were not limited to majority or 'mainstream' groups; perception of police procedural justice seemed to shape identification with the UK among a sample of young ethnic minority men living in London (see also Jackson *et al.* 2013).

Outwith the procedural justice paradigm, research has shown across multiple contexts that the experience, or perception, that authority figures such as police officers behave in a unfair manner can shake people's sense of self and shift their sense of inclusion and belonging. Blackwood and colleagues (Blackwood *et al.* 2013), for example, found that Muslim Briton's experiences of airport security processes resulted in a sense of misrecognition and official denial of their identities as British citizens. One young, Scottish-born, man included in their sample reported experiences at border points that resulted in him:

> being *made to feel* as the other … [and he stated that] 'for me to be singled out felt where am I now? This is my home, I consider Scotland my home. Why am I being stopped in my own house? Why am I felt, being made to feel as the other in my own house?'
>
> (Ibid.: 1098–1099, emphasis in original)

Importantly, this sense of exclusion and uncertainty can be triggered not only by experience of procedural unfairness but also by distributive unfairness and the suspicion of stereotyping (cf. Tyler and Wakslak 2004). The fact of being singled out for 'special' attention at an airport made another of Blackwood *et al.*'s Muslim respondents 'boil' with rage, 'because she was thinking "*why do they have to do it to me? Why don't they stop the Scottish woman*"' (Blackwood *et al.* 2013, 2015: 1102). The relevance here with police stops is obvious – the mere fact of having been stopped may affect the individual concerned in addition to or in interaction with their judgement of how the officer involved behaved.

This research, along with many other examples (e.g. Millings 2013; Parmar 2011; Sharp and Atherton 2007), focuses attention on the role of police and policing in 'misrecognition' (Millings 2013; cf. Honneth 2007). Police can often fail to behave in ways that accept that people from minority groups, in particular, belong to and have standing within the dominant culture or 'mainstream society', while at the same time acting in ways that denigrate or exclude minority identities. Such work is entirely congruent with the procedural justice perspective taken here. What the experience of unfairness can communicate to people is that they do not belong, that they are not valued, and that their status as citizens of a standing equal to others around them is not recognized (or is even denied). This exclusion or denial amounts to what Honneth (2007: 134) calls a moral injury caused by 'a disregard for aspects of our positive self-relation'. By 'self-relation' Honneth means a reflexive aspect of the self that refers to assessments of properly held capabilities and rights that is constructed inter-subjectively via 'agreeing or affirmative reactions on the part of other subjects' (ibid.). Police, that is, can like any other actor behave in ways that recognize those with whom they interact as effectual rights-bearing subjects (or they cannot). The symbolic and physical power of the police, it might be argued, likely serves to amplify such processes. Moral injuries, when they occur, 'impair our sense of being socially significant within a concrete community' (ibid.: 136).

Pertinent here is, first, that it is a concrete community that is at stake, and second just how widespread is identification with social groups the police might plausibly be said to represent. The 2009/2010 Citizenship Survey, for example (DCLG 2011) found that overall 87 per cent of people felt they 'very' or 'fairly' strongly belong to Britain, and that there was relatively little variation on this indicator by ethnic or religious group. Some 88 per cent of people with white ethnicities felt this way, compared with 87 per cent of people with Indian ethnicities, 90 per cent of those with Pakistani ethnicities, and 85 per cent of those with black Caribbean ethnicities. Similarly, 89 per cent of self-identified Christians felt this way, compared with 87 per cent of Muslims, 86 per cent of Hindus, and 84 per cent of those with no religion. Perhaps rather remarkably only 2 per cent of people felt they belonged to Britain 'not at all' strongly. This data suggests that to the extent that police denote 'Britain', then officer behaviour will be identity relevant to a very large proportion of those with whom those officers interact.

Indeed, one reason for the widespread existence of a 'procedural justice effect' may well be the strong association, in *many* social contexts, between the police and identities linked to nationhood, nationality, state and community (Bradford forthcoming; Emsley 1999; Loader and Mulcahy 2003; Taylor 1999). Identities associated with these types of groups, which to be sure are much more imagined than real (Anderson 1983), tend to be important to a large proportion of people in given national or local contexts. This is certainly the case in England and Wales, making police behaviour 'identity relevant' to large numbers of people.

To this can be added the notion that police can be said to represent, and certainly expend significant energy representing themselves as, the 'law-abiding'. From those elements of police culture which prioritize the 'thin blue line', establishing order in the face of chaos and protecting the innocent from the guilty (see Reiner 2010), to the imagery that shapes much of the promotional materials now produced by police organizations (Mawby 2002), there can be little doubt that the British police are concerned with promoting the message they are on the side of the 'law-abiding majority'. Equally pertinent, though, is the argument, expounded most forcefully by Loader and Mulcahy (2003), that a significant proportion of the public also uses the language and symbolism of police and policing to generate categories of meaning that take on, utilize and sometimes re-direct this message. The symbolic power of police (Bourdieu 1991) is such that this institution can insert itself into and provide a structure for processes of meaning production and identity formation within the wider population. The police, that is, can provide a crucible and a catalyst for the continuously ongoing generation and negotiation of identity within particular contexts (which is not to claim that many other institutions, behaviours and cultural tropes are not as or more important). That such processes almost inevitably involve the construction and enforcement of boundaries – social groups are constructed in relation to outgroups that are themselves defined during the process of identity formation – merely serves to underline the close affinity between policing and social identity.

Not only can police activity influence the subjective identities of the policed, then, but the latter can use the idea of police to articulate and make real who is 'us' and who is 'them', who is 'in' and who is 'out'. While the primary concern here is with a broadly inclusive identity, closely linked to the idea of the nation-state and membership thereof, it is important to remember that police can and do represent more exclusionary social categories, whether these are ethno-national, class-based or defined along some other axis. The 'we' represented by police can be significantly more limited and exclusive than any general notion of 'law-abiding' citizenship. Equally, in as much as police represent 'law-abidingness' to the policed, officer activity can position people on one or other side of this divide, too. It is a relatively rarely remarked upon but important implication of procedural justice theory that police can act, whether deliberately or not, in ways that communicate to people that they are on the 'wrong' side of boundaries established by identities that revolve around the idea of the law-abiding citizen. The classificatory aspects of police activity can serve not only to indicate status and inclusion inside the group, but also assignment to an outgroup. This is not to claim that those so assigned do not have a say in the matter – the police do not determine the subjective identities of the policed – but simply that police activity can be experienced in ways that have implications for how people position themselves in relation to the social groups involved.

Evidence from two studies

Two recent surveys allow consideration of a key question raised by the above and obviously pertinent in the overall context of this book: are perceptions of the procedural fairness of police stops associated with the identity judgements of those experiencing them? Answering this question is important if we are to properly understand the effect being stopped by police can have on the subjective identities of those subject to this form of police action and, perhaps, their subsequent behaviours.

Study 1: the Scottish Community Engagement Trial

The first survey was the Scottish Community Engagement Trial (ScotCET), already alluded to above. Funded by the Scottish Government this experimental study aimed to replicate the Queensland Community Engagement Trial (QCET) (Mazerolle *et al.* 2011, 2012), and tested whether enhancing procedural justice during routine encounters between police and citizens could influence public opinion and promote police legitimacy (see MacQueen and Bradford 2015 for full details). Data from this study allow for consideration of whether the experience of procedural (un)fairness during a police stop is associated with identity judgements. While unlike the remainder of the volume these data relate to Scotland, there is no reason to think they do not apply also to the rest of Great Britain (i.e. England and Wales).

The encounters included in the study were vehicle stops conducted during the Scottish Festive Road Safety Campaign 2013/2014. The 20 road police units in Scotland at the time were divided into 10 matched pairs according to geographical and other characteristics. Within each pair one unit was randomly assigned to the control group and the other to the treatment group. The control group conducted 'business as usual' stops throughout the campaign. After the initial stop – for which, under Scottish law, the police must have a reason – the encounters generally involved speaking with the driver of the vehicle to ascertain whether a breath test was appropriate and running a series of safety checks on the vehicle. Officers in the treatment group were instructed to 'deliver' enhanced procedural justice via the incorporation of key messages into their encounters that related to the key components of procedural justice: dignity and respect; equality; trustworthy motives; neutrality of decision making; clear explanation; and the opportunity for citizen participation or 'voice'. Motorists stopped by officers in the experiment group also received a leaflet, which was intended to emphasize the road safety concerns behind the campaign and assure drivers of the motives of the police.

All drivers stopped – in control and experimental groups – were issued with a self-completion questionnaire with a prepaid envelope to return to the researchers. An online alternative was also offered: 816 completed questionnaires were returned, providing an overall response rate of 6.6 per cent. Some 63 per cent of respondents were male, and the mean age was 50.7 (SD=14.8, min=17, max=87). Three-quarters (75 per cent) were homeowners; 40 per cent had a university degree or higher, while 12 per cent reported holding no qualifications. The majority were in employment (71 per cent), and 73 per cent were married or in a relationship.

Many items in the ScotCET survey were directly relevant to the issues at hand. First, drivers were asked how procedurally fair the police had been during the stop (via six items that covered questions such as whether the officers concerned were 'approachable and friendly', 'respectful', 'professional' and 'fair'). These six items all loaded very strongly onto one factor, which was extracted and save for analysis (mean=–0.1; SD=0.75; min=–3.1; max=1.2).

Second, four questions probed respondents' identity judgements (on five point agree–disagree scales):

- I see myself as a member of the Scottish community (53 per cent strongly agreed, while the remainder gave some other response)
- It is important to me that others see me as a member of the Scottish community (33 per cent strongly agreed)

- I see myself as an honest law-abiding citizen (72 per cent strongly agreed)
- It is important to me that others see me as an honest law-abiding citizen (53 per cent strongly agreed)

These four items also loaded strongly onto one factor, which was again extracted and saved for analysis (mean=0; SD=0.9; min=–4.5; max=1).

Third, the survey contained a number of variables suitable as control measures – not only age and gender, but also perception of social cohesion (represented by a scale constructed from three survey items), what might be termed 'belongingness' (respondents were asked whether they belonged to a church, a neighbourhood association, or other community group), and overall trust in police fairness and effectiveness (see MacQueen and Bradford 2015). All three correlate with both the identity measures and perceived procedural justice during the stop, and thus potentially confound the relationship between them (cf. Antrobus *et al.* 2015).

To assess the question posed above, a linear regression model predicting scores on the identity measure was estimated. Included as covariates were respondents' perceptions of the procedural fairness of the police during the stop, age, gender, perceptions of social cohesion and 'belongingness' (other socio-demographic variables, such as education and employment status, were also tested in the model, as was the measure of overall trust in the police, but none were found to be significant in the model).

The results from this model are summarized in Figure 8.1. There was a statistically significant and substantively quite strong correlation between stop procedural justice and identity judgements (β=0.24; p<0.0005). Holding constant the other variables in the model those who experienced unfair stops were significantly less likely to affiliate themselves with the 'citizen' identity defined above.

To further illustrate the nature of this association the four original identity measures were each dichotomized into new binary variables, coded such that 1 = a strongly agree response and 0 = all other responses. Four binary logistic regression models, predicting each measure in turn and with the same covariates as above were then estimated. Results from these models are summarized in Table 8.1, which shows the predicted probability of strongly agreeing to each identity statement, conditional on the other variables in the model, at three levels of stop procedural justice – low (2 standard deviations below the mean), mean, and high (1 standard deviation above the mean).

Stop procedural justice was a significant predictor of all four individual identity measures. People who experienced high procedural justice during the road traffic encounter were very much more likely to identify strongly across all four measures, while those who experienced low procedural justice were much less likely to strongly identify. Given the more or less standard nature of the encounters involved, and that the models control for some possibly confounding variables (and others were tested and found not significant) these results are striking. Respondents who experienced an unfair (low procedural justice) stop were half or less than half as likely to identify strongly across all four measures than those who experienced a fair (high procedural justice) stop.

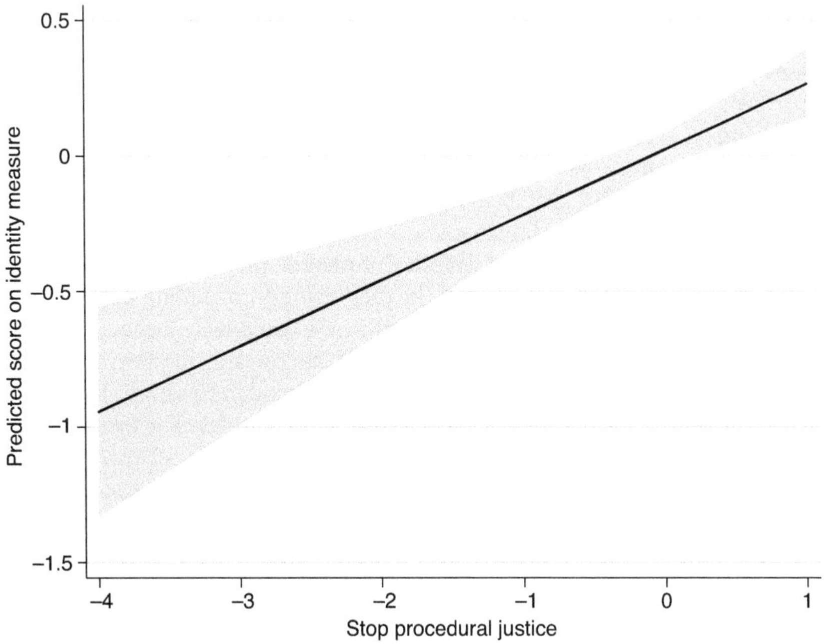

Figure 8.1 The experience of procedurally unfair stops was associated with weaker affiliation with a 'citizen' identity.

Source: ScotCET.

Table 8.1 Stop procedural justice is associated with identity judgements

Predicted probabilities generated from binary logistic regression models	*Stop procedural justice*		
	Low	*Mean*	*High*
I see myself as a member of the Scottish community	0.29	0.54	0.66
It is important to me that others see me as a member of the Scottish community	0.19	0.32	0.4
I see myself as an honest law-abiding citizen	0.48	0.75	0.84
It is important to me that others see me as an honest law-abiding citizen	0.31	0.55	0.66

Source: ScotCET.

Study 2: the Fiducia survey

The second study uses data from a survey of seven European countries conducted for the European Union FP7 funded FIDUCIA project (www.fiduciaproject.eu). The countries were Bulgaria, Finland, Germany, Italy, Lithuania, Turkey and the United Kingdom; these were selected on the basis that (a) partners in the project were based there and could manage the surveys locally and

(b) they represented a range of 'old' and 'new', north and south, European countries. However, I use here only the data from the UK survey – actually relating only to England and Wales – which was a random-digit dial telephone survey with a sample size of 1,004 (although the achieved response rate was less than 10 per cent, meaning the representativeness of the survey was rather questionable). Some 53 per cent of respondents were female; 24 per cent were aged over 65, compared with 13 per cent in the 18–24 category and 13 per cent in the 25–34 category; 42 per cent held degrees, compared with 12 per cent who reported that they had no qualifications.

The FIDUCIA surveys fielded identical measures (in translation) regarding police and the criminal justice system in each country, including contact with and trust in the police, police and legal legitimacy, compliance behaviour, willingness to cooperate with legal authorities, attitudes towards the law, and identity/citizenship (more details on the surveys can be found in Bradford, Jackson *et al.* 2015a). Of interest here are particular two sets of measures. The first set comprised four items concerning respondents' identity judgements. These matched closely the items used in the ScotCET survey, although the response scales were different (four-point scales, very important to not at all important). The individual items were:

- How important is being British to how you see yourself? (43 per cent said very important)
- How important is being a law-abiding citizen to how you see yourself? (76 per cent said very important)
- How important is it that others see you as British (32 per cent said very important)
- How important is it that others see you an honest law-abiding citizen (69 per cent said very important)

As in the ScotCET survey these four items also loaded strongly onto one factor, which was extracted and saved for analysis (mean=0; SD=0.4; min=–1.6; max=0.9).

The second set of measures comprised questions probing respondents' experience of being stopped and/or otherwise approached by police. The first asked 'In the past 2 years, have the police in your local neighbourhood approached you, or made contact with you for any reason?' (27 per cent had experienced such contact). Two further items then asked: 'Thinking about your experience with the police the last time this happened, how fairly did the police make decisions about what to do?'; and 'Again thinking about your experience with the police the last time this happened, how fairly were you treated by the police?'. Responses in both cases on five-point scales – 'very fairly' to 'very unfairly' – and other half (52 per cent) of respondents who had been stopped or approached by police felt they had been very fairly treated on both measures. To construct a measure of 'stop fairness' a simple three category response variable was created from these two items. This was coded 0 if the respondent had not been stopped or approached by police in the last two years, 1 if they had been stopped or approached and felt *very* fairly treated on both measures, and 2 if they had been stopped and felt less than very fairly treated on one or both measures. This approach allows comparison of views across people who had and had not experienced police-initiated contact as well as the statistical effect of fairness judgements on identity.

The Fiducia survey also contained a range of measures suitable as control variables: age, gender, educational attainment (three categories), ethnicity (dichotomized as white British vs. all others), perception of household income (four categories ranging from living comfortably to finding it difficult to live on present income), a measure of political affiliation (self-placement on a left–right scale), region of England and Wales and a set of rural/urban indicators.

To assess the nature of the correlation between police-initiated contact and identity judgements the identity measure outlined above was regressed on the contact measure and the set of control variables. Results from the analysis are summarized in Figure 8.2. There was a statistically significant, albeit substantively quite small, association between police-initiated contact that was experienced as less than fully fair and identity judgements. Compared with those who had not experienced this forms of police contact (the reference category) and those who had but experienced it as very fair, those who experienced less than fully fair contact affiliated themselves somewhat less strongly with the 'citizen' identity (β=–0.12; p=0.003). As a point of comparison, this was a similar

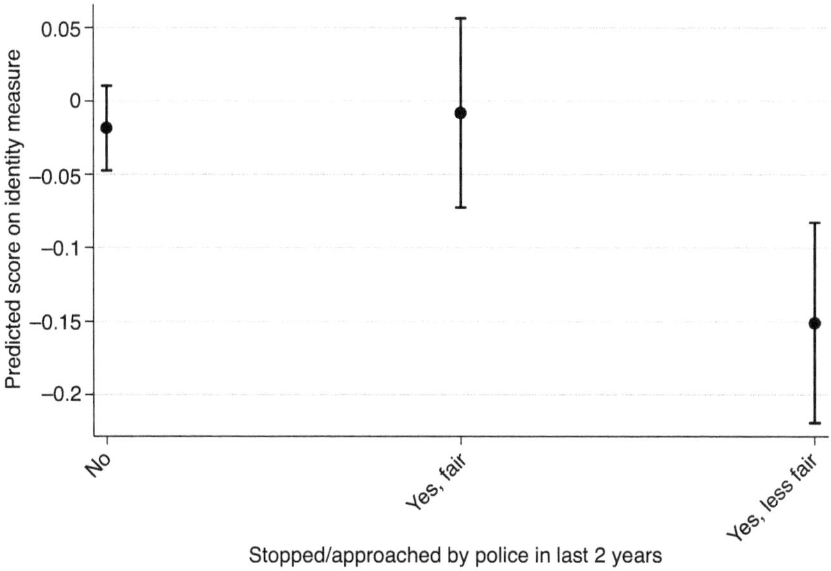

Figure 8.2 Respondents who experienced less than fully fair contact affiliated less strongly with a 'citizen' identity.

Source: Fiducia survey.

difference in predicted scores on the identity measure to that between respondents with a university degree and those with a lower qualification (β=0.13; p<0.0005).

To further probe the association between 'stop' experiences and identity judgements an interaction effect was also tested in the model, which allowed the statistical effect of stop experiences on identity to vary by ethnicity. This latter variable was, recall, dichotomized as white British/non-white British – this was simply because the small number of BME respondents in the Fiducia sample (n=118) made a more extensive categorization impractical. This interaction term proved to be significant, and demonstrated that it was *only among BME respondents* that there was a significant association between experiences of police-initiated contacts and identity judgements. BME respondents who had experienced less than fully fair police stops were significantly less likely than others to affiliate themselves with a 'citizen' identity. Among white British respondents, by contrast, the perceived fairness of police-initiated encounters had no significant association with identity judgements. One reason for this finding may be that people from ethnic minority groups tended to be more uncertain about their place in society and were thus more sensitive and responsive to the identity relevant content of police behaviour than their white British counterparts.

Results from the Fiducia survey therefore seem to correspond with those from the ScotCET survey. People who experience less than fair – or simply unfair – police behaviours associated themselves less strongly with a social identity the police might plausibly be said to represent. While these results are little more than indicative, since the analyses are based on cross-sectional data and therefore cannot estimate causal effects, and the effect sizes themselves are only small to moderate, they do tally with a growing volume of evidence linking judgements about the fairness of the police with identity judgements. While much more work remains to be done on these issues, most pertinently in relation to the direction of causality – it is perfectly possible, indeed likely, that affiliating more strongly with the group police represent motivates people to experience police activity as more fair – the potential for procedural unfairness to shift or modulate people's identity judgements is underlined by these results.

Yet the importance of these findings – and those of some of the other recent studies outlined above – should not be underestimated. At a time when the issue of alienation and 'radicalization' of young people, especially those from ethnic minority groups, is at the top of the political and policing agendas it matters a great deal that more or less mundane police activity, to the extent that it is experienced as unfair, may have an effect on people's identity judgements. Processes of alienation and exclusion do not just operate at bureaucratic and structural levels but also have experiential and subjective components. On the basis of the results presented above the way police officers interact with members of the public may have important implications for their sense of affiliation and belonging to a superordinate social category which links them in some way to many others in their social environment. Police unfairness may therefore not only serve to alienate people from the police, as shown in Chapter 7, but also from each other – or, at least, from the social 'mainstream'. Quotidian street-level police activity is thus identified as an important factor – among many others – that serves to push people to the margins of society, with potentially important implications for their future behaviours.

Further implications of being 'stopped'

Thus far the discussion has focused on the subjective or experiential effects of being stopped by police. It would be naïve however to omit consideration of the objective or perhaps 'bureaucratic' implications of such encounters for those who experience them. The record-taking and record-keeping processes that surround stop and search, in particular, open up the possibility for radical shifts in the subsequent experiences of those involved; in ways, moreover, that begin the blur the lines between the 'objective' and 'subjective'.

Most obviously, we know that a significant proportion of those stopped and searched under formal powers are subsequently arrested (and it seems likely that arrests can also stem from more informal stops, too). In 2014/15, for example, 14 per cent of the 541,000 stop/searches recorded in England and Wales resulted in an arrest (Home Office 2015). That this is an outcome of particular stops is of course inevitable and, to be clear, often desirable. While many arrests relate to the possession of small amounts of soft drugs – and thus constitute over-policing of trivial forms of deviance – some stop/searches do reveal stolen goods, larger amounts of hard drugs, weapons and other evidence of serious offending (see, for example, HMIC 2013: 42). To reiterate a point I have made throughout this book, the ability of police to stop and search can be a useful power. Equally, however, all those arrested have their details entered into a variety of databases and are labelled in many potentially consequential ways.

Moreover, while full data from all police forces was not available to the HMIC (2013), returns from 36 forces covering the 2014/15 period, suggested that a further 12–14 per cent of stop/searches resulted in some other outcome, such as, in the case of stops where drugs was given as the reason, a cannabis or khat warning (ibid.: 42; recall also that around half of stop/searches are conducted on the grounds of suspected possession of drugs). Here, though, the picture becomes a little murkier. Whether the provision of such disposals, which are given to people caught with small amounts of drugs that the officer involved is satisfied are for personal use only, is considered (a) an effective use of police time or (b) reflective of the extremely problematic drugs policies in place in England and Wales at the present time will presumably reflect the political and social priorities of the observer. What is certain, though, is that those subject to such warnings will have their details entered into local police databases and, in many cases, the Police National Computer (PNC). Not inconsequentially, such records are mandated by the official guidance around these types of warnings, which explicitly states that an individual can be given only one: if they are caught again in the future then police must escalate to a Penalty Notice for

Disorder (PND) or arrest (see MoJ 2013). It is therefore necessary that records be kept in order to facilitate this process. Receipt of a warning can also be disclosed for an enhanced Disclosure and Barring Service (DBS) check, which employers can obtain during recruitment processes. A similar set of provisions surround other non-arrest disposals available to police after a stop and search, such as community resolutions and Youth Cautions. The latter can be given to young people aged 10–17 by the police in the place of an arrest/prosecution for summary and 'triable either way' offences.

While the disposals outlined above require both an admission of guilt and the consent of the accused (in the case of Youth Cautions, parents/carers must be given full information in order that they can make an informed decision on the young person's behalf), it seems unlikely that many people, when given the choice, would opt for an arrest instead of a warning. This means that significant numbers of people are entering the criminal justice system – or at least the records thereof – as a result of these encounters (Sanders and Young 2007: 101–102), the outcomes of which are never tested in court and, perhaps more importantly, usually relate to extremely minor offences. Crucially, the ethnic disproportionality in the distribution of stop/search encounters, discussed in Chapter 5, mean that the probability of such 'entry' is not evenly spread across the population. Research by the drugs charity Release, published in 2013, showed that the stop and search rate in relation to drug searches, specifically, was 7 per 1,000 for the white population compared with 18 per 1,000 among those with Asian ethnicities and 45 per 1,000 among those with black ethnicities (Release 2013). Since a significant proportion of these searches result in an arrest, a PND or a cannabis warning, this means that despite there being no evidence that people from ethnic minority groups use drugs at a higher rate than those from the white British majority they are more likely, in an overall sense, to be caught with drugs by police and *records will be created* of these events. An important conclusion of the research conducted by Release was that black people are arrested for drug offences at six times the rate of white people, while Asian people are arrested at twice the rate (Release 2013: 12; see also May *et al.* 2010). One reason why arrest rates among minority populations might be greater may be that higher levels of prior stops result close down the possibilities of other disposals.

Of course, even when an arrest, PND, warning or other formal outcome does not transpire – as is the case in the majority of stop/searches – a bureaucratic record is still created. While the HMIC report of 2013 found that use of stop and search forms was extremely variable across different police force areas, it seems that in at least some areas the information recorded on them is entered into various databases in order, for example, to 'map the locations of the stops against recorded crime, or to link stop and search encounter to prosecutions and convictions' (HMIC 2013: 41). In some forces there are more or less automatic processes for entry of stop form data into intelligence databases.

Taken together these record-keeping processes provide multiple pathways through which people's bureaucratic and possibly subjective identities can be affected. The creation of administrative records around a search, warning or arrest involves, by definition, the assignment of the individuals concerned to categories suitable for entry into systematized record storage and retrieval systems. As Ericson and Haggerty (1997: 257) argue:

> Through the routine work of checking-off boxes on forms, and through what happens to that knowledge as it moves into various risk management contexts and panoptic sorting processes, the police help to force people into particular institutional identities. Far from being original and creative authors of this work, the police merely tailor people to fit the identity characteristics available within police classification formats. Moreover, the texts created by the police escape their grasp and move into new contexts in which a person's institutionally relevant identity is sorted and imprinted.

Police stop activity is indeed classificatory, ascribing the people with whom police interact to specific social categories. Moreover, while these may be relatively innocuous on their own ('male', 'young', 'black') they become deeply problematic when they co-occur, as will inevitably be the case in the kind of records created by stop/search activity, with the categories of 'suspect' and/or 'offender'. Not only is the individual stopped so labelled, but the other social categories within which they are placed by police likely become associated, via a self-reinforcing process, with the idea and connotation of offending. To the extent that police continue to disproportionately stop people from specific ethnic minority and other groups, the idea that membership of those groups is associated with offending will recur and maintain salience. The over-representation of people from minority groups in police databases and informal knowledge systems is one way that those groups as a whole become labelled as offenders, as the debates over the years, around drug, gang, knife and 'black on black' crime, have amply demonstrated (Hall *et al.* 1978; May *et al.* 2010; Release 2013).

Two important implications flow from this classificatory aspect of policing, particularly, it might be argued, in the context of stop and search. First, the process described above constitutes an example of the 'ratchet effect' described by Harcourt (2007). As people from minority groups are more likely to be stopped/searched they are more likely, despite the fact that overall offending rates are *not* higher in these groups, to appear in police record-keeping systems of various kinds. This means (a) that the individuals concerned may appear in intelligence briefings and so forth, becoming, eventually, the usual suspects; and (b) that the racial or ethnic categories to which they were assigned by police become associated with offending: both in an actuarial sense, since the police records appear to show that black people, for example, are disproportionately involved in drug crime; and at the level of the lived experiences of police officers, who internalize the idea that black people are more likely to use drugs (Glaser 2015; May *et al.* 2010; Quinton 2015). These factors seem likely, in turn, to affect the future behaviour of officers, which will be directed by formal and informal processes toward people from ethnic minority groups, thus triggering the creation of more records and the commencement of another turn of the ratchet.

Second, individuals assigned to administrative or bureaucratic identities by police can begin to take on or absorb aspects of those identities into their sense of self. Ericson and Haggerty (1997: 257–258) invoke Giddens (1990), Bauman (1992) and Beck (1992) in defence of this position, arguing that individuals are not simply free to choose identities but must in an important sense select from those made available to them by the 'strategies and notions provided by abstract systems' (Giddens 1990: 124) such as the police and criminal justice system. On this account the classificatory aspects of police activity serve not only to produce a range of identities towards which the people officers encounter are pushed, but also, potentially, to inhibit the possibility of taking on and living other identities, as might well be the case for example if an individual with a record of a cannabis warning is turned down from a job on the basis of a DBS check.

This, clearly, is a labelling perspective, which envisages that people take on and begin to act in congruence with identities they are ascribed by powerful bureaucratic processes, not least because those same processes have blocked the potential for other sources of identity formation and meaning. Yet it equally clearly relates to some of the key themes in procedural justice theory. In both cases the identities of those who encounter police are altered by this experience, and the extent to which an individual experiences a shift in their sense of self is thought to be linked to their future behaviour. It is this last point that I now turn.

The effects of differential social categorization

There is much to suggest, then, that police stops can not only undermine perceptions of the fairness *of* police, and the extent to which legitimacy is conferred *on* police, but that they can also exert influence on the social identities, and perhaps subsequent behaviours, of the people stopped. The power to stop, question and perhaps search can thus be positioned as one aspect of wider processes of social exclusion and a set of experiences that, particularly in much as they trigger the creation of bureaucratic records concerning the people stopped, have both subject and objective components and consequences. Individuals caught up by this practice will, on average, experience an attenuation of links to superordinate social categories and, possibly, will be motivated to take on alternate labels such as 'non-citizen', 'suspect' or 'offender'. This, it seems to me, is perhaps the most destructive aspect of the police power to stop and/or search, since it relates not to people's relations with the police but their relations with each other, and, at least on the account provided above, with social groups to which all have a valid claim of membership.

What might be the implications of this process (Bradford *et al.* 2014: 531–532)? McAra and McVie (2007, 2012) describe a significant body of international research that suggests 'system contact', such as involvement with the youth justice system and in particular experience of more severe forms of sanctioning, is as likely to result in enhanced offending as in diminished offending (e.g. Farrington 1977; Farrington *et al.* 1978; Huizinga *et al.* 2003; Tracy and Kempf-Leonard 1996; Slocum *et al.* 2016; Wiley and Esbenson 2016). Much system contact research has used longitudinal survey designs, and complex statistical techniques such as propensity score matching, to reach its conclusions (which nevertheless are far from conclusive – see Bernberg 2009), and the data available for the studies included here cannot match those that have been used elsewhere. Yet, procedural justice theory may be able to supply a plausible causal mechanism for labelling theory, which often seems to rely (a) on the idea that labelling closes down life chances, making offending more likely/desirable and/or (b) that the labelled accept, take on and begin to live to negatively valorized, delinquent, social categories (ibid.). Both ideas may be in some sense correct, but neither can explain why some people labelled by criminal justice agents go on to offend (more) and some do not (although see Sherman 1993). It may be that it is not the fact of system contact that is important so much as the subjective experience of procedurally unfair treatment, which undermines trust and legitimacy and therefore removes or diminishes the effect of normative guidelines for behaviour (that it is right to defer to legitimate authority, and right to obey to the rules the authority embodies). And has described above, procedural (in)justice may also influence people's identities in a direct sense. Such an experience may lead not only to a de-legitimation of the police – representing one pathway to an increased likelihood of offending – but also a withdrawal from social identities associated with the police and a re-focusing of identity onto alternate sources of value and meaning which may, as McAra and McVie (2012) describe, be themselves 'offending identities'.

This immediately recalls the 'asymmetry' effect in contacts between police officers and citizens (see Chapter 7). Encounters with police officers judged favourably (which occurs primarily when they are judged to be fair – Tyler and Fagan 2008) can have a positive effect on trust and legitimacy and thus, potentially, on people's decisions to offend. However, encounters judged unsatisfactory (largely, unfair) seem to have a much larger negative effect, leading to a net negative association between contact with the police, trust, and legitimacy. If this association plays out in relation to the fairness, *identity* and legitimacy pathway, then we would expect some people who come into contact with the criminal justice system to come away with a decreased propensity to offend (if they were treated fairly, felt included, and granted the police more legitimacy), but others, who felt they were treated unfairly, would come away with an enhanced propensity to offend (because they felt excluded, began to de-legitimize the police, and perhaps turned to other sources of social identification): the latter would outweigh the former, leading to the net increased level of offending described in the system contact literature.

A further implication, as noted, is that police contact judged to be unfair, demeaning and exclusionary can alienate people not only from the police but also from each other. In England and Wales, and Scotland, it can be claimed that (a) police represent a social identity to which a large majority of people feel some sense of connection or affiliation, and that (b) this identity has the potential for forming an important affective bond between those who feel they share it. Policing can serve to make people feel more included and secure within these imagined communities, and therefore bolster their sense of 'we-feeling' in relation to others around them (Bradford 2014; Loader and Walker 2007). Yet, processes that involve the generation of 'we' imply the formation of group boundaries and, therefore, the definition of 'them'. Police are not neutral arbiters in such processes – to the extent that they choose to interact with different people in different ways officers assign those individuals to distinct social categories, in the process creating and reproducing boundaries of various forms. Policing can also serve to indicate people are on the 'out' side, making them less inclined to feel a sense of shared group membership not only with police but also, perhaps, other members of the group the police represent.

Justice and Meares (2014) have recently outlined a distinctive and novel iteration of the argument laid out above. Distinguishing between the 'overt' and 'covert' curriculum of criminal justice, they describe how police activity can fit one or other of these categories. Curriculum is defined by reference to educational theory – as a set of 'structured experiences' (ibid.: 163) through which people, whether school children or not, pass as they are made into citizens and taught what good citizenship entails. The overt curriculum refers to the constrained use of police power, the protection of individual rights, and the collective endeavour of creating security. This is the way that policing is presented on an ideological level and, to be sure, the way it is actually experienced by significant numbers of citizens. Here, people are socialized, in part by the actions of police officers and other legal authorities, to believe everyone should be treated as a 'valued citizen' (ibid.: 173) who is equal before the law. Procedural justice in the interactions between police and policed generates a sense of shared interests, aim and means, and promotes forms of social capital that might allow people to pursue such interests (for example by reassuring them that they are valued members of society protected by legitimate authorities).

The covert curriculum 'sends the opposite message, showing certain citizens clear signals that they are a special, dangerous, and undesirable class' (ibid.: 173). This aspect of the criminal justice curriculum is hidden precisely because it goes against the dominant understanding – the overt curriculum – that police (for example) should treat everyone in as procedurally just manner as possible. Justice and Meares are concerned primarily with the United States, where the evidence clearly shows that this is not the case, and moreover that the experience of procedural injustice is concentrated in specific areas and on specific groups and types of person. Yet the resonance with the situation in England and Wales is strong. We saw above that police stops were disproportionately directed against people from marginal social categories (Chapter 5). More important, however, was that the experience of negative encounters was concentrated within the same categories (Chapter 7). People who were already in some sense on the margins of society were more likely to have had negative encounters with the police that, if the ideas outlined above are correct, will have served to push them yet further 'out'.

This points to something of a paradox in terms of the aims and outcomes of policing. In *The Fabrication of Social Order* (2000) Neocleous takes a position on 'police' strikingly similar to Dubber's (2005) concept. He also argues forcibly that policing is not simply about reproducing social order: police also construct order of particular kind, most importantly via the constitution of orderly subjects through the imposition of the habits and values of work. This idea runs through many accounts that have considered police power in the wider sense used by Dubber and Neocleous, not least Foucault:

> Police is the totality of measures which make work possible and necessary ... the question Voltaire would soon formulate, Cobert's contemporaries had already asked: Since you have established yourselves as a people, have you not yet discovered the secret of forcing all the rich to make all the poor work? Are you still ignorant of the first principles of the police?
>
> (Foucault 1967: 44, quoted by Neocleous 2000: 18)

Much of the discussion above has revolved precisely around the idea that policing can serve to make people into, or at least motivate them to feel that they are, law-abiding citizens, part of a group (or a 'people') and willing to work within and on behalf of it. This process can be painted in both positive and negative lights. As Justice and Meares describe, criminal justice processes that encourage people to feel they are valued rights-bearing citizens of a society with a shared set of aims and interests have the potential to produce many socially beneficial outcomes. Yet the encouragement of 'we-feeling' may come at a price, in terms both of people's relations with those placed on the wrong side of the boundaries that are inevitably drawn and their willingness to support within-group structures and processes that are not aligned with their objective, or even subjective, best interests or desires. There is much to suggest, for example, that people who feel they are treated or governed in a procedurally fair manner are more accepting of outcomes unfavourable to themselves or others (MacCoun 2005). The extent to which such processes create 'docile bodies' (Foucault 1977) not merely amenable to governance but self-governed by internalized norms and group related values, has yet to be fully explored.

These issues would need a quite different book to properly investigate. The paradox they illuminate is however significant. If policing aims at a fundamental level to produce orderly, well-functioning and socially embedded citizens – however this process is construed – the extent to which one of its more important modalities interferes with this end is striking. When it comes to police stops the asymmetry effect means that the covert curriculum holds sway. This mode of policing, when it does effect change across the axes of status, inclusion and belonging, seems more often to exclude rather than include and to inhibit rather than encourage the creation of orderly citizens. Seen in this light police stops are not, to put it bluntly, effective disciplinary tools.

One resolution to this paradox would be the idea that policing has also at its root an exclusionary purpose, and that it is concerned not only with the creation of productive citizens but also with the labelling and exclusion of the unproductive. Police function not only to discipline and to bring the recalcitrant back into the fold, but also to delineate those who cannot be brought back in and who must therefore be dealt with in some other way. The policing of race in the United States has been theorized in exactly this way (Alexander 2012). Equally, the group or 'people' involved in such processes may be an exclusionary rather than an inclusionary category, with the police functioning to patrol its boundaries. On this account there is in fact no paradox, since exclusion or marginalization is itself an aim of policing, and police stops are effective way of demarcating those placed on the outside.

Another response to the paradox would be to accept its existence and seek to minimize its implications. The claim here would be not that there is something inherently exclusionary about policing in general, but rather that police stops in particular hold the potential for such outcomes. Regardless of the wider aims and functions of police, this mode of activity will always throw up difficult encounters and problematic consequences, and the task is to implement it in the least damaging way possible while accentuating other forms of policing that have less deleterious implications for those who experience them. Procedural justice theory has much to offer such efforts. Indeed, one might go further, and claim that the use of procedural justice before, during and after street stops can not only mitigate their negative implications but serve actively to enhance legitimacy and perceptions of belonging. It may not be 'police contact per se' that is the problem, but rather 'the style of policing through which contact occurs' (Tyler *et al.* 2015: 630).

Would making contacts between police and public 'better' (fairer) merely constitute a salve obscuring underlying structural inequalities that would otherwise be thrown into sharper relief? Or do such contacts constitute and alter citizen's locations in various social, economic and cultural hierarchies, such that improvements to the quality of police/public interaction would shift underlying inequalities? The extent to the symbolic and practical power vested in the police suggests that the later process is certainly possible – police can and do materially alter the life chances of those they encounter while, at the same time, shaping the way those individuals feel about themselves and others around them. To reiterate Neocleous' point, police do not merely reproduce social order but also constitute it, and if this is the case then inequalities can be alleviated – and not simply obscured – by changing police practice in the way Tyler and colleagues suggest.

Summary

It seems, then, that police stops can be exclusive in two distinct but interrelated ways. On the one hand they can serve to reinforce, and even extend, objective or structural inequalities by switching and diminishing life chances. On the other hand they can alter the subjective experiences and identities of those targeted, making them *feel* less wanted and included. To the extent that identities shape behaviour, those so treated may go on to 'act out' in ways that have important implications for their lives further down the line. Because only a small proportion of stops result in a criminal justice outcome the latter process may be the more important. Or at least, *any* individual who is stopped may be exposed to the identity threatening aspects of police behaviour, whereas only a proportion enter into the criminal justice system or the records thereof. It is this fact that opens up the possibility noted by Tyler *et al.* (2015). Because the main or most important effect of stops is experiential or subjective, the use of procedural justice *may* encourage, among some individuals at least, a firmer sense of status and belonging. Policing, when it is done right, can include rather than exclude. Moreover, to this might also be added the claim that stops conducted in a procedurally fair manner should be less likely to be unjustified and mis-targeted – because decisions reached would be a made in neutral, unbiased manner – thus minimizing their 'net-widening' or 'ratcheting' effect. If all this is true, of course, the question naturally arises as to whether, and how, police behaviour can be calibrated to produce such outcomes.

References

Akers, R.L. (1999). *Criminological Theories: Introduction and Evaluation*. Abingdon: Routledge.

Alexander, M. (2012). *The New Jim Crow. Mass Inceration in the Age of Colorblindness*. New York: The New Press.

Anderson, B. (1983). *Imagined Communities. Reflections on the Origin and Spread of Nationalism*. London: Verso.

Antrobus, E., Bradford, B., Murphy, K. and Sargeant, E. (2015). Community norms, procedural justice and the public's perceptions of police legitimacy. *Journal of Contemporary Criminal Justice* 31(2): 151–170.

Bauman, Z. (1992). Life-world and expertise: Social production of dependency, in Stehr, N. and Ericson, R.V. (eds) *The Culture and Power of Knowledge: Inquiries into Contemporary Societies*. Berlin: Walter de Gruyer.

Beck, U. (1992). *Risk Society: Toward a New Modernity*. London: Sage.

Becker, H. (1963). *Outsiders: Studies in the Sociology of Deviance*. New York: Free Press.

Bernberg, J.G. (2009). Labelling theory, in Krohn, M.D., Lizotte, A.J. and Hall, G.P. (eds) *Handbook on Crime and Deviance*. New York: Springer.

Blackwood, L.M., Hopkins, N. and Reicher, S.D. (2013). 'I know who I am, but who do they think I am?' Muslim perspectives on encounters with airport authorities. *Ethnic and Racial Studies* 36(6): 1090–1108.

Blackwood, L.M., Hopkins, N. and Reicher, S.D. (2015). 'Flying while Muslim': Citizenship and misrecognition in the airport. *Journal of Social and Political Psychology* 3(2): 148–170.

Blader, S.L. and Tyler, T.R. (2003). A four-component model of procedural justice: Defining the meaning of a 'fair' process. *Personality and Social Psychology Bulletin* 29: 747–758.

Blader, S. and Tyler, T.R. (2009). Testing and expanding the group engagement model. *Journal of Applied Psychology* 94: 445–464.

Bourdieu, P. (1991). *Language and Symbolic Power*. Cambridge: Polity.

Bradford, B. (2014). Policing and social identity: Procedural justice, inclusion, and cooperation between police and public. *Policing and Society* 24(1): 22–43.

Bradford, B. (forthcoming). The dog that never quite barked: Social identity and the persistence of police legitimacy.

Bradford, B., Hohl, K., Jackson, J. and MacQueen, S. (2015). Obeying the rules of the road. *Journal of Contemporary Criminal Justice* 31(2): 171–191.

Bradford, B., Jackson, J. and Hough, M. (2015). *Trust and Attitudes to Justice Abroad. Testing the legitimacy model on "new-crimes" and addressing supra-national trust and institutional legitimacy*. Fiducia Project.

Bradford, B., Jackson, J. and Stanko, E.A. (2009). Contact and confidence: Revisiting the impact of public encounters with the police. *Policing and Society* 19(1): 20–46.

Bradford, B., Murphy, K. and Jackson, J. (2014). Officers as mirrors: Policing, procedural justice and the (re)production of social identity. *British Journal of Criminology* 54(4): 527–550.

Burke, P.J. and Stets, J. (2009). *Social Identity Theory*. Oxford: Oxford University Press.

Chainey, S. and Macdonald, I. (2012). *Stop and Search, the Use of Intelligence and Geographic Targeting: Findings from Case Study Research*. London: NPIA.

DCLG (2011). *Citizenship Survey 2009/10*. London: Department of Communities and Local Government.

De Cremer, D. and Tyler, T.R. (2005). Am I respected or not?: Inclusion and reputation as issues in group membership. *Social Justice Research* 18(2): 121–153.

Dubber, M.D. (2005). *The Police Power. Patriarchy and the Foundations of American Government*. New York: Columbia University Press.

Emsley, C. (1999). *Gendarmes and the State in Nineteenth Century Europe*. Oxford: Oxford University Press.

Ericson, R. (1975). *Criminal Reactions: The Labelling Perspective*. London: Ashgate.

Ericson, R.V. and Haggerty, K. (1997). *Policing the Risk Society*. Toronto: University of Toronto Press.

Farrington, D.P. (1977). The Effects of Public Labelling. *British Journal of Criminology* 17: 112–125.

Farrington, D.P., Osborn, S.G. and West, D.J. (1978). The persistence of labelling effects. *British Journal of Criminology* 18: 277–284.

Foucault, M. (1967). *Madness and Civilisation: A History of Insanity in the Age of Reason*. London: Tavistock.

Foucault, M. (1977). *Discipline and Punish*. London: Penguin Books.

Giddens, A. (1990). *The Consequences of Modernity*. Cambridge: Polity.

Glaser, J. (2015). *Suspect Race*. New York: Oxford University Press.

Hall, S., Critcher, C., Jefferson, T., Clarke, J. and Roberts, B. (1978). *Policing the Crisis*. London: Macmillan.

Harcourt, B.E. (2007). *Against Prediction. Profiling, Policing and Punishing in an Actuarial Era*. Chicago: Chicago University Press.

HMIC (2013). *Stop and Search Powers: Are the Police Using Them Effectively and Fairly?* London: Her Majesty's Inspectorate of Constabulary.

Home Office (2015). *Police Powers and Procedures England and Wales, Year Ending 31 March 2015*. London: Home Office.

Honneth, A. (2007). *Disrespect. The Normative Foundations of Critical Theory*. Cambridge: Polity Press.

Huizinga, D., Schuman, K., Ehret, B. and Elliot, A. (2003). *The Effects of Juvenile Justice Processing on Subsequent Delinquent and Criminal Behaviour: A Cross-National Study*. Washington, DC: Final Report to the National Institute of Justice.

Huo, Y.J. (2003). Procedural justice and social regulation across group boundaries: does subgroup identity undermine relationship-based governance? *Personality & Social Psychology Bulletin* 29(3): 336–348.

Jackson, J., Bradford, B., Hough, M., Myhill, A., Quinton, P. and Tyler, T.R. (2012). Why do people comply with the law? Legitimacy and the influence of legal institutions. *British Journal of Criminology* 52(6): 1051–1071.

Jackson, J., Bradford, B., Stanko, B. and Hohl, K. (2013). *Just Authority? Trust in the Police in England and Wales*. London: Routledge.

Justice, B. and Meares, T.L. (2014). How the Criminal Justice System educates its citizens. *The Annals of the American Academy* 651, January: 159–177.

Loader, I. and Mulcahy, A. (2003). *Policing and the Condition of England*. Oxford: Oxford University Press.

Loader, I. and Walker, N. (2007). *Civilising Security*. Cambridge: Cambridge University Press.

McAra, L. and McVie, S. (2005). The usual suspects? Street-life, young people and the police. *Criminology and Criminal Justice* 5(1): 5–36.

McAra, L. and McVie, S. (2007). Youth Justice? The impact of system contact on patterns of resistance from offending. *European Journal of Criminology* 4(3): 315–345.

McAra, L. and McVie, S. (2012). Negotiated order: Towards a theory of pathways into and out of offending. *Criminology and Criminal Justice* 12(4): 347–376.

MacCoun, RJ (2005). Voice, control, and belonging: The Double-edged sword of procedural fairness. *Annual Review of Law and Social Science* 1(1): 171–201.

MacQueen, S. and Bradford, B. (2015). Enhancing public trust and police legitimacy during road traffic encounters: results from a randomized controlled trial in Scotland. *Journal of Experimental Criminology* 11(3): 419–433.

Manning, P.K. (2010). *Democratic Policing in a Changing World*. Boulder: Paradigm Publishers.

Mawby, Rob. (2002). *Policing Images: Policing, Communication and Legitimacy*. Cullompton: Willan Publishing.

May, T., Gyateng, T. and Hough, M. (2010). *Differential Treatment in the Youth Justice System*. London: Equalities and Human Rights Commission.

Mazerolle, L., Bennett, S., Antrobus, E. and Eggins, E. (2011). *Key Findings from the Queensland Community Engagement Trial*. CEPS Briefing Paper June 2011.

Mazerolle, L., Bennett, S., Antrobus, E. and Eggins, E. (2012). Procedural justice, routine encounters and citizen perceptions of the police: Main findings from the Queensland Community Engagement Trial (QCET). *Journal of Experimental Criminology* 8(4): 343–366.

Millings, M. (2013). Policing British Asian identities: The enduring role of the police in young British Asian Men's situated negotiation of identity and belonging. *British Journal of Criminology* 53 (6): 1075–1092.

MoJ (2013). *Quick Reference Guide to Out of Court Disposals*. London: Ministry of Justice.

Myhill, A. and Bradford, B. (2012). Can police enhance public confidence by improving quality of service? Results from two surveys in England and Wales. *Policing and Society* 22(4): 397–425.

Neocleous, M. (2000). *The Fabrication of Social Order*. London: Pluto Press.

Oliveira, A. and Murphy, K. (2015). Explaining negative attitudes toward police: Does race or social identity matter more? *Race and Justice* 5(3): 259–277.

Parmar, A. (2011). Stop and search in London: Counter terrorist or counter-productive? *Policing and Society* 21(4): 369–382.

Quinton, P. (2015). Race disproportionality and officer decision-making, in Delsol, R. and Shiner, M. (eds) *Stop and Search*. Basingstoke: Palgrave Macmillan.

Reiner, R. (2010). *The Politics of the Police* (4th edn). Oxford: Oxford University Press.

Release (2013). *The Numbers in Black and White: Ethnic Disparities in the Policing and Prosecution of Drug Offences in England and Wales*. London: Release.

Sanders, A. and Young, R. (2007). *Criminal Justice* (3rd edn). Oxford: Oxford University Press.

Sharp, D. and Atherton, S. (2007). To serve and protect? The experiences of policing in the community of young people from black and other ethnic minority groups. *British Journal of Criminology* 47(5): 746–763.

Sherman, L.W. (1993). Defiance, deterrence, irrelevance: A theory of the criminal sanction. *Journal of Research in Crime and Delinquency* 30: 445–473.

Skogan, W.G. (2006). Asymmetry in the impact of encounters with police. *Policing and Society* 16: 99–126.

Slocum, L.A., Wiley, S.A. and Esbensen, F.-A. (2016). The Importance of Being Satisfied: A Longitudinal Exploration of Police Contact, Procedural Injustice, and Subsequent Delinquency. *Criminal Justice and Behavior* 43(1): 7–26.

Sunshine, J. and Tyler, T.R. (2003). Moral solidarity, identification with the community, and the importance of procedural justice: The police as prototypical representatives of a group's moral values. *Social Psychology Quarterly* 66(2): 153–165.

Taylor, I. (1999). *Crime in Context*. Cambridge: Polity Press.

Tracey, R.E. and Kempf-Leonard, K. (1996). *Continuity and Discontinuity in Criminal Careers*. New York: Plenum Press.

Tyler, T. (2006). *Why People Obey the Law* (2nd edn). New Haven: Yale University Press.

Tyler, T.R. and Fagan, J. (2008). Legitimacy and cooperation: Why do people help the police fight crime in their communities? *Ohio State Journal of Criminal Law* 6: 231–276.

Tyler, T.R. and Huo, Y. (2002). *Trust in the Law: Encouraging Public Cooperation with the Police and Courts*. New York: Russell Sage Foundation.

Tyler, T.R. and Wakslak, C.J. (2004). Profiling and police legitimacy: procedural justice, attributions of motive, and acceptance of police authority. *Criminology* 42: 253–281.

Tyler, T.R., Jackson, J. and Mentovich, A. (2015). The consequences of being an object of suspicion: Potential pitfalls of proactive police contact. *Journal of Empirical Legal Studies* 12(4): 602–636.

Wiley, S.A. and Esbensen, F.-A. (2016). The Effect of Police Contact: Does Official Intervention Result in Deviance Amplification? *Crime and Delinquency* 62(3): 283–307.

9 Conclusion

As a multi-purpose tool that can respond to almost any circumstance and be turned to almost any purpose, police stops in general and stop and search in particular are important ways in which police exercise power. They can serve as the first – and in many cases the primary or even sole – step in asserting or re-asserting order, control and/or discipline. In Chapter 5 we saw that a number of different theoretical paradigms seemed to have something to offer in terms of explaining the empirical distribution of police stop activity – conflict theory, implicit bias and stereotyping, and, to the extent that it is indeed also directed toward crime, consensus theory. But none achieved primacy. Given the diversity of uses to which this power will inevitably be put, and the scale of its use, it is perhaps hardly surprising that none of these paradigms could on their own account for its distribution. What is needed to explain this phenomenon is an understanding of the way policing as a formative social practice is constituted and enacted.

Police stops and police power

In the preceding chapters I have argued that police stops can be seen as an example of police power in the sense developed by Dubber (2005), who describes police – as a noun and a verb – as state action oriented toward the reproduction of normative social order. Police power is both general, in that it is intended to provide order and stability for all citizens, and specific, in that it is intended to reproduce extant notions of right and existing social hierarchies. Policing in this sense is about the reproduction, or assertion, of 'normality'. While anyone, and anything, can pose a potential threat to existing social relations and concepts of order, and thus properly be the objects of police, there are regularities in the exercise and targeting of this power that mean certain groups and types of people are more likely to be the objects of police attention. As well as those who engaged in illegal behaviour (drug use), the young, men, the socially marginal (the unemployed, those in poor health, recent victims of crime), black Caribbeans, Asian Muslims, those using the public highway and those available to police (that is, those out of their homes, possibly at night) were consistently more likely to be stopped by police.

These categories resonate with the historical notion of police power theorized by Dubber. From its inception as a mode of governance it was directed against those who threatened existing social hierarchies and proprieties: individuals and groups who did not 'fit' and which were therefore in need of discipline and control; vagrants, the landless, disturbers of the peace. Fast forward to the present day, and we have a new set of threats to social order – the young as a constant source of trouble and disorder, young men in particular as potential criminals in a society often obsessed with crime, black Caribbeans as idealized offenders (Hall *et al.* 1978), Muslims as a new suspect community (Pantazis and Pemberton 2009). Yet there are also continuities with earlier eras. Police stops are still directed at the poor, particularly the unemployed (Neocleous 2000), and those who use public space in a certain way or who are seen as disorderly or, at best, less than respectable (Young 1999). The apparently self-evident fact that people who use cars are more likely to be stopped by police also corresponds with the eighteenth-century emphasis on police as a mechanism for controlling flows of people and for enabling traffic and commerce (Hunt 2006).

Policing is therefore directed toward both behaviours in need of regulation (e.g. using the road) *and* types of person considered a threat (e.g. the poor). Important here, though, is the idea that the categories of person constituted as a threat do not simply pre-exist the attention of the police. Nor are police necessarily directed toward such individuals by external forces, although this will certainly be the case on occasion. These are categories that are also created and reproduced by and through the practice of policing itself, even more so perhaps when we define police in Dubber's very wide sense. On this argument, police do not stop and search black Caribbean people more than others because officers are necessarily racist, or biased, or because black Caribbeans pose a greater 'group threat' than other minority groups (or indeed any threat at all), or because there is political pressure to do so – although, to reiterate, these things may all be true in some times and places. Rather, police stop black Caribbean people more than others because they have come to be positioned, over many decades, as suitable objects of the disciplinary power exerted via this type of police activity. Indeed, since the 1950s, black Caribbean people – men in particular – have been defined as problematic social group in large part *by the behaviour* of the police (Hall *et al.* 1978; Gilroy 1987; Keith 1993; cf Epp *et al.* 2014: 148–150). While the salience of this process might have waxed and waned over the years it has remained relevant right up to the present day, as almost continuously recurring concerns about 'knife crime' and 'gangs' in London and other cities attest (e.g. Sveinsson 2008).

Muslims are, arguably, subject to a more recent instantiation of the same process (Mythen *et al.* 2009; Pantazis and Pemberton 2009), although here the extent to which police and policing are caught up in a much wider set of judicial, legal and indeed political processes is equally apparent. The targeting of Muslim Britons by the state is a process far more extensive than the activity of the uniformed police. Yet police nonetheless contribute to these processes as well as being influenced by them. Officers may respond to external stimuli – legal, political or of some other kind – by (excessively) targeting people with Asian Muslim ethnicities, but they also by their actions contribute to and reproduce discourses that position Asian Muslims as dangerous or 'other'.

Harcourt (2001), in his critique of broken windows theory, suggests a highly analogous process. Arguing that zero-tolerance, order maintenance or quality of life styles of policing are problematic in their assumption that 'disorder' and 'disorderly' people are naturally occurring or socially fixed categories to which the police simply respond, Harcourt suggests instead that these categories are 'constructed in part through lengthy process of policing and punitive practices' (2001: 161). Developing a Foucauldian analysis of police practice, he stresses its generative or productive aspects, and the extent to which disciplinary processes both create and solidify the social categories over which they seek to exert control. Central to Harcourt's argument is the idea that it is the category, or the characteristics, of the person themselves that come to be marked as disorderly, not the acts they may, or may not, commit (ibid.: 162). The resonance with the findings presented in Chapter 5 is again strong – recall that it was their personal characteristics, rather than behaviours, that tended to be the most important predictors of an individual's chances of being stopped by police. It is further notable that a key feature of zero-tolerance and related policing styles is, of course, stop and frisk.

There are two important provisos to be made here. The first is that with the exception of ethnicity many of the characteristics associated with a greater chance of being stopped are also associated with a greater risk of offending. While the regression models described in Chapter 5 controlled for an important aspect of such behaviour, use of illegal drugs, there may be other, unobserved offending behaviours that may have influenced the findings. This is likely to be a particularly pertinent factor in relation to issues of youth, gender and possibly victimization. An important reason why police stop young men more than others is surely that young men commit more crime, and it is important to remember that crime-related concerns are important in explaining the distribution of stop and search. But there are other, equally important factors in play, and it seems to me that the extent to which *the police* concentrate on both crime and 'disorderly people' can also be understood in light of the more expansive notion of *police* as developed by Dubber and others (Bradford and Loader 2016). Use of this concept, that is, can help explain the full distribution of police stop activity, not just one aspect of it. Crime is not the only threat to social order in which police take an interest, nor is offending the only form of behaviour police seek to regulate.

The second proviso is that the account provided above does not negate the relevance of police stereotyping or the potential effect of differential policing styles in different areas. These and other factors help explain the empirical distribution of police stop activity. Rather, the claim I am trying to make is that while the social and spatial distribution of such activity is associated with the proclivities of particular officers, organizational factors and wider processes of discrimination and exclusion, these sit after, and moderate or mediate, something that as a fundamental aspect or expression of police power is to a certain extent independent of them. The urge to police – the institutional imperative to not only deal with issues of crime and to maintain order but also (perhaps more importantly) order and discipline marginal social categories – is prior to the agency of individual officers, organizations and indeed specific modes or ideologies of discrimination. The question of who is subject to any particular mode of policing (such as police stops) and why, cannot therefore be answered solely or even primarily by factors operating at the level of individual police officers or organizations. This argument runs close to the claim that was is at stake here is a pure form of institutional racism, since it suggests that there is something intrinsically discriminatory about policing and that people from ethnic minority groups – and others – are targeted simply on the basis of their difference.

Stops and police legitimacy

In addition to exploring the social and spatial distribution of police stop activity the analysis presented in the preceding chapters, in line with much other research, further suggested that the net effect of being stopped (and searched) on public trust and police legitimacy is negative. If the core predictions of procedural justice theory are correct, this will in turn undermine public deference toward officers, cooperation, and possibly even compliance with the law. Additionally, and importantly, we saw that people from different social groups and types of person seem to react in very similar ways to police contact. The association between unsatisfactory police contact and lower levels of trust, legitimacy and propensity to cooperate with police was broadly speaking invariant across a range of different social categories. This is a power that risks damaging trust and legitimacy wherever and whenever it is used.

Police stop activity, as I have defined it here, is fundamental to the practice of policing in a country such as England and Wales. Indeed, it is very hard to imagine modes or styles of policing where officers were not entitled, empowered and expected to stop people going about their business and direct, question and/or search them in some way. Yet this practice generates in an equally fundamental sense challenges to the legitimacy of the police: not because most people stopped by officers react badly – as described in Chapter 7 most are satisfied with the way police behave – but because those who are not happy react so strongly to these encounters. Importantly, dissatisfaction with police behaviour during stops is not evenly distributed across those stopped but is concentrated among particular groups and categories, which I have characterized as being marginal in Young's (2011) sense. The challenge to legitimacy generated by stop activity is thus concentrated within particular sections of the population, very often those who might wish or require more positive relationships that would enable to them to turn to police in times of need. It was particularly concerning, for example, to find that victims of crime were more likely to be stopped, were more likely to have bad experiences when this occurred, and were less likely to trust police. The barrier stop activity can place between police and policed is therefore likely to much wider and higher among some communities than others, and it is likely tallest among those most in need of the help. People stopped by officers are often also those most affected by crime and who almost certainly have the least amount of social, economic and other forms of capital that might enable them to deal with this experience, making them more in need than others of police assistance.

Why then do police in England and Wales use stop and search, specifically, as much as they do? Why in a general sense do police engage in stop activity that undermines the trust and legitimacy upon which they depend? There are a number of possible responses to this question (see also Bradford and Loader 2016). First, as noted above, police stops are a fundamental aspect of the practice of policing, a behaviour undertaken by, in this case, agents of formal social control that is oriented toward the reproduction of normative social order, where the nature of such order is a socially constructed phenomenon that favours dominant social groups (those with economic, political, social and cultural capital). Policing is not just directed against crime. It is also disciplinary action that is directed primarily at the socially marginal, the excluded, and the 'difficult', and which simultaneously helps generate and reproduce these as problematic social categories that are threatening and in need of discipline (Brogden and Ellison 2012; Choongh 1997; Harcourt 2001). Police stop particular groups or types of people on the street or in public spaces, question them, and possibly search them because this is in a sense what it is *to police*, at least as this aspect of state practice has come to be understood in England and Wales.

Second, police officers believe in stop and search. They do so for a number of reasons, some entirely understandable (police stops do produce arrests, cautions and intelligence), and some that make most sense when stop and search is seen as an aspect of the fundamental work of policing as described above. Particularly relevant here may be the frequently aired police opinion that stops and cognate practices are vital for keeping order on the streets and showing 'them' who is in charge (Choongh 1997; Hough 2013). Third, and relatedly, the public and politicians support the power to stop and search in general, if not always specific, terms. People *want* proactive policing that seems in control, asserts order, and maintains social discipline, and street and traffic stops often seem to fit with this vision.

It is on this last point that the tensions created by police stops become apparent. Street and traffic stops are a basic mode of policing. There is also little doubt that there are significant social pressures promoting visible, proactive, even at times forceful policing that gives the appearance of control and which suggests social order is adequately maintained, and that the incidence and distribution of police stop activity is affected by these pressures. Yet, there is a desire also for fair policing, that takes account of community wishes at the local level and which is conducted in ways that seek to promote, not undermine, trust and legitimacy – but this is precisely the effect stop/search seems to have. These tensions shape the way debates around stop and search, to take the most obvious and high profile example, play out criminologically, socially and politically. They are,

I believe, acute, and in all likelihood very difficult to reconcile (although see Bradford *et al.* 2014) because police stop activity taps into and speaks to two important visions of what policing is *for*.

On the one hand policing can be seen as concerned to an important extent with the demarcation and control of people from marginal social categories and the maintenance of extant social hierarchies. This is primarily a socio-structural position. It concerns the actual function of policing, which may be independent of people's experiences of it or ideas about it. Indeed, it is probably true to say that relatively few people would consciously *wish* for policing to be about control in this sense (although some may). At stake here are the actual ends of policing and the role police play in propping up the existing order (broadly defined).

On the other hand, are more overtly social – verbally expressed, discussed, debated and indeed desired – conceptualizations of policing stress crime, its control and the requirement for police to 'fight' it. On this account policing is primarily or even solely about crime. The objectives of the police comprise in the first and most important instance the detection of crime, the sanctioning of offenders and the maintenance of order (narrowly defined as the absence of disorder). Wider social or political factors are downplayed and even considered irrelevant.

These two visions have no necessary connection. It is perfectly possible to envisage policing that is directed toward one set of ends in preference to the other, or even one to the exclusion of the other. Police could be 'successful' in relation to one of these accounts with, or without, being successful in relation to the other. Yet there is a strong affinity between them. While they can be seen as two sides of a dialogue or even debate (is policing about social control or is it about crime) answers to 'the problem of crime' are often framed in terms of the need to control problematic populations, demonstrate force, and maintain a narrow version of order. People defined as disorderly are classed as criminals, while to commit a crime is almost by definition to be disorderly. Given these contrasting yet arguably complementary visions of policing and its objectives it is perhaps not surprising that stop and search and cognate practices are so frequently deployed. They enable the pursuit of both sets of ends, offering a sense of discipline and control and constituting a tool in the fight against crime.

There is another vision of policing, however, that moves beyond a narrow focus on crime and order to take a much wider view of the extent to which policing can enable, even free, individuals, and promote democratically justifiable and socially desirable modes of order maintenance (Loader and Walker 2007). Here, policing is not simply, or even primarily, about controlling deviant populations, and maintaining negative freedoms. It is also concerned with promoting positive freedoms, and it endeavours to 'draw' people toward developing a sense of shared aims and objectives, based on the articulation of collective identities, that is oriented toward the reproduction of collectively validated norms of security and order (ibid.). Procedurally just policing, which both motivates a sense that police are legitimate and encourages a sense of shared group membership between police and policed, and possibly among the policed, fits well with this alternative vision of policing. Excessive use of the power to stop and/or search does not – not least, of course, because stop and search seems, on average, to damage trust, legitimacy and propensities to cooperate among those who experience it.

This crystalizes the 'wickedness' (Fleming and McLaughlin 2010) of the problem at hand. Stop and search is used to further the fight against crime, and it may have some utility in this regard. Police stops, in a general sense, contribute to both crime and order-maintenance related ends. Yet the net effect of police stops is to undermine public cooperation and perhaps even to motivate offending. If the patterns described in the present volume and elsewhere, generally derived from survey research and self-reported offending, find purchase in terms of 'real' crime, police stop activity, in as much as it considered unfair and is undermining of legitimacy and common, shared, social identities, *inhibits* the ability of the police to achieve crime-reduction ends. Even if we accept the value of the 'fight against crime', stop/search is problematic. If we believe that policing can and should move beyond such metaphors and transcend the urge to control in order to achieve the modalities envisaged by Loader and Walker (2007), then it becomes almost imperative to reduce reliance on such an apparently counterproductive practice.

Since the underlying problem here has causes other than the behaviour of individual police officers and organizations, procedurally just or process-based styles of policing can alleviate but not dispel the tensions outlined above. Policing is in a fundamental sense about controlling marginal populations, and because police activity inevitably contains an element of confrontation, unhappiness with police is always likely to be concentrated within certain population groups, generating localized legitimacy problems that cannot be dealt with simply by enhancing procedural justice. While police action contributes to the creation of marginality it is surely not the only or the most important force in play, and host of economic, social and political factors come together to make people into suitable objects of police attention. Wider social change is needed to shift, recalibrate and diminish the social hierarchies that mean some people are more likely to be stopped than others. In a sense the real problem here is much larger than can be solved by simply 'reforming' the police.

However procedural justice theory still has much to add to this debate. Most importantly perhaps it adds agency to the structural position outlined above (cf. Giddens 1979). While the underlying purpose of policing may direct police officers towards certain groups and individuals, predispose particular forms of treatment for them, and thus continuously throw up legitimacy problems, individual officers and organizations retain the ability to modulate, redirect or amend their behaviours. They can act in ways that either reinforce the challenge to legitimacy generated by stop activity or that ameliorate, diminish or perhaps even reverse it. Likewise, policing can be more or less exclusionary and even, potentially, inclusionary (Bradford 2014; Tyler *et al.* 2015). Police stops can therefore be handled in such a way as to either exacerbate or alleviate the inevitable tensions they create. Applying procedural justice principles means that when people are stopped they are treated as full members of society deserving of dignity, respect and the other rights afforded to them as citizens. *Because* the police create as well as reproduce hierarchies and boundaries, encounters between officers and citizens contain at least the potential for positive change. Equally, though, procedural justice can have a soothing effect on difficult, conflictual encounters. For both normative and instrumental reasons, then, when police do stop people they should treat them as procedurally fairly as possible, given the circumstances.

The idea that the problem is structural does not therefore absolve the police from responsibility for their actions. Individual officers and police organizations have agency, and much room for manoeuvre, and they can elect to act in legitimacy enhancing or undermining ways and to promote or suppress processes of marginalization. Police choose who to stop and how to treat them, and these street-level choices and actions feed into the processes described above.

Managing the tension?

Which brings me, finally, to the policy lessons of all this – although I have little to say that has not, I suspect, been said before (see, for example, Bradford and Jackson 2016; Delsol and Shiner 2015; Hough 2013). It seems imperative on the basis of the evidence presented here that police use stop and search powers to the minimal degree possible and in order to further carefully defined ends. The evidence that targeted applications of stop and search can 'work' in terms of dealing with crime in local areas is compelling. Along with the concern about what police would do if they did not have a diffuse non-arrest based power to stop and question people in the streets this obviates, to my mind, calls to 'ban' stop and search. This is a useful power for police to have, but the problem seems often to have been that they do not recognize its extent or import. Representing the unbridled power of the state to intervene and direct the lives of citizens, stop and search might be described as a very heavy hammer that has often been used to break some rather small nuts. More attention, inside and outside the police service, needs to be directed toward decisions concerning when, why and how this power should be exercised. There are encouraging signs that such attention is increasingly evident, as witnessed for example by the marked decline in the use of stop and search in the last few years, reports from HMIC (2013, 2014) and efforts by the College of Policing to guide the debate around and training on stop and search. Take, for example, the latter's 'Best use of stop and search' scheme, which aims to:

> achieve greater transparency, community involvement in the use of stop and search powers and to support a more intelligence-led approach, leading to better outcomes, for example, an increase in the stop and search to positive outcome ratio.
>
> (College of Policing 2014: 2)

Key provisions in the Best use guidance include enhanced data recording, lay observation policies, a 'community trigger' that requires police to explain to community groups how powers are being used if and when a certain level of complaints has been reached and new policies that aim clearly at reducing the use of s.60 stops (ibid.). In addition, more emphasis on training in procedural justice and, particularly, the minimization of implicit bias, is also needed, and again there have been some encouraging moves in this direction.

The broader and more or less informal power to 'stop', as I have described it here, would plainly be harder to control and constrain in the same way – or, at least, such issues blur into the much bigger question of how to control police power in a general sense. Be that as it may, each and every use of legal, extra-legal or pre-legal use of the power to stop and question members of the public should be carefully considered by the officers concerned. The possible effects on the individual stopped are significant, and police need to be more aware of this. One area for policy-makers and police managers to address might indeed be fostering greater awareness among officers of the extent of the symbolic as well as material power vested in them. It is this that makes people so attuned to police behaviour, and so sensitive to the way they are treated by officers. It is easy for people working within an organization to forget how those outside it view them, particularly, perhaps, as perceptions move up and down a steep power gradient such as that which separates police officers and most of those they police. Perhaps more effort is needed in terms of reminding police officers about the effect their words and actions can have on all with whom they interact.

Welcome also would be a shift away from a narrow focus (on all sides of the debate) on stop and search per se and a greater emphasis on, precisely, the wider category of 'police stops'. There are, again, encouraging signs, for example in relation to traffic stops. In March 2016 the Home Secretary announced that rules governing the recording of stop and search would be extended to vehicle stops carried out under the Road Traffic Act (BBC 2016), a development presented as a direct response to emerging evidence of the extent of ethnic disproportionality in this kind if encounter. Yet at the time of writing no firm timescale for this move has been forthcoming, something that may point to a challenge facing all attempts at reform in this area. Stop/search and related issues are high on the political agenda, something almost certainly linked to although not wholly causative of the decline in the use of stop and search powers since 2010 (see Chapter 2). This amplified level of debate seems to have served to both shift police practice and encourage other potentially desirable outcomes (as for example the Best Use of Stop and Search Scheme, as well as the recording of traffic stops). However, we have in a sense been here before. The use of stop and search dipped in the aftermath of the Stephen Lawrence Enquiry, something commonly attributed to the increased attention focused on police practice at the time. Yet, again as seen in Chapter 2, as time went by use of the power increased again, and indeed soon surpassed previous levels.

So perhaps the most important lesson of all this is that debate and political attention is needed not only to drive reform but also to ensure that positive change persists (Bradford and Loader 2016; Delsol and Shiner 2015; Lennon and Murray 2016; Murray and Harkin 2016). Absent such pressure it seems likely that previous patterns and ways of working will reassert themselves – it is for this reason that the absence of a timetable for the recording of traffic stops is concerning, since it leaves open the possibility for drift and inertia. The idea that police stop (and search) is a fundamental aspect of policing explains, at least in part, this potential. This is a mode or practice so closely woven into both the aims of policing and the means for achieving these ends that it would hardly be surprising if it resurfaced after periods during which, for whatever reason, its use became more difficult. Given that the evidence presented in Chapter 6 suggests that at least part of the decline in stop and search since 2010 will be simply the decline in police numbers (albeit that this evidence is far from conclusive), it will be interesting to see whether the decline in stop and search halts, then reverses, once those reductions are over. The challenge to legitimacy generated by police stops is such that continued vigilance, from all parties, is required.

References

BBC (2016). Police stop-and-search rules to apply to vehicle stops. *BBC News* www.bbc.co.uk/news/uk-35904025 (Last accessed May 2016).

Bradford, B. (2014). Policing and social identity: Procedural justice, inclusion, and cooperation between police and public. *Policing and Society* 24(1): 22–43.

Bradford, B. and Jackson, J. (2016). Enabling and constraining police power: On the moral regulation of policing, in Jacobs, J. and Jackson, J. (eds) *Routledge Handbook of Criminal Justice Ethics*. Oxford: Routledge.

Bradford, B. and Loader, I. (2016). Police, crime and order: The case of stop and search, in Bradford, B., Jauregui, B., Loader, I. and Steinberg, J. (eds) *The SAGE Handbook of Global Policing*. London: SAGE.

Bradford, B., Jackson, J. and Hough, M. (2014). Police legitimacy in action: Lessons for theory and practice, in Reisig, M. and Kane, R. (eds) *The Oxford Handbook of Policing*, pp. 551–570. Oxford: Oxford University Press.

Choongh, S. (1997). *Policing as Social Discipline*. Oxford: Clarendon Press.

College of Policing (2014). *Best Use of Stop and Search Scheme*. London: Home Office.

Delsol, R. and Shiner, M. (eds) (2015). *Stop and Search*. Basingstoke: Palgrave Macmillan.

Dubber, M.D. (2005). *The Police Power. Patriarchy and the Foundations of American Government*. New York: Columbia University Press.

Ellison, G. and Brogden, M. (2012). *Policing in an Age of Austerity: A Postcolonial Perspective*. London: Routledge.

Epp, C.R., Maynard-Moody, S. and Haidar-Markel, D. (2014). *Pulled Over. How Police Stops Define Race and Citizenship*. Chicago: University of Chicago Press.

Fleming, J. and McLaughlin, E. (2010). 'The public gets what the public wants?' Interrogating the 'public confidence' agenda. *Policing: A Journal of Policy and Practice* 4(3): 199–202.

Giddens, A. (1979). *Central Problems in Social Theory*. London: Macmillan Education.

Gilroy, P. (1987). *There Ain't No Black in the Union Jack*. London: Routledge.

Hall, S., Critcher, C., Jefferson, T., Clarke, J. and Roberts, B. (1978). *Policing the Crisis*. London: Macmillan.

Harcourt, B.E. (2001). *Illusion of Order: The False Promise of Broken Windows Policing*. Cambridge: Harvard University Press.

HMIC (2013). *Stop and Search Powers: Are the Police Using Them Effectively and Fairly?* London: Her Majesty's Inspectorate of Constabulary.

HMIC (2014). S*top and Search Powers 2: Are the Police Using Them Effectively and Fairly?* London: Her Majesty's Inspectorate of Constabulary.

Hough, M. (2013). Procedural justice and professional policing in times of austerity. *Criminology and Criminal Justice* 13(2): 181–197.

Hunt, A. (2006). Police and the regulation of traffic: Policing as a civilizing process?, in Dubber, M.D. and Valverde, M. (eds) *The New Police Science: The Police Power in Domestic and International Governance*. Stanford: Stanford University Press.

Keith, M. (1993). *Race, Riots and Policing: Lore and Disorder in a Multi-Racist Society*. London: UCL Press.

Lennon, G. and Murray, K. (2016). Under-regulated and unaccountable? Explaining variation in stop and search rates in Scotland, England and Wales. *Policing and Society* Advance access.

Loader, I. and Walker, N. (2007). *Civilising Security*. Cambridge: Cambridge University Press.

Murray, K. and Harkin, D. (2016). Policing in cool and hot climates: Legitimacy, power and the rise and fall of mass stop and search in Scotland. *British Journal of Criminology* Advance Access.

Mythen, G., Walklate, S. and Khan, F. (2009). 'I'm a Muslim, but I'm not a terrorist': Victimization, risky identities and the performance of safety. *British Journal of Criminology* 49(6): 736–754.

Neocleous, M. (2000). *The Fabrication of Social Order*. London: Pluto Press.

Pantazis, C. and Pemberton, S. (2009). From the 'old' to the 'new' suspect community: Examining the impacts of recent UK counter-terrorist legislation. *British Journal of Criminology* 49(5): 646–666.

Sveinsson, K.P. (2008). *A Tale of Two Englands – 'Race' and Violent Crime in the Press*. London: Runnymede Trust.

Tyler, T.R., Jackson, J. and Mentovich, A. (2015). The consequences of being an object of suspicion: Potential pitfalls of proactive police contact. *Journal of Empirical Legal Studies* 12(4): 602–636.

Young, I.M. (2011). *Justice and the Politics of Difference*. Princeton: Princeton University Press.

Young, J. (1999). *The Exclusive Society*. London: SAGE.

Index

Page numbers in *italics* denote tables, those in **bold** denote figures.

For Product Safety Concerns and Information please contact our EU representative GPSR@taylorandfrancis.com
Taylor & Francis Verlag GmbH, Kaufingerstraße 24, 80331 München, Germany

www.ingramcontent.com/pod-product-compliance
Ingram Content Group UK Ltd.
Pitfield, Milton Keynes, MK11 3LW, UK
UKHW021302190926
475701UK00009B/575

* 9 7 8 0 3 6 7 2 2 6 1 9 0 *